Adapting Government to Regional Needs

INSTITUTE OF GOVERNMENTAL STUDIES
University of California, Berkeley
1971

Adapting Government to Regional Needs

Report of the Conference on Bay Area Regional Organization
April 18, 1970

STANLEY SCOTT and HARRIET NATHAN
Editors

262858

International Standard Book Number (ISBN) 0-87772-079-7

Library of Congress Catalog Card Number 72-634806

$5.50 per copy

CONTENTS

FOREWORD   ix
   Regional Mileposts: The View in 1971

PART ONE: WHY WE ARE HERE
   Background and Purpose   3
   Eugene C. Lee

   Where We Are Now: The Rhetoric and the Reality   8
   Ignazio A. Vella

   The Constitutional Issues in Bay Area Regional
     Organization   12
   John T. Knox

PART TWO: THE GOVERNMENTAL JOBS TO BE DONE IN
   THE REGION
   Background Paper: Regional Organization in
     the San Francisco Bay Area--1970   19
   Ora Huth

   Panel: Moderator, *Stanley E. McCaffrey*,
     Members, *Frank M. Stead, Joseph E. Bodovitz,*
     John C. Beckett, John J. Miller   61

PART THREE: ORGANIZATION, POWERS AND REPRESENTATION
   Background Paper: The Regional Jobs to be Done
     and Ways of Getting Them Accomplished   87
   Stanley Scott

   Lessons from the Twin Cities   105
   James L. Hetland, Jr.

   Panel: Moderator, *Ira Michael Heyman*,
     Members, *T. J. Kent, Jr., Don Fazackerley,*
     Mary W. Henderson, Joseph P. Bort, Donald
     P. McCullum   123

PART FOUR: FINANCING THE JOBS THAT NEED TO BE
   DONE: WHO PAYS AND FOR WHAT?
   Background Paper: Financing a Regional
      Organization in the Bay Area: A Way of
      Thinking about the Problem   163
   Leslie E. Carbert

   Panel: Moderator, *William L. C. Wheaton*,
   Members, *Ralph Anderson, Leslie E. Carbert,
   Earl R. Rolph*   174

PART FIVE: SUMMARY AND COMMENTARY
   Eugene C. Lee   201

   John T. Knox   203

   Ignazio A. Vella   205

APPENDICES

I   Comparative Analysis of Three State Legisla-
     tive Proposals for Bay Area Regional Organi-
     zation   211
     AB 1846 (Bagley) 1969
     AB 711 (Knox)   1969
     AB 2310 (Knox)   1970
     Ora Huth

II   To Create a Bay Area Home Rule Agency   225
     1969 Proposal: AB 1846
     Ora Huth

III To Establish a Regional Government of the
     Bay Area   239
     1969 Proposal: AB 711
     Ora Huth

IV   To Establish a Conservation and Development
     Agency of the Bay Area   251
     1970 Proposal: AB 2310
     Ora Huth

V   The Metropolitan Council of the Twin Cities
     Area   259
     Stanley Scott

VI   Choosing Representatives for a Bay Area
         Umbrella Agency: Another Possibility . . . 263
         Stanley Scott

VII   A Bay Area "Regional Budget" 275

VIII Representative Local Government: from
         Neighborhood to Region 278
         Victor Jones

TABLES

Discussion
I   Who Is Doing the Governmental Work on the
       Environment? 67

Background Papers
I   Tally of Regional Problems and Report
       Sources 88

Appendices
I   Electoral Units for a Bay Area Umbrella
       Agency 264

II 1971 Bay Area Legislative Delegation and ABAG
       Executive Committee 266

MAPS

I   Bay Region Assembly Districts 273

II Bay Region Senate Districts 274

INDEX 299

FOREWORD

Regional Mileposts: The View in 1971

1971 is likely to be viewed as one of the most
crucial periods in the Bay Area citizenry's long-term
effort to "write a constitution" for the governance of
its nine-county region. In a vague way this process can
be said to have begun decades ago with formation of subregional bodies such as the East Bay municipal utility
and regional park districts (1923 and 1934 respectively)
and the Golden Gate bridge district (1928). But the
conscious attempt to design an interrelated regional
governmental framework can probably be dated from the
formation of the nine-county regional air pollution control district in 1955, and the five-county BART district
in 1957--later reduced to three counties.

The tempo of these efforts quickened in the 1960's.
ABAG was formed in 1961, and the growing strength of the
environmentalists emerged with the establishment of a
temporary Bay control agency in 1965. In 1969 BCDC was
made permanent. Meanwhile the concept of a multipurpose
regional government for major regional functions, which
for many years had received only intermittent attention, and that primarily in academic circles, came increasingly into public view and gained acceptance. By
1967 there appeared to be general recognition that a
multipurpose regional agency was needed, but controversy
continued over its powers and fiscal basis, and especially over the composition of its governing body.

The degree of consensus had increased by 1970. The
idea of a mixed governing body had originally been suggested by BCDC in 1968-69, as a compromise between the
conservationists and others who demanded direct election,
and the ABAG-formula proponents, many of whom had in-
sisted with equal fervor on constituent-unit

ix

representation. The "umbrella-agency" concept emerged, envisioning a regional agency with effective overall *planning* powers, but with few if any direct *operating* responsibilities.

These concepts appeared during a period of increasing public realization that the new agency would not necessarily need significant new monetary sources in order to have a crucial impact on local and regional developments in the region. It would only need adequate staffing and sufficient authority to influence ways of spending the existing streams of money that sluice into governmental coffers from federal, state and local sources.[1] For this, the umbrella agency would not need to raise large sums from new tax sources.

Thus proponents agreed that in a very real sense, a comparatively tiny monetary "tail" could wag a huge and otherwise unwieldy regional dog. In fact, the public seemed to realize that an effective umbrella agency could be worth its salt even if it only managed to keep the existing regional and local governments from getting in each other's way and stepping on each other's toes.

In fairly rapid fashion, at regional conferences in September 1968[2] and April 1970,[3] at a series of "summit" sessions at the Berkeley campus faculty club in the fall of 1970, and in numerous other forums, the lineaments of a consensus emerged. Principal areas of difference were narrowed to the crucial question of representation: who would be in the driver's seat?

---

[1] See Appendix VII, "A Bay Area 'Regional Budget,'" pp. 275-276, this report.

[2] See *Toward a Bay Area Regional Organization: Report of the Conference, September 14, 1968*, eds. Harriet Nathan and Stanley Scott (Berkeley: Institute of Governmental Studies, University of California, 1969).

[3] As reported in this volume.

The chief regional governmental proposal of 1971, Assembly Bill 1057, called for a Conservation and Development Agency of the Bay Area. It was introduced in March by Assemblyman John Knox, with Senator Milton Marks as co-author. As introduced, the bill provided for a 40-member governing body, directly elected from equally apportioned districts. By the end of July, the need both for compromise and for insuring broad representation produced a key amendment to add 43 members, giving the proposed body a total of 83 members.

Forty of the additional 43 would be city councilmen and county supervisors, distributed among the 9 counties roughly according to population. Alameda and Santa Clara counties would have 8 representatives each; San Francisco, 6; Contra Costa and San Mateo counties, 4 each; Sonoma and Marin counties, 3 each; and Napa and Solano counties, 2 each. Finally, one member each would be selected by and from the membership of the governing boards of the regional air pollution control district, the regional water quality control agency, and the Bay Conservation and Development Commission.

Much of the regional agency's business would be conducted by a 10-member executive committee, with 6 affirmative votes required to pass agency measures. The executive committee would consist of the agency president plus 9 members appointed by the agency board from its membership, including 4 city and county representatives, 4 directly elected representatives, and one selected from among the 3 special district representatives.

The agency's principal power would lie in the adoption of five mandatory regionwide resource plans within three years. First, the San Francisco Bay plan of BCDC would be adopted as is, and BCDC would remain intact as a separate commission. Second, a transportation plan would include highways, bridges, mass transit, airports, seaports and any related facilities. The agency would take over the functions of the recently activated Metropolitan Transportation Commission. Third, an environmental quality plan would be adopted for the control of

air, water and land contamination. Fourth, a regional
open space plan would be required. Fifth, there would
be a regional parks plan.

All of the plans except the first, for the Bay itself, would be implemented by agency ordinances prescrib-
ing rules and regulations to be complied with by private
persons and by Bay Area local governmental bodies. The
agency would also review applications for federal and
state grants by any local agency in the region. The plan
for the Bay would continue to be enforced by BCDC. The
regional agency could finance its administrative and
planning efforts through imposition of a small documen-
tary transfer tax of 4 cents per $100 market value of
real estate at the time of sale. The tax would raise
approximately $700 thousand per year. This is a minute
fraction--a little over 1/100th of one percent--of the
current rate of all governmental spending in the Bay
Area.

At this writing--mid-August 1971--it is not yet
clear whether the Knox Bill, AB 1057, will pass and be
signed by the governor. But the measure is closer to
enactment than any other in the history of the Bay Area.
Many of the elements underlying its conception are
sketched in the papers and discussions reported in this
account of the regional conference of 1970.

Other related Bay regional bills were also under
consideration in 1971. Another Knox measure, Assembly
Bill 2867, would establish a Bay Area Sewer Services
Agency (BASSA) to develop a regional water quality plan
in the nine-county area, and provide for its implementation. The bill was the result of "Phase I" recommendations included in the report of the Bay-Delta Study
Program, submitted by the State Water Resources Control
Board in April 1971. Except for San Francisco, with its
peculiar problem of sewer inadequacy, there appears to
be little opposition to the bill. It leaves options
open for the development of programs of transportation,
dilution or reclamation of wastes or otherwise maintaining water quality, while handling wastes from some 150
dischargers in the region.

xii

BASSA would have a 21-member governing board appointed by county supervisors from nominees selected by mayors and board members of water quality control and management districts in each county, from among members of the district boards and city and county governing bodies. BASSA board membership would be allocated geographically as follows: the counties of Alameda and Santa Clara, 5 each; San Francisco, 3; Contra Costa and San Mateo, 2 each; and Marin, Napa, Solano and Sonoma, one each.

BASSA would be empowered to review local plans and to require conformity with the regional plan, to review and comment on grant requests related to water quality management, and under certain conditions to construct and operate facilities.

A third measure by Assemblyman Knox, Assembly Bill 515, was endorsed by the Association of Bay Area Governments as their 1971 "home rule" legislation. AB 515 would provide for establishment by July 1972 of environmental planning councils in regions designated by the state Council on Intergovernmental Relations, and would require adoption of advisory regional interim environmental quality plans within two years. The bill has no provisions for plan enforcement. Hence, it would simply continue ABAG as the Bay Area's advisory regional planning body.

Also of regional interest is the proposed 1971 California Coastal Zone Conservation Act, Assembly Bill 1471, introduced by Assemblyman Alan Sieroty, and its initially identical companion, Senate Bill 1555 by Senator Alfred Alquist. This is a strengthened version of a 1970 proposal by Assemblyman George Milias, which was drafted by coastal legislation experts and patterned after the successful BCDC legislation. Sieroty's bill would create a strong California Coastal Zone Conservation Commission and 6 regional commissions, to regulate development along the coastline and protect access to beaches until 1975, when a coastal development master plan would be completed.

The 12-member state-level commission would have 6 public members chosen 2 each by the governor, speaker of the assembly, and the Senate Rules Committee, and 6 members representing the 6 regional coastal commissions established under the act. The regional commission would also have 12 members, 6 chosen 2 each by the governor, speaker and Rules Committee, and 6 representing cities and counties in the region. The regional coastal agencies would have interim permit power to regulate coastal development over an area extending from three miles at sea to 1,000 yards inland, while a detailed plan for the future use of the 1,100 mile California shoreline to five miles inland is under preparation.

* * *

With few exceptions, the central themes in the debate over environmental policy control, and their resolution, were clearly outlined in the background papers and discussion at the regional conference of 1970, reported in full herein. This volume thus becomes both a major progress report on regional consensus and a basic document on governmental philosophy for restructuring the region to fit the needs of the final third of the 20th Century.

In this endeavor the editors have received substantial assistance from persons too numerous to name, both in the Bay Area and in Sacramento. Ora Huth, our colleague on the staff of the Institute of Governmental Studies, deserves special mention, however, because she was principal organizer of the April 1970 Conference, a major contributor of background material, and an essential aid, guide and critic in the preparation of this document. The enterprise also benefitted from the sustained interest and enthusiasm of the Institute's Director, Eugene Lee, who was a prime mover in setting up the conference, and who served as its general chairman. We also gratefully acknowledge the expert editorial assistance of Louise Howe, and the skill and patience of Nancy Maslin and Judy Rasmussen in typing the manuscript.

Stanley Scott and Harriet Nathan
Editors

Part One:

Why We Are Here

BACKGROUND AND PURPOSE

Eugene C. Lee

Director, Institute of Governmental Studies
University of California, Berkeley

Welcome to the 1970 Conference on Bay Area Regional Organization. About 18 months ago many of you gathered with us on this campus to explore some aspects of the same problems we will be discussing today. One of our goals is to learn how far we have come since then and to try to understand where we should be going next.

Today is not only 18 months since our previous conference, but it is also the 64th anniversary of San Francisco's famous 1906 earthquake. And it is just about a year since we were shaken up again, if only fictionally, by what might be termed "the Curt Gentry phenomenon."

In *The Last Days of the Late, Great State of California*, Gentry imagines that another earthquake took place in 1969, during which half of California tumbled into the sea. He shows, very perceptively I believe, that the greatest irony of the tragedy was that no earthquake or act of God was needed to destroy California. Man, with his great ingenuity, was managing to do that all by himself.

In Gentry's book what really shocked the nation about California's end was not that it happened, but that it happened so suddenly. It took only one hour and 57 minutes, and so it was considered an unprecedented tragedy. But while California was slowly being destroyed over the course of the years, we virtually ignored the process.

3

A NEW REALITY

A few years ago Gentry might well have been writing about the Bay Area, and to some extent he still is. But your presence here today underscores a new reality: citizens of the Bay Area are determined not to let their magnificent region slip into an ocean of smog, pollution, garbage, Bay fill, traffic, congestion or sprawling slurbs. What we still must decide, however, is how to best organize ourselves to insure that our determination becomes a vehicle for change.

This conference has been planned on the basis of a set of common assumptions. We do not demand that you fully accept all of them, although we do believe that they are valid. As a starting point from which the conference can begin its deliberations, we pose them here as "givens" and ask the participants to proceed on the basis that the assumptions are understood and accepted.

ASSUMPTION 1: REGIONAL PROBLEMS EXIST

Our first assumption is that there *are* regional problems. We need not spend a substantial amount of time telling this audience that an environmental crisis exists, or that the region's population is increasingly stratified in terms of race and income, or that there are 101 problems confronting the region, and all of them could be detailed. Numerous meetings and publications on these subjects have all made the point that we are confronted with major public issues that are beyond the scope of existing public institutions. We start with that assumption today.

ASSUMPTION 2: REGIONAL GOVERNMENT EXISTS

The second assumption is that there *is* regional government, or regional organization, now. In this conference we do not have to convince you that a host of

regional agencies, including departments of federal and
state government, are daily making and implementing critical policy decisions affecting the Bay Area and your own
life.

ASSUMPTION 3:   DECISIONS CAN BE MADE IN THE REGION

We believe, some with more confidence than others,
that the regional decisions confronting us should not all
be made in Sacramento or Washington. Why do we believe
this? Because of a long-standing American conviction
that political power in our society should be divided
to the maximum extent possible.

ASSUMPTION 4:   THERE IS MERIT IN ALTERNATIVES

We assume that there is merit in having alternative
ways of doing things, of permitting *choices* in the public
as well as in the private marketplace, of securing maximum political participation and access of different
groups to political power.

Negatively, we have a stake in avoiding some of the
rigidities and costs of a huge state or federal bureaucracy. We also need to limit the occurrence of irre-
trievable errors in political judgment.

ASSUMPTION 5:   REGIONAL PROBLEMS NEED REGIONAL SOLUTIONS

For all of these reasons and more, we believe we
should try as much as possible to handle regional problems on a regional level and not leave them to our representatives in state and national government.

ASSUMPTION 6:   MANY DECISIONS WILL CONTINUE TO BE MADE
                IN SACRAMENTO AND WASHINGTON

The other side of the political coin is that many
decisions affecting our lives and our regional and local

agencies will still be made in Sacramento and Washington.
Therefore, we need to have an effective regional voice
in these two capitals. We now lack such a voice.

ASSUMPTION 7:   THE STATUS QUO IS INADEQUATE FOR THE
                SEVENTIES

Finally, we believe that the existing course of
action, with each regional problem now being handled by
one or more separate agencies with little or no coordination, is not the best way to organize the region.
What is wrong with large, separate and specialized regional agencies? Our panels may touch on this question,
and I hope they do. For the moment, I submit that such
agencies are difficult for the public to control effectively, that they pose critical and unresolved problems
of coordination, and that they fragment the political
power of the region vis-à-vis state and national government.

In short, I pose to you as a final assumption that
the status quo is not adequate to the needs of the
1970's.

We have, then, seven assumptions in all: (1) Regional problems exist; (2) Regional government exists;
(3) Decisions can be made in the region; (4) There is
merit in alternatives; (5) Regional problems need regional solutions; (6) Many decisions will continue to be
made in Sacramento and Washington; and (7) The status
quo is inadequate for the seventies. With these assumptions as our starting point, what do we hope to accomplish?

CONFERENCE GOALS

During the day we will be listening to three panels,
each with a different goal. Panel One has as its goal
an analysis of the functions of the existing regional
organizations, their relationships with each other,

with state and federal government and with local agencies. Hopefully, we will achieve a better understanding of the gaps, overlaps and jurisdictional conflicts that now exist.

With this as background, Panel Two will discuss the alternative organizational approaches to the problems posed by Panel One. We hope when it concludes to have a clearer picture of the political consequences of various approaches to regional organization.

Finally, Panel Three will grapple with one of the most difficult subjects of all. Its goal is to help us understand the fiscal realities of the regional approaches that have been discussed by the two preceding panels. How much will it cost to do the job that needs to be done?

These, then, are some of the assumptions and goals of this conference. We do not expect to find the final answers to all of our questions or the total solutions to all of our problems. Far from it. We do hope that when this meeting adjourns in about six hours that we will each leave with a renewed sense of the need to move ahead and with greater knowledge of how and where we should be moving.

WHERE WE ARE NOW: THE RHETORIC AND THE REALITY

Ignazio A. Vella

Supervisor, Sonoma County and
President
Association of Bay Area Governments (ABAG)

I am here today, to use a baseball analogy, in the guise of a pinch hitter. The original speaker--Mayor Jack Maltester of San Leandro, who is president of the National Conference of Mayors--is far more versed in the problems of the Bay Area, having been enmeshed in them far longer than I. But one of the things that a manager very often asks of a pinch hitter is that he do something to shake up the ball game, and so, with your permission, I am going to attempt to do just that.

In writing to me about this conference, Professor Lee, near the end of his letter, says: "To repeat, we are not trying to do the same old things again, but to break new ground and advance the discussion one step nearer a meaningful solution." Then he proceeds to send me the agenda (which I think has a great deal of the same old story in it), and the background material, and I find we are rehashing the very same thing.

Therefore I decided, for better or for worse, to take an entirely different tack this morning. For I am sure that you would not be here if you did not already have some smattering of ideas about regional government, or if you did not have some interest in what is happening in the Bay Area. For me to rehash that and claim that I am laying a foundation for the rest of the day would be to waste your time. So let me use the approach of a pinch hitter.

UNDERSTANDING AMERICA

It is the contention of a number of world-famed historians that the United States has produced only three historians whose works have aided in the understanding of the American nation. One is Frederick Jackson Turner, whose original research and subsequent essays on the influence of the frontier in America were not only startlingly original in concept, for his day, and even for our day, but were also sociologically oriented.

The second historian of worldwide stature is Herbert Eugene Bolton, of this very campus, whose original research and resultant hypothesis have led us to a new appreciation of the Indians of the southwest and their civilization. The third is Walter Prescott Webb, whose untimely death in 1963 deprived us of several volumes of monumental writing. However he did live to promulgate in his first book, *The Great Frontier*, the thesis that I wish to discuss today.

Webb's thesis was that the discoveries of Christopher Columbus touched off a 400-year-long boom that, in turn, made possible private capitalism, representative democracy and what he aptly termed "the other parallel institutions of the United States of America." Now that the bloom of the boom has passed, he held, the world was experiencing the upheaval of vast change without knowing toward what it was adjusting. In other words, we now have the task of turning from an outward looking people to an introspective people. This is difficult enough for us as individuals, let alone as a nation.

Another factor that I believe merits consideration is the effect upon the people of the United States of the generation of '29. In Spain, following the debacle of losing a war in 1898 to what was considered a fourth-rate fledgling power--the United States--a great wave of pessimism swept the Spanish empire--or at least what was left of it.

YESTERDAY AND TODAY

I think that there is a parallel between the generation of '29 and today's generation. I was born in 1928, and I have never seen my generation out of a crisis. There was the crisis of the Depression, followed by the cataclysm of World War II, followed by the atomic and hydrogen bomb era, followed closely by the debacle of Korea, and now by the present status of Vietnam.

Throughout these years we have been kept in constant ferment and crisis, and this fact, in my opinion, has molded much of this generation's youth. I don't think you can keep people constantly in ferment and then expect them to do great things in literature, or in any of the arts that man needs to satisfy his soul. What you get instead--and this is exactly what we did get--is a great buildup in technology, engineering and research because these are direct answers to a crisis.

But the most glaring defect of the moment, I think, is that we are attempting to approach the 1970's with a local government structure modeled on the California Constitution of 1879. No businessman, no engineer--nobody--would attempt to tackle 1970's problems with an 1879 solution, and yet that's what we are doing day after day. And then we wonder why we are not solving our problems.

POLICIES AND REALITY

One of the points mentioned by Mr. Lee this morning is that the federal government and the state government are exercising a great deal of influence in our area already. Yet, as a local government official, I have been handicapped by the lack of a set policy either in Washington or in Sacramento upon which I could build. There have been five changes in five and a half years of policies.

I do feel that conferences such as this are very good for an exchange of views, but I would counsel you that unless you are able to relate these views to reality--the reality of the political arena, the reality of selfishness, ambition, outright greed, despoliation, the reality of all the despicable things that we talk about when we worry about the environment--unless you are able to compute these factors as well, then you will have nothing but an elegant, academic exercise.

If we do not begin to sublimate some of our personal desires, some of our ambitious greed, to the greater mission of the common good, we will succumb to the Marxist threat of class against class. There is another danger too--the danger of zoning ourselves into separate little islands.

Hopefully during this day we will examine ourselves and evolve some practical ideas with which we can move forward into the 1970's. And then perhaps, in the words in the preface to *The Great Frontier*, "The citizenry of this age will only look wistfully to the past knowing that mankind will not pass these windfall ways again."

THE CONSTITUTIONAL ISSUES IN BAY AREA
REGIONAL ORGANIZATION

John T. Knox

*Assemblyman, Richmond; Chairman, Committee on
Local Government, Joint Committee on Bay Area
Regional Organization (BARO), and
Joint Committee on Open Space Lands*

If Supervisor Vella is the pinch hitter, I suppose
I am the bat boy today. I'm very pleased to be here in
any case. I had the occasion just the other day to think
about the people in the Bay Area and the troubles we are
having in getting ourselves organized, while I was putting forward a modest proposal to raise the revenues
available to the Bay Area Air Pollution Control District.

That lovable, crusty old curmudgeon, Frank Lanterman,
chairman of the Assembly Ways and Means Committee, was
also on the Transportation Committee and, although he
is favorable to the bill, he said: "What's the trouble
with you people in the Bay Area that you can't raise
enough money to have a proper air pollution program?"
And I replied that his remark reminded me of the problem
detailed in *Brave New World*.

You'll recall that in the world Huxley set up there
were various classes of people: the Alphas, the Betas,
the Deltas and so forth. The Alphas were the most intelligent group and the highest class, but they found
when they tried to put them alone on an island, the Alphas were totally unable to govern themselves. As I suggested to Frank Lanterman, that may be the same difficulty
we are having in the San Francisco Bay Region.

THE CURRENT PUSH

However, I do think progress is being made in Sacramento. Last year, because of the crisis around San Francisco Bay, we worked mostly on the Bay Conservation and Development Commission program. Therefore we were not able to push the regional organization bill. This year we are trying to move ahead on a number of fronts. For one thing, the BARO bill has been reintroduced. It is in essentially the same form as last year except that, in an effort to reach a compromise, we have suggested that 20 of the 40-member legislative body be appointed under the system espoused by ABAG and 20 be directly elected. This is probably the best way to succeed in getting everybody angry at us instead of just the half we had before, but nonetheless, that's the compromise we've put in the bill.

We are obviously open to further discussion and compromise, but our hope is to pass a bill this year if humanly possible, because the problems are not getting any better--they are getting worse. Although we are spending more and more money, we stand a substantial risk of becoming even more fragmented in our regional affairs in the future than we are today.

SEPARATE APPROACHES

For example, in the area of *transportation* Assemblyman John Foran of San Francisco has a very ambitious and in many ways an excellent program for the solution of regional transportation problems.

A number of us also have proposals relating to *open space* lands. (Senator Milton Marks has introduced a bill; I have eight bills on the subject; and many others have regional programs as well.) Moreover, the Speaker's Select Committee on the Environment has its own regional approach as part of its recommendations.

In addition, because I'm worried that if we don't get a regional program going this year our *sewage* situation will get worse than it already is, I have suggested in still another bill that the Bay Conservation and Development Commission be empowered to set up the regional sewer district areas that are espoused also in the regional government bill. Further, I have suggested that the BCDC be ordered to come up with a plan to connect into a directly elected body, after they have had a chance to study this possibility for a year.

What else? Assemblyman Willie Brown of San Francisco has a bill to make the governing board of the Bay Area Air Pollution Control District directly elected. That bill came out of my committee and will be on the floor of the Assembly next week.

So, we are moving very rapidly in about eight different directions--and this may be therapeutic. It may be a helpful way for things to take place, but we really do have to finally arrive at some conclusion as to what we want to do. And I think we can. I think there are people of good will in the Bay Area, both in and out of government, who are willing to arrive at some solutions so that we can move ahead in our regional affairs in some rational fashion.

AN OBVIOUS ANSWER

Let me conclude with a rather interesting incident, at least from a governmental point of view. When Governor Reagan first took office I asked for time with him to explain what we are trying to accomplish in regional government, and he very kindly granted me a substantial amount of time: I went down to his office and talked *at* him for about half an hour. He was extremely polite and listened very carefully. I told him about all of the problems we are facing in the Bay Area, all of the governmental entities that exist, all of the organizational difficulties we are having. And when I finished, his first reaction was fascinating. He said, "John, the answer is obvious. Why don't you form it all into one county?"

And that *is* an obvious answer, an impossible answer but an obvious one; it gives us food for thought. As a matter of fact, I'm thinking very seriously of trying to set up a commission to reconsider the county lines that were drawn in California in 1879 to see whether we *can* have a more rational organization of our governmental structure.

The State of California's local government is built on a county basis. Our ports are organized that way, as are many of our governmental functions. The tradition of identifying ourselves as being from Contra Costa or Alameda or Napa--or wherever--is an old one, and I understand all that is attendant upon it. Nevertheless, that tradition may well be one of the most expensive traditions we have in California, and perhaps in the 1970's we should take another look at it as well.

Part Two:

The Governmental Jobs to be Done in the Region

Background Paper:

REGIONAL ORGANIZATION IN THE
SAN FRANCISCO BAY AREA--1970

Ora Huth

Research Associate
Institute of Governmental Studies

Significant new developments that occurred after
the conference for which this paper was originally produced, appear throughout in boxed sections. References in the Appendices add more
detailed information on relevant state legislation.

There is ample evidence of continuing concern in
the San Francisco Bay Area about the quality of life and
environment of the region. While no big groundswell may
be in prospect, like the one that helped push through the
1969 legislation to continue the Bay Conservation and
Development Commission as a permanent agency, Bay Area
citizens are now actively seeking ways to influence decisions being made on a number of current environmental
issues.

For example, conservationists are protesting: the
placement of power lines in a scenic section of a regional park in Contra Costa County, the planned construction of a high dam on a creek to provide water for "intensive development" of a sparsely settled section of San
Mateo County, and an "agreement" authorizing dredging for

forty years at the mouth of a river on the Sonoma County coastline. The citizen pressure being applied at Briones, Pescadero and Jenner is part of the current wave of concern for preservation of the Bay Area environment. Recently, this has been accompanied by a demand for more effective regional solutions to such functional problems as water and air pollution, open space preservation and parks.

As we enter the 1970's, the 9-county Bay Area is continuing to experiment with a variety of approaches to regional problems, especially environmental problems. Recent state legislative activity includes the introduction of proposals to change the method of selection of several existing regional governing boards, to establish two new Bay Area single-purpose agencies, and to create a limited-function regional government. A brief summary of the establishment of regional governmental agencies in the Bay Area follows.

REGIONAL PLANNING OR STUDY GROUPS

Council of Governments

The *Association of Bay Area Governments* (ABAG) is a voluntary organization formed in 1961 under the Joint Exercise of Powers Act. ABAG membership currently includes 84 of the Bay Area's 91 cities and 8 of the 9 counties. The association conducts special studies, and provides its members with a forum for the discussion of mutual problems and a mechanism for cooperation. Since 1964, ABAG has been designated by the United States Department of Housing and Urban Development (HUD) as the agency responsible for review of applications for federal financial grants in the Bay Area. Currently it is completing an advisory comprehensive land use plan for the region, begun in 1964. The plan is to be submitted to the membership later this year. (1970)

The ABAG General Assembly is composed of one representative chosen by the governing body of each member

city and county. The 31-member executive committee includes a president and vice president, chosen by the ABAG
membership, 13 county representatives and 18 city representatives.

A proposal to transform ABAG into a regional organization responsible for several functions was introduced
but not enacted in the 1967 legislative session. In 1969
a revised measure, Assembly Bill 1846 (See Appendix II)
introduced by Assemblyman William Bagley was referred
to interim study. Under its provisions ABAG would have
been responsible for the Bay Conservation and Development
Commission's functions, as well as regional solid waste
disposal, open space, parks, airports, transportation,
air pollution control and criminal justice planning programs. The measure would have permitted financing by
bonding approved by 60 percent of the voters, a business
privilege tax, and a regional income surtax, not to exceed ½ of one percent of the state income tax.

Additional Developments through 1970

The Solano County Board of Supervisors is continuing discussion on proposed action to bring the county
into the Association of Bay Area Governments. Impetus
is likely to be added to the debate by recent ABAG Executive Committee action, disapproving a $150 thousand
Solano County federal transportation grant application
because the county is "failing to participate in areawide transportation planning either financially or by
cooperative policy body participation." To date the
county has also failed to pay required grant application review fees.

The Association of Bay Area Government's General
Assembly approved the ABAG Regional Plan 1970-1990 at
its July 30, 1970 meeting. The plan is scheduled for
review "at intervals of not less than five years...."

Transportation Planning

The *Regional Transportation Planning Committee* (RTPC) as successor to the Bay Area Transportation Study Commission (BATS), assumed responsibility for Bay Area transportation and land use planning in 1969 under a joint agreement between ABAG and the state Business and Transportation Agency. The committee is to study and submit reports on transportation planning, policies and development, plus all other matters assigned by ABAG, "or as may be needed to meet state or federal requirements." The agency is governed by a 10-member board composed of elected officials from each of the 9 Bay Area counties (appointed by ABAG), and one member appointed by the state Business and Transportation Agency. Recent ABAG Executive Committee action proposed expanding the RTPC to include 3 additional voting members representing the Division of Highways, the Bay Area Rapid Transit District, and all other operating transit agencies (to be chosen by the agencies).

Financial support comes mainly from federal funds available for a regionally directed transportation planning program. The committee has been awaiting federal funding and accepting temporary state support, due to delays in appropriation since the old HUD-BATS contract expired in September 1969.

Additional Developments through 1970

The ABAG Executive Committee action proposing expansion of the RTPC, described above, was unacceptable to the state Business and Transportation Agency. However the transit agencies and the Division of Highways were invited to appoint representatives to serve on the RTPC Technical Advisory Committee (TAC).

With these additions, TAC presently has 14 voting members and 3 ex officio members. Thus the advisory committee represents a cross section of transportation interests in the Bay Area. The committee has established an ad hoc subcommittee, the Bay Area Mass Transit Group (BAMTG), composed of representatives of Bay cont'd

Area transit agencies and the City of San Jose. This committee is looking into possibilities for a region-wide transportation development program to advise the TAC. The 3 currently vacant positions on TAC may be filled by one representative each of the new San Francisco Airport Commission, HUD, and the Urban Mass Transportation Administration.

To maintain the eligibility of the Bay Area for available state and federal grants-in-aid programs under required federal clearinghouse procedures, the Regional Transportation Planning Committee was designated by the ABAG Executive Committee as the agency to carry out the technical review of grant applications in terms of transportation planning.

The functions of the RTPC were to be assumed by the Metropolitan Transportation Commission (MTC) created by the 1970 state Legislature shortly after the agency became effective in late November, 1970. The MTC is expected to hold its first meeting early in 1971. (See page 39.)

Regional Organization

The Legislature established the *Joint Committee on Bay Area Regional Organization* (BARO) in 1967, with membership composed of senators and assemblymen from the Bay Area and Assemblyman John T. Knox (Richmond) as chairman. The committee's assignment was to study the governing of regional functions in the region and report to the 1969 Legislature.

In 1969, the committee introduced Assembly Bill 711 (See Appendix III), authored by Assemblyman Knox, following 16 months of study and hearings. No action was taken, and the proposal was sent to interim study. AB 711 would have required Bay Area citizens to vote on the creation of a "Regional Government of the Bay Area." The government would have been responsible for regional planning, especially transportation planning, Bay conservation and development, Bay-Delta water quality (sewage disposal) programs and facilities, and parks and open space planning and programs. The 36-member governing board would have been selected in nonpartisan elections, one from each of 36 districts having approximately 100,000 population. Members would have served 4-year terms and been paid $6 thousand annually, plus a per diem payment at a level set by the board. A president and vice president, selected by the board from among its members, would have appointed a 6- to 10-member executive committee.

Powers would have included review of applications for state and federal grants for regional projects, authority to make joint agreements with other governments, and planning to include elements for Bay conservation and development, regional transportation, environmental quality, parks and open space, and major public utilities.

To implement the plan the agency would have been directed to adopt the plans of BCDC, the BATS, and that of the Bay-Delta sewage disposal project. Adoption of comprehensive general plans by local governments would have been required. The agency would also have had authority to act as a clearinghouse for manpower information on job training and placement programs.

Financing authority would have included: (1) a personal income surtax levy not to exceed one percent of the state income tax; and (2) a business privilege tax imposed at the same level. These were to provide for the annual budget, with excess tax revenue to be returned to local governments. Property taxes could have been levied for debt service on bonds and for special purposes in designated areas. Service charges, certain environmental quality fees, and voter-approved general obligation and revenue bonds would have been authorized.

Unless there are new moves to continue it, the joint committee is scheduled to go out of existence at the end of the 1970 legislative session.

Additional Developments through 1970

> Legislation to extend the life of the Joint Committee on Bay Area Regional Organization--ACR 182 (Knox)--died in the Assembly Committee on Rules, and the life of the BARO committee was not extended.

Water Quality Control

The *San Francisco Bay-Delta Water Quality Control Program* was established in 1965 under the State Water Resources Control Board. The program focused primarily on technical and engineering aspects of the sewage disposal problem, and was directed to (1) study the effects of waste and drainage discharges into and affecting the Bay and the Sacramento-San Joaquin River Delta region, (2) develop a comprehensive plan for water pollution control, and (3) consider future waste water disposal needs. A report was to be made to the 1969 Legislature.

The final recommendations were not acted upon, presumably because legislators thought the plan represented only half of a system and failed to give ample recognition to the need for pursuing reclamation as an alternative solution. The 1969 Legislature continued the program only through last-minute legislation and with a minimal budget. The continuing study is advised by an 11-member San Francisco Bay Water Quality Group.

The 1969 report recommended construction of a 12-county integrated sewage treatment and disposal system over the next 50 years, at a projected cost of $2.5 billion. It suggested the project be included under a limited-function regional agency, or a separate 12-county agency constituted for this purpose. The report further recommended that the implementing agency be given the power to (1) tax, (2) issue bonds for capital costs, (3) build and operate waste water collection, treatment and disposal facilities, (4) enter into cooperative agreements with local agencies, and (5) approve local sewage disposal plans.

Additional Developments through 1970

> The Bay-Delta study report is expected to be sub-mitted to the 1971 Legislature in April. The report from the State Water Resources Control Board will in-clude a proposal for implementation of the Bay-Delta plan. Past studies indicate the proposal will suggest creation of a single-purpose agency to carry out the plan.
>
> The Bay-Delta Water Quality Control Program is continuing with work in four areas: (1) further stud-ies of the dispersion capabilities of San Francisco Bay, initiated in January 1970 and expected to continue until February 1971; (2) a study of the toxicity and biostimulation of San Francisco Bay (begun in March 1970 and likely to continue until November 1971); (3) a study of local liquid waste discharging problems in Contra Costa County (begun in January 1970); and (4) a study of liquid waste discharging problems in the ex-treme south Bay (begun in August 1970). The small Bay-Delta study staff has continued to advise the State Water Resources Control Board regarding technical as-pects of all public agency programs having an impact on the Bay. The study continues to be assisted by the ad-visory San Francisco Bay Water Quality Group.

Earthquake Hazards

A study is now in progress under the 8-member *Joint Committee on Seismic Safety*, chaired by Senator Alfred Alquist (Santa Clara County). The joint committee was created by the Legislature in 1969 to study and report in 1974 on earthquake hazards, and on methods of mini-mizing their potentially catastrophic effects through-out California, and particularly in the Bay Area. With the help of 5 advisory groups, comprising 75 members in all, the study will look into building locations, dam specifications, construction on fill and hillsides, and fault zone planning and zoning. The committee will also recommend ways of implementing its programs and propo-sals.

Additional Developments through 1970

> Successful legislation, SCR 60 and SCR 70 by Senator Alquist, appropriated funds to keep the Joint Committee on Seismic Safety alive and to continue its work.

REGIONAL GOVERNMENTAL SERVICE AND CONTROL AGENCIES

Conservation and Development

The San Francisco Bay Conservation and Development Commission (BCDC) was established by the Legislature in 1965 to operate until 1969, to make a study of the Bay, prepare a comprehensive and enforceable plan, and recommend the appropriate agency to carry out the plan. The commission was given responsibility for protecting the Bay shoreline during the study and planning period, plus power to issue or deny permits for projects involving fill or extraction of material from the Bay. In 1969 the Legislature amended the BCDC law to continue the commission indefinitely, require adherence to the Bay Plan, and provide limited jurisdiction over a 100-foot shoreline band.

The 27-member commission includes appointed federal, state, local governmental, and public representatives. The BCDC Bay Plan calls for reserving about half of the 276-mile Bay shoreline for 5 priority uses: ports, water-related industry or recreation, airports and wildlife preserves. The agency is financed by a state appropriation.

Water Quality Control

The *San Francisco Regional Water Quality Control Board* is one of 9 regional regulating agencies in California (created by the Legislature in 1949), within the State Water Quality Control Board and the State Resources Agency. The board regulates wastes discharged into public waters within its jurisdiction, which includes part

of each of the 9 Bay Area counties. The board coordi-
nates the action of private, state and local agencies,
and individuals on all matters related to abatement,
prevention and control of water pollution.

The agency is governed by a 9-member board, appointed by the governor from within the region, and having special interests related to water quality control.
It is financed by state appropriations and federal assistance grants.

In January 1970, two water quality experts were
added to each regional board and new control powers went
into effect, providing increased penalties for polluters.
These include imposition of fines up to $6 thousand per
day levied on industries, public agencies or individuals, who also are responsible for the cost of cleaning
the polluted water. The new law presumably could restrict the volume, type and concentration of wastes that
may be added to a community's sewage system.

Air Quality Control

The smog that came to the Bay Area in the 1950's
led to legislative establishment of the *Bay Area Air
Pollution Control District* in 1955 to control stationary
sources of air pollution. Six counties are currently
participating in the district. The remaining 3 counties
may activate the district in their respective areas if
their boards of supervisors decide to do so.

The 12-member governing board consists of 2 elected
officials from each county: one, a supervisor selected
by the board of supervisors, the other, a councilman or
mayor, selected by the city selection committee in the
county.

Regulations enforced in the district include (1) a
prohibition against industrial smoke, dust and certain
visible chemicals; (2) a prohibition against open dump
and backyard burning; and (3) restrictions imposed on
agricultural burning.

Revenue, within a legal limit, comes from a property tax levy. It is apportioned one-half according to
the relative value of the real estate, and one-half according to the county's population in proportion to the
population of the district as a whole.

Transit and Transportation

The Bay Area Rapid Transit District (BART) was established by the Legislature in 1957 to plan, build and
operate a rapid transit system in the Bay Area. It includes Alameda, Contra Costa and San Francisco counties.
When formed, BART included San Mateo and Marin counties,
but they withdrew in 1962.

The 12-member governing board consists of 4 members
from each county, 2 chosen by the supervisors and 2 by
the mayors serving as the city selection committee in
each county. Members may be elected local officials,
but are not required to be.

BART is financed by a voter-approved $792 million
general obligation bond issue, federal grants, bridge
tolls to pay for the under-the-Bay tube, and a recently
effective ½ cent levy on the sales tax in the district,
authorized by the 1969 Legislature.

The 72-mile, 34-station system, including under-
ground and aerial sections and a 3.6-mile underwater
tube, is scheduled for completion in 1972, with plans
for some trains to run in the East Bay in 1971.

The *Golden Gate Bridge, Highway, and Transportation
District* was established in 1928 to build and operate a
bridge over the Golden Gate. A $35 million bond issue
was approved by the voters in 1930. The district includes Mendocino and Del Norte counties, in addition to
the Bay Area counties of Marin, Napa, San Francisco and
Sonoma.

The 18-member governing board, appointed by the
supervisors of member counties includes 9 San Francisco

representatives, 3 each from Marin and Sonoma counties, and one each from Napa, Mendocino and Del Norte counties.

1969 legislation added "transportation" to the district's title, allowed establishment and operation of "any and all modes of transportation," directed the district to develop a transportation facilities plan by 1971, and changed the representation formula from "either/or" with respect to supervisors and laymen to require that, by 1972, both supervisors and lay representatives serve on the board. Since the bridge was completed in 1937, all costs, including bond redemption, have been financed by bridge tolls.

The *Alameda-Contra Costa Transit District* was established in 1956 by legislative act, and by a referendum in the two counties. The district operates a 3-county bus system that includes the principle cities in the western sections of Alameda and Contra Costa counties, and traverses San Francisco Bay to San Francisco.

The 7-member governing board includes 5 directors elected from wards, and 2 elected at large for 4 year terms. The district is financed by voter-approved general obligation bonds, revenue from fares and a levy on the property tax (for which there is no legal limit).

Parks

The *East Bay Regional Park District* was formed in 1934, as a result of the efforts of interested citizens and a vote of the electorate in the area concerned. It was established under provisions in the Public Resources Code to develop and maintain regional parks and other recreation facilities. The district includes Alameda County, with the exception of Murray Township, and Contra Costa County, with the exception of Liberty Union High School District.

The 7 members of the governing board are elected from wards for 4-year overlapping terms. The district is financed by a levy on the property tax and income from revenue-producing facilities.

Municipal Utilities

The *East Bay Municipal Utility District* was formed by the voters of 9 East Bay cities in 1923 for water supply in a 282-square mile area in Alameda and Contra Costa counties. The district added sewage treatment in 1944, following a vote of the electorate in the 6 cities affected, and began recreation activity in 1958.

The 5-member board is elected at large from among nominees from wards within the district. Financing depends on a voter-approved bond issue, rates charged to customers served by the district's programs, and a levy on the property tax (with no legal limit).

The *Valley Community Services District* was established in 1953, and activated in 1960 by voters in the district. It provides municipal services in an unincorporated area and has approximately the same powers as a sixth class city. The 5-member governing body has jurisdiction over part of the San Ramon Valley in Contra Costa County and the Old Rancho San Ramon in Alameda County. The district is financed by a levy on the property tax.

RECENT BAY AREA REGIONAL PROPOSALS AND DEBATE

The most consequential 1969 legislation for the Bay Area strengthened and made permanent the San Francisco Bay Conservation and Development Commission. Two important regional organization bills were proposed to create agencies responsible for several functions (AB 711 and AB 1846). Both were sent to interim study. Several proposals of significance to the future of the Bay Area have been introduced this year, but so far none has been enacted.

Regional Organization

Assembly Bill 2310 (Appendix IV) was introduced by Assemblyman Knox in early April 1970. The measure

proposed the establishment of an "umbrella" regional
agency in the 9-county Bay Area, and was similar in many
respects to AB 711, introduced the previous year and sent
to interim study. Significant changes in AB 2310, as introduced and compared with AB 711, modified the composition of the governing body and deleted some of the operating programs. (See Appendix I) For instance, AB 2310
had no provision for bonding or for construction of the
Bay-Delta sewage disposal facilities. It originally
called for a 40-member governing board composed of 20
members directly elected from equally apportioned districts, and 20 members who must be elected local mayors,
councilmen, or supervisors, chosen under a constituent-
unit formula. The agency would be responsible for preparation of a general regional plan, and would have the
power to force compliance and prevent action inconsistent
with the plan.

Another proposal, AB 1310 (introduced by Assemblyman
Knox in March 1970) would authorize a takeover by BCDC of
the Bay-Delta Study Program. It would continue research,
make further studies to complete the plan, and use the
1969 Bay-Delta report to the Legislature as a guide. For
these purposes, its jurisdiction would include the 9-
county Bay Area. BCDC would be required to submit a plan
to the 1973 Legislature, recommending the implementing
agency and powers needed "to finance, construct, operate
and maintain" facilities outside the responsibility of
existing waste water dischargers. Plans of agencies proposing construction of new or enlarged waste water treatment, reclamation or disposal facilities would be subject
to review and comment by BCDC. No new financial appropriations were proposed in the measure.

Additional Developments through 1970

Only slight attention was given by the Legislature
to AB 2310, and the measure died late in the session in
the Senate Committee on Governmental Organization.
Amendments introduced by the author in an effort to win
support for the bill changed the measure to provide
for: (1) a 40-member directly elected regional board;
(2) legislation establishing agency election districts

formerly in AB 2348 to be incorporated into AB 2310;
(3) deletion of provisions for a regional personal income tax; (4) completion and adoption of regional plans
in a 3-year, rather than a 5-year period; (5) deletion
of provisions requiring adoption of comprehensive local
general plans by local agencies; (6) deletion of provisions for acquisition, construction, financing, maintaining or operating any facilities, or acquiring any
real or personal property; (7) deletion of provisions
for review by the agency of street, highway and freeway
construction proposals for the region; and (8) addition
of provisions for $2,400 plus expenses as compensation
for board members.

AB 1310 died in the Senate Committee on Governmental Organization in late August 1970. On August 6 the
Bay Conservation and Development Commission voted to
oppose the bill. To explain the action the commission
chairman said BCDC had its hands full with present responsibilities and did not have time to administer the
Bay-Delta Program.

SB 1055 by Senator Richard Dolwig, the companion
bill to Assemblyman Knox's AB 1310, died in the Senate
Committee on Governmental Organization.

AB 2345 by Assemblyman Knox would have directed
cities and counties to establish regional environmental
planning councils in regions designated statewide by
the state Council on Intergovernmental Relations. The
measure declared that it is the policy of the state to
set up planning programs and require preparation and
maintenance of long-term plans to guide the conservation and development of resources of the region. The
regional resources plan was described as being useful
as a guide for state and local planning and policy and
for providing the state with information about the region's problems and priorities.

The planning councils, to have been set up by
January 1, 1971, could have been established by a joint

cont'd

powers agreement, or under legislation providing for
regional planning districts, area planning commissions,
special planning districts, or "any agency established
by legislative act to perform general environmental and
resources planning within any of the regions of the
state." There was to be only one environmental quality
planning council in each region.

An interim environmental quality plan was to be
adopted by July 1, 1972 for general waste disposal for
air, land and water; and plans were also to be adopted
for open space, transportation, regional land use and
conservation. If an interim plan was not adopted by
July 1, 1972, the state Council on Intergovernmental
Relations could adopt a plan for the region to be effective until the regional council adopted one of its
own. The councils would have been designated as the
agencies to review state and federal grant applications. Provisions to finance the regional councils'
planning program were eliminated by amendments while
the bill was being considered in the Assembly Committee
on Natural Resources and Conservation.

To the extent reasonable, the planning would have
been required to contain advisory statements and estimates of: (1) an intermediate program of specific public actions; (2) the amounts, types, characteristics
and general locations of land to be acquired by public
agencies and the expected impact of the acquisition on
public facilities and people; (3) development controls
and additional personnel required; (4) the costs of acquisitions, development, and enforcement of development
controls and the sources of public funds available; (5)
the social and economic consequences of the intermediate program of public actions including the impact on
population distribution by characteristics and income,
employment and economic condition; and (6) the assumptions on which the intermediate program is based as it
relates to private development and future development
for public use by public agencies. (These provisions

cont'd

were also included in AB 711 and AB 2310. See Appendix
I.) The open space plan would have been required to be
consistent with and implement the state's open space
policy.

AB 2345 was supported in principle by the state
Council on Intergovernmental Relations and the Association of Bay Area Governments. The measure passed in
the Assembly and on August 21, on a motion by Senator
Lewis Sherman (Oakland), it was sent to the Senate in-
active file where it died. The author said later that
he was forced to let the bill die because it contained
interlocking provisions with the Metropolitan Transportation Commission legislation, which might have allowed
ABAG to establish itself as a multi-functional regional
government with authority to take over the transportation commission and transportation planning for the
region.

Conservation and Development

AB 1200, also introduced in March by Assemblyman
Knox, would require BCDC to formulate and recommend to
the 1971 Legislature a procedure for direct election of
the members of the commission. The legislative recommendation would include the number of members, method
of election, and the electoral areas or districts within
the 9-county Bay Area.

Additional Developments through 1970

AB 1200 was amended by the author on June 24,
1970 to delete provisions requiring BCDC to recommend
procedures for direct election of commission members
and provide instead for extension of the date when the
commission must file a resolution fixing water-related
priority land uses within the Bay's shoreline band.
This changes the date from November 10, 1970, to December 1, 1971. The measure was passed and signed by
the governor on September 14.

cont'd

During voting in the Senate on sections of the state budget, the Senate by an overwhelming voice vote rejected a proposal by a Los Angeles County senator to delete all funds for BCDC. The $265 thousand appropriation remained in the budget.

Another successful bill was AB 1771 by Assemblyman John Dunlap, which allows BCDC commissioners to send proxy members with full voting rights to commission meetings. The alternates must be confirmed by the body that appointed the commissioners. This measure was signed by the governor on September 15.

Also enacted was AB 1971 by Assemblyman John Vasconcellos, extending BCDC jurisdiction to portions of 7 rivers and creeks flowing into the Bay. This gives BCDC permit authority over dredging and filling operations on the Napa and Petaluma rivers, the Plummer, Coyote, Redwood, Tolay and Sonoma creeks. The measure was signed by the governor on September 16.

SB 1110 by Senator John McCarthy had provisions similar to AB 1971. The McCarthy measure died in the Senate Committee on Governmental Organization.

SJR 35 by Senator Milton Marks, requesting all federal agencies to submit plans for Bay shoreline development to BCDC, was adopted by the Legislature and filed with the secretary of state on August 19.

A related measure, SR 225, also by Senator Marks, was adopted by the Senate on June 22. The resolution urged the navy to comply with Bay fill and development guidelines of BCDC despite its not being legally bound to do so.

Water Quality

Additional Developments through 1970

SB 277 by Senator John Nejedly described various legislative findings and declarations regarding maintenance of water quality in the Bay-Delta system in connection with state and federal water projects. The measure died in the Senate Committee on Water Resources.

SB 187 by Senator Nejedly would have prohibited the state Department of Water Resources from spending money to build the Peripheral Canal around the Sacramento-San Joaquin Delta unless the project specifically had legislative approval. The measure died in the Senate Committee on Water Resources.

SB 86 by Senator Nejedly would have banned oil and gas exploration and drilling in the tidal and submerged lands of San Francisco Bay and the Delta. The measure died in the Senate Finance Committee.

AB 684 by Assemblyman William Bagley specifies that until March 1, 1975, all state-owned tidal or submerged lands in San Mateo, San Francisco, Marin, Sonoma, Napa, Alameda, Santa Clara and Del Norte counties, and in Solano and Contra Costa counties (except the tidal and submerged lands east of the Carquinez Bridges) may not be leased by the State Lands Commission for oil and gas purposes, except under certain conditions. The same provisions apply to the taking of cores or other samples by drilling operations. The measure was signed by the governor on September 17, 1970.

Open Space

SB 1400 introduced by Senator Marks in early April, would create the *San Francisco Bay Open Space Commission* to plan for preservation of undeveloped land within the jurisdiction of the 9 Bay Area counties. The proposal,

patterned after successful 1969 legislation establishing
BCDC on a permanent basis, is based on the report of
the People for Open Space Project Committee, chaired by
T.J. Kent, Jr. of Berkeley. The report documented the
critical need for the preservation of open space in the
Bay Area and proposed a plan to save this scenic
resource.

Under the proposed measure open space in the Bay
Area would be analyzed, planned, preserved, developed
and regulated as a unit. There would be provisions for
an inventory and analysis of areas to be designated for
recreation, agriculture, forestry, watersheds, wildlife
conservation, climate control, urban area and compact
development. The agency would study land needs projected to the year 1990, study the economic means available for preservation and development of regional open
space, and prepare an enforceable regional open space
plan to be submitted to the Legislature in 1972. The
27-member commission would include appointed representatives of federal, state and local government agencies,
and the public. It would go out of existence after the
1972 legislative session. The commission would have
permit authority over any construction initiated after
January 1, 1970 within prescribed open space areas. An
unspecified sum would be appropriated for commission
expenditures during 1970-1971.

Additional Developments through 1970

Senator Marks accepted a number of amendments to
SB 1400, hoping to gain legislative approval. Significant amendments directed the open space commission
to use the ABAG Regional Plan's open space element as
a guide, and to submit its study findings to ABAG for
review and comments. Amendments also stipulated that
the commission could not recommend a new single-purpose
agency to implement its plans, and provided for expand-
ed membership to make the agency a 31-member commission.
Massive citizen support for this measure, which would
have established the commission for a 2-year period at
a cost of $250 thousand did not get it out of the
Senate Finance Committee. With 12 of the 13 committee

cont'd

members present, the vote on the bill brought only 6 favorable votes, whereas 7 were needed. The author was unable to bring the bill to another vote and it died in committee.

One amendment to SB 1400 changed its funding from the State General Fund to the California Environmental Protection Program Fund to be established by SB 262. This measure, also by Senator Marks, passed and was signed by the governor August 21. It makes possible the purchase of personalized license plates for an additional $35 fee, with proceeds to go to the environmental fund. It is expected to bring in approximately $2.2 million annually.

Transportation

A proposal introduced in January, AB 363 by Assemblyman John Foran, to establish a Metropolitan Transportation Commission (MTC) in the 9-county Bay Area is similar to the Metropolitan Transportation Authority measure he introduced in 1969. The MTC would assume the planning and related responsibilities of the Bay Area Transportation Study Commission and its successor, the Regional Transportation Planning Committee. The MTC would be given responsibility for adopting a transportation plan for the region and for operation, construction or modification of highways, transbay bridges, mass transit facilities and the interfacing of transportation in the Bay Area.

The BATS Plan would be considered, as well as the effect of the transportation plan on housing, employment, recreation, environmental quality, local and regional land use policies, the "economically deprived," and other related economic and social factors. The MTC would be required to indicate regional transportation priorities 10 years in advance, would prepare a financial plan, and would be responsible for review of applications for federal assistance grants to determine the consistency of the project with the regional transportation plans. The role of harbors and airports would be studied, and a report would be made to the 1973 Legislature.

Financing would come mainly from federal and state support expected to be available for transportation planning, plus contributions from local agencies. The commission and the state Business and Transportation Agency would negotiate contracts or agreements with appropriate agencies for contributions of funds and services.

The 19-member commission would be an appointed board representing the 9 counties in the Bay Area, with one representative each from ABAG, BCDC, the state Business and Transportation Agency, the federal Department of Transportation and HUD. Representatives of the last 3 agencies would be nonvoting.

The MTC would be required to join a multifunctional regional government one year after such an agency is organized.

A proposal presumably designed to change the BART governing board, AB 725 by Assemblyman Carlos Bee, was killed in March in the Assembly Committee on Local Government. It would have required members of transit district boards, or of boards and commissions set up under a joint powers agreement, to be elected public officials.

Additional Developments through 1970

AB 363 moved easily through the Legislature and was signed by the governor on September 14. The most important amendments (1) clarified provisions allowing the State Highway Commission to deviate from the "schedule" and "priorities" of the MTC transportation plan; (2) directed the commission to report to the Legislature by January 1973 rather than by January 1972; (3) established the Bay Area Rapid Transit District as the operator of the BART system; and (4) provided that the California Toll Bridge Authority be

cont'd

responsible for bridge planning begun after 1965 and
before the MTC effective date. The author of the legislation stated recently that "Washington is very much
in favor of the change," which takes transportation
planning away from ABAG and its Regional Transportation
Planning Committee and gives it to the MTC, because
"ABAG had no teeth, no power to make anyone listen to
it...."

In March AB 725 appeared to be dead in the Assembly Committee on Local Government. It survived and
emerged with new provisions and a new author, Assemblyman Ken MacDonald. As amended, the bill provides
that officers of joint powers agencies, acting as audi-
tors or controllers for the agency and also for the
county, should follow the uniform accounting procedures prescribed by the state controller. This measure
was signed by the governor on July 13.

AB 647 by Assemblyman Don Mulford, authorizing the
Bay Area Rapid Transit District to establish its own
security force, passed and was signed by the governor
on September 18. A similar measure, SB 48 by Senator
John Nejedly was also successful and was signed by the
governor on September 18.

Another BART bill, AB 1984, by Assemblyman John
Foran was successful and signed by the governor on September 14. It allows BART to pledge income from property taxes to pay for revenue bonds or equipment trust
certificates.

ACR 40, also by Assemblyman Foran, was adopted in
both the Assembly and the Senate and requests the state
in cooperation with BART and other agencies to study
the feasibility of extending the BART system to Sacramento.

AB 2459 by Assemblyman Frank Belotti adds one member of the Sonoma County Board of Supervisors to the

Golden Gate Bridge, Highway and Transportation District board. It passed and was signed by the governor on September 14.

Another successful bill, SB 793 by Senator Alfred Alquist, limits the property taxation power of the Santa Clara County Transit District to purposes of bond redemption. Creation of the district was an issue on the ballot in Santa Clara County in November. The bill was approved by the governor on August 12, but then failed in the November general election.

SB 708 by Senator Lewis Sherman proposed that a Bay Bridge commuters' fund be established and allocated to the Alameda-Contra Costa Transit District in order to provide free commuter transportation. Early in the session it was assigned to the Senate Committee on Transportation, where it died.

Several bills were concerned with a southern crossing over San Francisco Bay:

ACR 26 by Assemblyman Robert Crown passed the Assembly and the Senate. It requests the California Toll Bridge Authority to reconsider its earlier decision to construct a southern crossing.

SB 331 by Senator Alquist, a proposal to delay construction of a new bridge for automobiles from the East Bay to San Francisco until at least 1972, died in the Assembly Transportation Committee. It would have provided for a joint legislative committee study of the impact on the environment and possible competitive damage to BART.

ACR 97 by Assemblyman Carl Britschgi and SCR 24 by Senator Richard Dolwig to create a Joint Committee on the Southern Crossing died in the Assembly Committee on Rules.

cont'd

ACR 182 by Assemblyman John Knox would have extended the life of the Joint Committee on Bay Area Regional Organization and ordered the committee to study
the proposed southern crossing. The measure died in
the Assembly Committee on Rules.

Air Quality

AB 479, introduced in February by Assemblyman Knox,
would require Napa, Solano and Sonoma counties to join
the Bay Area Air Pollution Control District in 1971.
Recent amendments would allow the state Air Resources
Board to approve transfer of part of a county to another
air pollution control district, and to provide for establishment of "enforcement zones" and "taxing zones" within
the district.

AB 641, introduced by Assemblyman Willie Brown, Jr.
in February, would change the Bay Area Air Pollution
Control District governing board from an appointive to
an elective body beginning January 1, 1973. The membership would be elected at large from each participating
county, for 2-year terms, with one member for each 200
thousand of county population. Each member would be
required to run for a particular seat on the board.

Additional Developments through 1970

AB 479 was signed by the governor on September 16.

AB 641 died in the Assembly Committee on Local
Government.

AB 16 by Assemblyman William Ketchum, prohibiting
local and regional authorities from completely banning
all agricultural burning, was signed by the governor
on September 20.

AB 108 by Assemblyman Earle Crandall, repealing
the civil penalty provisions of the Bay Area Air Pollution Control Law and authorizing a penalty (of not less

cont'd

than $200 nor more than $6000 per day in which viola-
tions of any air pollution abatement orders occur) died
in the Assembly Committee on Transportation.

AB 215 by Assemblyman John Vasconcellos, requiring
the Bay Area Air Pollution Control District to publish
notices of hearings to consider a variance from established antipollution requirements, was signed by the
governor on September 16.

AB 357 by Assemblyman John Burton, a measure to
allow the Bay Area Air Pollution Control District to
charge industry for smog control inspections, died in
the Senate Committee on Health and Welfare.

AB 387 by Assemblyman Burton, requiring the BAAPCD
to set odor emission standards, was signed by the governor September 16.

AB 477 by Assemblyman John Knox, a measure to
allow the BAAPCD to register and charge fees against
equipment creating air pollution, died in the Senate
Committee on Health and Welfare.

AB 478 by Assemblyman Knox, increasing the BAAPCD
levy on the property tax from 1.3 cents to 2 cents for
support of the district in 1971-72 and 1972-73, was
signed by the governor September 17.

AB 642 by Assemblyman Willie Brown, Jr., changing
the composition of the membership of the Bay Area Air
Pollution Control Advisory Council as of January 1,
1971, was signed by the governor August 14.

ACR 41 by Assemblyman Burton, relating to a legis-
lative study of the administration of the Bay Area Air
Pollution Control Law, died in the Senate Committee on
Rules.

SB 62 by Senator John Nejedly, requiring the
BAAPCD Legal Counsel to be responsible to and report

cont'd

directly to the district board, died in the Senate Committee on Local Government.

SB 77 by Senator Tom Carrell, allowing the BAAPCD, certain county air pollution control districts and regional air pollution control districts to require crankcase and exhaust emission devices on 1955 to 1965 model automobiles, was signed by the governor on September 14. The exhaust emission control devices may not be required until one year after the State Air Resources Board determines such devices are available for installation.

Representative Don Edwards introduced a bill in Congress August 5 requiring all federally subsidized antismog agencies to make public the sources of all commercial and industrial pollution. The legislation is the outgrowth of a lawsuit initiated in February against the BAAPCD by 3 University of Santa Clara law students. They lost the lawsuit, but the district did voluntarily release the names of the major Bay Area polluters. Rep. Edwards said this was "a token gesture" because the names of polluters operating under variance permits from the district were not included. The legislation would apply to all of California's 9 air pollution control agencies receiving federal grants. They would be required to submit periodic reports to the Department of Health, Education and Welfare (HEW) for publication in the *Federal Register*.

Parks

Additional Developments through 1970

AB 2077 by Assemblyman Knox, authorizing an increase in the maximum tax rate the regional parks can impose (from 5 cents to 10 cents per $100 of assessed value of real property within the park district), was signed by the governor August 10. It thus allows the East Bay Regional Park to raise its tax rate.

cont'd

> SB 980 by Senator Nicholas Petris, authorizing regional park districts to plan, adopt, improve, and maintain trails, natural areas, and ecological and open space preserves, and authorizing the board to submit tax overrides to voters to finance them, was signed by the governor on September 8.

Earthquake Hazards

Additional Developments through 1970

> SCR 60 and SCR 70 by Senator Alfred Alquist appropriated $22,790 and $10,667, respectively, to keep the Joint Committee on Seismic Safety alive and to continue its work. SCR 60 and SCR 70 were adopted by the Senate and Assembly and filed with the secretary of state on September 23 and May 27, respectively.

1970 STATEWIDE LEGISLATION OF REGIONAL SIGNIFICANCE: COASTAL CONSERVATION AND DEVELOPMENT

Statewide proposals likely to affect development and conservation along the Bay Area coastline were introduced in February 1970 in both the Assembly and the Senate. AB 640, by Assemblyman George Milias of Gilroy, would create a California Coastal Conservation and Development Commission and 5 regional commissions. They would be responsible for preparing a comprehensive plan for California's coastal zone, defined as that portion of the coastline between Oregon and Mexico extending one mile inland and 3 miles seaward. Any area under BCDC's jurisdiction would be excluded. The 31-member state commission and the 5 regional commissions would include representatives of federal, state and local government agencies, as well as marine commercial and development interests, marine scientific interests and the public. The commissions would be required to report to the 1973 Legislature, and would go out of existence at the end of that session. No funds are provided in the Assembly proposal.

AB 818 and a companion bill, AB 1247, introduced by Assemblyman John Briggs, would establish a state power plant authority to review and approve sites for the location of nuclear, coal, oil or gas power generating plants and provide for a 20-year power plant development plan to be carried out by the state Resources Agency.

SB 371, by Senator John Nejedly, would create a Seacoast Conservation and Development Commission based in San Diego, similar to the commission proposed in AB 640, but establishing 6 regional commissions. The commissions would be required to report annually to the Legislature, and within 2 years would be required to prepare and adopt a plan for the coastline. Neither appropriations nor termination for the commissions would be provided in the bill.

In March, Senator Nejedly introduced SB 687, which would create an interregional conservation district to include the entire state. It would be responsible for providing for the construction, operation and maintenance of new major water resources and conservation projects for the good of the state as a whole.

Additional Developments through 1970

Three similar coastal protection bills were merged into one proposal, AB 2131, in June in an effort to win legislative approval: AB 640 by Assemblyman Milias, AB 730 by Assemblyman Alan Sieroty, and AB 2131 by Assemblyman Pete Wilson. The measures for coastline conservation and development were similar but differed in the distance inland to be controlled under statewide plans by zoning authorities. AB 2131, the Wilson bill, would have called for plan development at the local level with local agencies producing the plans for the areas under their jurisdiction.

AB 640 and AB 730 died in the Assembly Committee on Natural Resources. The Wilson bill passed the Assembly but was killed in the Senate in an unusual way: it was scheduled for a hearing in the Senate Committee

cont'd

on Governmental Organization August 20th, the last possible date for consideration, but died when Senate
President pro tem Jack Schrade abruptly canceled a
scheduled hearing on the bill. Senator Schrade explained that he canceled the meeting because he wanted
all senators on the Senate floor to vote on the large
number of bills requiring action by the deadline of
August 21.

SB 371 by Senator Nejedly died in the Senate Committee on Governmental Organization after considerable
opposition from utility companies.

SB 687 also by Senator Nejedly, died in the Senate
Committee on Rules.

AB 818 by Assemblyman John Briggs, was amended
considerably to make the measure more acceptable to
conservationists, local agencies and other opponents.
Successful amendments provided that local zoning bodies
would not be superseded by the proposed agency. Conservation spokesmen said the bill was not strong enough
to prevent ecological damage due to power plant siting.
The measure died in the Senate Committee on Rules.

AB 1247 introduced by Assemblyman Briggs as a companion bill to AB 818, requires the state Resources
Agency, in cooperation with affected public utilities
and the Public Utilities Commission, to draw up a 20-
year plan for the location of new electric power plants
and additions to old plants with recommendations on
environmental considerations. The plan is to be submitted to the Legislature by the fifth legislative day
of the 1973 session.

AB 1247 was signed by the governor on September
19.

AB 1942 by Assemblyman Briggs directs the state
Resources Agency to conduct research and studies concerning the siting of power plants. It appropriates

cont'd

$150 thousand from the California Environmental Protection Program Fund and assigns it to the state Resources Agency in order to support the bill's provisions. AB 1942 was signed by the governor on September 17. The Environmental Protection Program Fund was created by SB 262 (Marks) and approved by the governor on August 21.

AB 2463 by Assemblyman Sieroty would have financed a program of beach and coastline preservation by providing state bond funds to be voted on in the election of November 1970. The measure died in the Assembly Committee on Ways and Means.

SB 1082 by Senator Robert Lagomarsino with provisions identical to AB 2131 (Wilson) died in the Senate Committee on Rules.

SB 1354 by Senator Anthony Beilenson, creating a state coastline conservation and development commission, died in the Senate Committee on Insurance and Financial Institutions.

SB 1321 by Senator Clair Burgener provides that when the Legislature revokes, amends or modifies a grant of tidelands, there is to be no impairment of the rights or obligations of those who enter into leases or contracts with the grantee. The measure was approved by the governor on September 19.

AB 493 by Assemblyman John Dunlap requires subdividers of coastal lands to provide for public access to ocean beaches and tidelands from highways, unless reasonable access is otherwise available. The measure was signed by the governor on September 17.

NEW FEDERAL GRANT REVIEW REQUIREMENTS

Although there have been cutbacks in a number of federal programs, the Bay Area is continuing to receive federal financial assistance for state, regional and local qualifying projects and federal development programs. There are 49 different federal assistance programs offered by 8 federal departments or offices available in the region, and these are covered by requirements outlined in the Bureau of the Budget Circular A-95, which became effective in October 1969.

Since 1962, ABAG has been designated by the Department of Housing and Urban Development (HUD) as the review agency for federal grant-in-aid programs. Major changes were made in grant requirements in 1966 by Section 204 of the Model Cities and Metropolitan Development Act and Bureau of the Budget Circular A-80.

Further modifications were included in Section 201, Title IV, of the Intergovernmental Cooperation Act of 1968. The significant new areawide planning requirements in the 1968 act were outlined in Bureau of the Budget Circular A-95. These describe the process, agencies affected, and substantive requirements that, along with other directives, require ABAG to take into account all pertinent findings and decisions by Bay Area special planning and regulatory agencies and local governments.

Applications for federal assistance are to be reviewed on the basis of the following considerations listed in Sections 401 and 402 of the 1968 act: land use, conservation and natural resources, balanced transportation, outdoor recreation and open space, protection of special areas, planned community facilities, good design standards, viewpoints of other governmental agencies, relationship to local planning, and the fact that the federal government will give preferential consideration to cities and counties over special districts.

Circular A-95 also lists guidelines for implementing the 1968 act. They add programs for review purposes; establish new application requirements; describe the procedure for bringing the state into the review process; and emphasize the coordination and cooperation required for the grant program. The procedures direct ABAG to cooperate with the state clearinghouse for review purposes (the state Office of Intergovernmental Management) located in the lieutenant governor's office and to notify all interested agencies of each pending application, before formal application to the federal government and review by ABAG. Newly listed as subject to review are activities concerned with planning for new communities, community renewal, urban mass transportation, solid waste disposal, air pollution control, comprehensive areawide health needs, economic development and technical assistance, and community action programs. The Circular also places review of all federal development projects without exception, and acquisition, disposal, and use of federal lands under the regional clearinghouse requirements. Federal projects are reviewed to determine their consistency with other regional plans, using the same criteria that apply to federal grant review.

HUD Circular MD 6410, dated July 1969, notified ABAG of new requirements for Bay Area programs qualifying for water and sewer assistance grants. There are further descriptions in HUD Circular MD 6415.1,2, and 3, dated August 1969. Requirements for continuing to qualify as the review agency are spelled out for ABAG, along with new provisions for including representatives of the poor and of minority groups on the policy-making body reviewing applications for water and sewer grant assistance. The Bureau of the Budget accepted ABAG as the review agency pending certification, on the basis of the ABAG areawide planning; stated regional goals; and the preliminary comprehensive general plan. The original certification date, October 1, 1969, was postponed to October 1, 1970. Presumably it will depend upon ABAG fulfillment of several HUD planning requirements, one of which is completion and adoption of the regional plan.

In addition, there is a statement that

> specific provision shall be made to include persons from disadvantaged low-income and minority groups where the

selection arrangement would not result
in their inclusion on the policy-making
body. In those instances where such
provision for the inclusion of persons
from disadvantaged low-income and minority groups on the policy-making body
cannot be fulfilled at the time of certification, specific provision must be
made to include such persons prior to
recertification. At the end of the
first 180 days of the certification
period, documentation must be submitted
to the HUD Regional Office indicating
action taken to accomplish such representation. (HUD Circular MD 6415.1,
August 28, 1969, pages 7 and 8)

Another HUD directive, Circular MD 60441, Chapter 1,
Section 3, Citizen Participation, requires applicants
for assistance grants to ensure

effective citizen participation...
which will directly involve residents
of the planning area...in the planning
process.... The citizen participation
mechanism should have clear and direct
access to the decision-making process
of the grant recipient.... The views
of low-income and minority groups must
be explicitly solicited and recognized
through whatever mechanism the grant
recipient designates to fulfill the
citizen participation requirement.

Additional Developments through 1970

A major revision of Bureau of the Budget Circular
A-95, currently underway, is planned for completion
early in 1971. According to advance reports, the revision will not change the process but will include directives requiring review by the regional clearinghouse
(ABAG) for 93 federal grant programs. The added review

cont'd

responsibilities will probably include programs for new public housing, urban renewal, HUD-supported college housing and Model Cities supplementary grants.

Approval of the ABAG Regional Plan 1970-1990 in July 1970 allows ABAG to continue to function as the clearinghouse for federal grant applications for Bay Area open space and water and sewers. The October 1, 1970 certification date was extended until October 1, 1971 by a rider attached to the Emergency Community Facilities Act of 1970 by Congressman Wright Patman. ABAG is required to include a functional water and sewer element in the ABAG Regional Plan by the new re-certification date in 1971.

The requirement to provide for representation of disadvantaged low-income and minority groups in HUD Circular MD 6415.1 dated August 28, 1969, was changed by the July 31, 1970 HUD Circular MPD 6415.1A. The latter supersedes all prior provisions, guides and procedures for HUD areawide planning requirements covering planning jurisdictions, organizations and comprehensive planning for the Water and Sewer Facilities Grant Program and the Open Space Land Program. Pages 6 and 7 of the circular cover requirements for the policy body composition. These direct that "Except where specifically prohibited" by state law:

> (1) *Area Representation.* Membership in the APO (Area Planning Organization) should include all units of general local government within the APJ (Area Planning Jurisdiction).
>
> (2) *Representation on Policy Body.*
>
> > (a) *Representation of Local Government.* At least two-thirds of the voting membership of the policy-making body of an APO

cont'd

shall be composed of or responsible to the elected officials
of a unit or units of general
local government within the
planning jurisdiction. Such
persons include mayors, city or
county managers, city councilmen, or others of similar rank
and breadth of responsibility.

(b) *Representation of Citizen
Interest.* The balance of the
full voting membership of the APO
policy-making body should be
composed of persons representing
major areawide citizen interests.
Citizen interest representatives
should typically be persons with
special knowledge or authority
to speak for the major areawide
citizen interest they represent.
Examples of such representatives
are *persons representing low-
income and minority groups*, and
persons having special famil-
iarity with community issues
such as housing, education, economic development, transportation, health, recreation, and
environmental problems.

(c) *Executive Committees.* Where
there is an executive committee
or similar group which performs
decision-making functions for
the policy-making body, its composition should reflect a representational balance comparable
to that of the policy-making
body. [Emphasis added]

cont'd

Presumably ABAG is currently proceeding under the assumption that these new requirements specify that whatever "state law sets forth" will determine the method of selection of representatives serving on the governing body of the review agency. Provisions in the Government Code (Chapter 5. Article 1. Section 6506) covering joint exercise of powers agreements set California policy in this regard. The pertinent section of the law reads:

> 6506. The agency or entity provided by the agreement to administer or execute the agreement may be one or more of the parties to the agreement or a commission or board constituted pursuant to the agreement or a person, firm or corporation designated in the agreement. One or more of the parties may agree to provide all or a portion of the services to the other parties in the manner provided in the agreement. The parties may provide for the mutual exchange of services without payment of any consideration other than such services. (Added by Stats. 1949, Ch. 84; amended by Stats. 1957, Ch. 330, and by Stats. 1963, Ch. 990.)

It should be noted the Joint Exercise of Powers Act does not require the policy-making body established by the agreement to be composed of signatories and gives the parties to the agreement authority to decide who shall serve and the method of selection.

Page 16 of HUD Circular MPD 6415.1A also outlines directives for public official and citizen participation. These require ABAG to:

> Secure wide and meaningful public official and citizen participation in both

56

cont'd

the comprehensive and functional planning
process. Public officials representing
the public agencies responsible for the
various functional components considered
in the comprehensive planning process
should be included in such participa-
tory groups. In order to ensure that
the planning process is responsive to
the objectives and values of citizens
affected, there should be an organizational structure, mechanism, or other
formalized process which will *directly
involve residents of the APJ, including low-income and minority groups,*
and public officials responsible for
various functional elements dealt with
in the planning process. Participants
should be provided with full information to enable them to make knowledgeable reactions and suggestions. Participation should be solicited and ob-
tained in all major phases of the process prior to the period when decisions are formalized or adopted and,
specifically, during preparation of
(1) the overall program design, (2)
goals and objectives, and (3) major
proposals, including those contained
in the functional planning and pro-
gramming.

Existing citizen participation organization should be used whenever possible. At the areawide level, representatives should be solicited from
local citizen participation organizational structures, *including locally
recognized organizations created
through Federal programs, e.g., Model
Cities, Workable Program, Urban Renewal
Program project advisory committees,
etc.* [Emphasis added]

cont'd

These provisions require ABAG to submit documentation to HUD at the end of the first 180 days following
October 1, 1970 (about April 1, 1971), indicating the
action taken to develop the required operable citizen
participation mechanism as specified above, although
certification has been postponed. In relation to this,
a citizen participation report prepared by a consultant to ABAG in the summer of 1970, is under consideration in the ABAG Regional Planning Committee. At this
writing ABAG staff has said that the report is not in
a form that can be made available to the public. However, several citizens' groups have indicated an interest in its recommendations. Among these are the
Spanish-Speaking Unity Council, the East Oakland Fruit-
vale Planning Council, and the League of Women Voters
of the Bay Area.

To fulfill the responsibility to review and comment on federal projects and on the acquisition, disposal and use of federal lands (spelled out in Bureau
of the Budget Circular A-95 and recent federal management procurement regulations issued by the General Services Administration), ABAG has declared an interest
in the projects of the U.S. Army Corps of Engineers,
U.S. Coast Guard and the Federal Aviation Administration, as well as the recently announced future disposal
of sections of Camp Parks.

Impact on the environment is an important consideration in the review of federal projects. Pertinent
guidelines are provided in the environmental impact
statement in the Environmental Quality Act of 1969 (PL
91-190). The act also established the Federal Environmental Quality Council, presently chaired by Russell
Train. The council conveyed to the Office of Management and Budget (formerly the Bureau of the Budget) its
views on the directives in A-95 (particularly the environmental aspects). The council advised the office
to direct the regional clearinghouse (ABAG) to measure
the environmental impact of federal projects "in a
flexible manner." Additional guidelines concerning

cont'd

environmental impact appeared in Russell Train's statement published in the *Federal Register* of May 12, 1969.

The U.S. Army Corps of Engineers is engaged in two
navigational study projects jointly costing $7.5 mil-
lion and looking into questions of environmental
impact: the "in depth" study of San Francisco Bay and
the "triple S" study of San Francisco, Suisun and San
Pablo Bays.

On July 13, 1970 the Regional Transportation Planning Committee was authorized by the ABAG Executive
Committee to undertake the technical transportation
planning review on behalf of ABAG. Such a review is
required in the Bureau of Public Roads (BPR) Inter-
agency Memo 50-2-65, because the Bay Area is currently
classified as a Class B area by the BPR with regard to
California applications for federal highway funds. It
is anticipated that technical review will no longer be
required when the transportation plan becomes part of
the regional comprehensive plan and a Class A classi-
fication is established. This review assigned to the
RTPC covers certain highway development projects previously reviewed by ABAG in its capacity as the areawide clearinghouse.

FUTURE ORGANIZATION TO SOLVE BAY AREA
REGIONAL PROBLEMS

Looking ahead to the organizational mechanisms
likely to be governing the Bay Area 10 years hence can
be a fascinating mental exercise. What will the region
be like in the 1980's? Certainly by then solutions
will have been found for the southern crossing dilemma,
for the interfacing of BART with feeder lines, and for
completion of the San Francisco Davis Street station,
by whatever agency is handling transportation planning
in the 1970's. But how will some of the other knotty
regional problems be resolved: (1) The one-man-one-vote

question; (2) representation of minority groups; (3) the problem of federal initiative, which begins programs, then cuts them back; (4) the social problems of jobs, housing, education, health services, racial conflict, law enforcement and administration of justice; and (5) the environmental problems of open space, air quality, water quality, sewage and solid waste disposal?

Some observers predict that acceptable local and regional solutions will not be found, and that the state and federal governments will be responsible for more and more programs concerned with the quality of life and the environment. How long a list of federal programs will require regional review in 1980?

A proposal introduced recently in the U.S. Senate by Senator Henry M. Jackson of Washington is one of many indications as to what the future may have in store. As chairman of the Senate Interior Committee, Senator Jackson noted the "total zoning anarchy at the local level" and introduced a bill to establish a National Land Act because this is "absolutely essential" to the preservation of our environment. He said land use is directly related to air and water pollution. With some "80,000 political subdivisions responsible for zoning" in the country, Senator Jackson says planning is either nonexistent or mired in confusion and working at cross purposes. As introduced, the national act would require each state to inventory its land resources and pass legislation for statewide zoning.

Additional Developments through 1970

In August 1970 the ABAG Executive Committee approved a recommendation that ABAG apply for a $120 thousand HUD demonstration grant to pay the full cost of conducting a one-year study of the feasibility of establishing a regional development agency to implement the recently approved "Regional Plan 1970-1990." The proposal for the new agency was prepared by Eckbo, Dean, Austin & Williams and Volt Information Sciences. The study will attempt to find ways to coordinate effort on

cont'd

the local and regional levels to combat the "enormous inefficiency, sprawl, and chaotic land use patterns" that take place when the private developer makes the decisions on when and where development should take place. In applying for the grant ABAG stated "...the legal approaches to planning development (through zoning and subdivision standards)" have led to "...mediocrity and dull uniformity."

It is proposed to look into the possibilities for (1) a new regional agency to supplement existing governmental units with funding that would not become a public burden; (2) development of legislative and economic proposals for the agency; and (3) setting up a pilot program to solve problems in Santa Clara and Sonoma counties.

The San Francisco Planning and Urban Renewal Association (SPUR) has begun an 18-month solid waste study financed by a $50 thousand Ford Foundation grant. The study will be especially concerned with institutional constraints on regional solid waste disposal programs. SPUR has contracted with Planning Research Associates to do the study, which will be directed by Frank Stead, environmental quality specialist.

Assemblyman John Knox, commenting on the failure of the Legislature to pass AB 2310, said he expects to reintroduce the measure in 1971 and that he will include the provision for a 40-member directly elected regional government board and will not include a provision for a referendum to establish the agency.

ABAG is currently discussing the possibilities for regional organization legislation in 1971, including the introduction of a bill similar to AB 2345 (Knox, 1970). The measure, as last amended before it died, approximates the 1969 "home rule" bill, AB 1846. (See Appendix II, page 225.)

THE GOVERNMENTAL JOBS TO BE DONE IN THE REGION

Moderator: Stanley E. McCaffrey, *President, Bay Area Council*

Panel: Frank M. Stead, *Consultant in Environmental Management*

Joseph E. Bodovitz, *Executive Director, San Francisco Bay Conservation and Development Commission*

John C. Beckett, *Government Relations Manager, Hewlett-Packard Co.; former Com., Bay Area Transportation Study Commission (BATS)*

John J. Miller, *Assemblyman, Berkeley; Chairman, Subcommittee on Welfare Reorganization; and Vice Chairman, Committee on Criminal Procedure*

Stanley E. McCaffrey

The first of the seven assumptions set forth by Eugene Lee was that we do have regional problems. In this panel we will carry that assumption a bit further by describing what we believe some of those problems are. With this background, we will be better able to identify the specific governmental jobs that are needed in the region.

I don't know when the existence of regional problems was first recognized, but certainly the particular problem noticed first was air pollution, a problem

McCaffrey, cont'd

that transcended city and state boundaries and yet did
not, at least initially, seem to require federal action.
Since that first and classic regional problem of air
pollution was recognized, we have become familiar with
many others. Indeed the entire subject of environmental quality is now recognized as a matter of regional
concern. We have asked Frank Stead, one of the first
to warn of the growing dangers, to describe what the
subject really includes.

Frank M. Stead

ENVIRONMENTAL PROBLEMS AND GOVERNMENTAL LEVELS

One of the most frequently heard comments about
environmental matters in the Bay Area is that the problems of air, water and solid waste are regional in scope
and nature, and thus need to be brought under the man-
tle of a regional management program. With this basic
thesis I certainly concur, but it is much too simplis-
tic an answer.

FOUR PROBLEMS

As we begin to grapple with the thorny task of
bringing about a regional program, we find we have to
take a far closer and more discerning look at each of
the problems involved. For example, once we start to
really look at the problems of air, water and solid
waste (which are themselves only one aspect of the total fabric of environmental problems), we find that we
are dealing not with just three problems, but with four.
This is because the problems relating to water have two
distinct aspects to them; one--primarily a quantitative
problem--has to do with the development and distribution of the water resources of the state; the other--
a qualitative problem--has to do with how the used
waters of the state are disposed of. So, you see, we
are talking about four problems, not three.

Stead, cont'd

FOUR ENVIRONMENTAL SCALES

Moreover, when we talk about these four problems, we find that there is an inherent environmental scale, or geographic scale, that is different in each case. For example, the environmental scale of air pollution is most logically that of an air basin, and in the San Francisco Bay this is the topographic air shed of the Bay itself, although a great deal of the problem spills over into the next topographic basin, the Central Valley.

On the other hand, water resource management, the quantitative aspect, has no fixed geographic limits. The size of this system is determined by our own decisions about the areas of origin and transport of water. The water resource system of California's Bay Area may be all of Central Valley; it may be the Columbia River; and it may even extend to the polar region itself, depending upon how political and technical decisions are made. But in *no* sense can a water resource system for the Bay Area be considered to be confined to the topographic basin of the Bay itself.

The scale of the water pollution, or the liquid waste aspect of the system, depends upon the technology used to deal with it. If the technology is to dispose the liquid waste into receiving waters for assimilation and dispersion, then the size of the receiving waters (namely San Francisco Bay and its tributaries) is the key. If we move toward reclamation of water, involving direct recycling on land, then we have a terrestrial land base scale of the system that is smaller, yet still expensive, and tied to the total hydrologic distribution of waters in the area.

Finally, when we get into the question of solid waste, we need not have even as large an area as the 9 Bay Area counties to have a viable, environmental scale. One only needs an area big enough for economies of scale and to tie together in a community of economic interest

the urban area and the countryside adjacent to it, since
these two areas produce the streams of solid waste that
must be handled as a single program.

FOUR KINDS OF EFFORTS

So our four environmental programs--air pollution,
water resources, water pollution and solid waste--have
four entirely different natural boundaries. On top of
this fact, there are four different levels of governmental effort involved with each of the four matters.
In deciding how to manage our problems, the choice must
be made among these four levels or combinations of them.

The top level--the one we need before we can begin
to understand how the total program is to be carried
out--is the enunciation of the basic principles, standards, precepts, criteria and concepts that must guide
us.

Next comes the matter of bringing into being the
actual plan for the management of the resources. Then
comes the governmental function of regulation. And last
comes the construction and operation of the physical
facilities themselves.

To show how this works, I would like to quickly run
through for you a box score of how the three levels of
government--state, regional and local (forgetting for a
moment the federal level, although we know it exists)--
are deployed in these four areas in each of our four
programs.

(1) *At the top level of conceptual control, the
development of the basic principles and precepts to
guide the program*: In all the four programs, this function is now filled by the state itself. In three of the
programs, this function is deeply imbedded in basic statutes such as the Health and Safety Code, the Water Code,

Stead, cont'd

and the Fish and Game Code. In the field of solid
wastes, we have the weakest program, but such as it is,
the overview function is filled by the state.

(2) *Bringing forth a plan*: In the field of air
pollution, the state performs this function with respect
to motor vehicles; regional and local government perform
it with respect to stationary sources. A very awkward,
arbitrary arrangement, but it is understandable because
of the lines of jurisdiction.

In the field of water resources management, the
state develops the plan for the wholesale, overview program of the state. Individual cities and districts carry
out the localized application. (The best examples here
in the Bay Area are the San Francisco Public Utilities
Commission and the East Bay Municipal Utility District.)

For water pollution control, the state performs
the planning function, but discharges it through a regional arm of the state, and this is different from a
regional agency responsive and answerable to the citizens of the region. In the field of solid waste, the
development of a plan is carried out by local groups
and agencies.

(3) *Governmental regulation*: With respect to air
quality, the situation is again divided, with the state
occupying the field with respect to motor vehicles, and
local agencies with respect to fixed emissions.

In the field of water resource development, the
state occupies the entire field, as it also does with
water pollution control, but with pollution it again
discharges the function through a regional branch of
the state.

Finally, in the field of solid wastes, governmental
regulation is carried out primarily by local agencies,
principally health departments.

Stead, cont'd

(4) *Construction and operation of facilities*:
Here's where the money is, and in the field of air pollution, there is a fascinating convergence. Industry
constructs the units that discharge pollutants in the
motor vehicular field, and private citizens operate them.
On fixed emissions, industry builds, industry pays and
industry operates.

In the field of water resources management, again
a strange dichotomy exists. The state is in the construction and operation business itself with respect to
the state water project, while local city and district
governments are in charge of the actual movement, cap-
ture and distribution of water.

In the field of water pollution control, the local
agencies, sanitary districts and cities construct the
sewage disposal facilities, while industry constructs a
majority of the special industrial waste facilities.

Finally, in the field of solid wastes, construction
and operation are local functions divided between cities
and private enterprise in the form of private scavengers.

SIXTEEN OPTIONS

Now, if we pool these figures together we come to
a very interesting discovery. (See Table I) From the
four programs and various levels and combinations, we
get a total of 16 options. Of these, the state is now
occupying 11; truly regional agencies, 2; and local
agencies, 9, of which 4 are private enterprise.

If you stand back and look at the total picture,
you see that the upper levels of this spectrum--the
conceptual job, the drafting of the guidelines, the
drafting of the rules of the game--tend to be performed
by the higher levels of government, state and federal.
The construction and operation functions tend to be

TABLE I

WHO IS DOING THE GOVERNMENTAL WORK
ON THE ENVIRONMENT?

This matrix shows the governmental entities, state, regional and local, that are charged with different levels of responsibility for each of the four environmental problem areas: air pollution, water resources, water pollution and solid wastes.

Levels of governmental responsibility	Environmental Problems			
	Air pollution	Water resources	Water pollution	Solid wastes
Development of basic concepts	State	State	State	State
Planning	State Local	State Local	State Region	Local (indus- try)
Regulation	State Local	State	State Region	Local
Construction and operation	Local (indus- try)	State Local	Local (indus- try)	Local (indus- try)

68

Stead, cont'd

local or private matters. It is in the middle range
of planning and regulation that the greatest aggrega-
tion of regional efforts is to be found.

Since the choice must be made as to where the regional entity should enter the field, it should be
realized that the higher up you are on this scale of
four, the greater the influence on the course of events
you will have, as well as the greater the opportunity
to bring under a single conceptual umbrella these interrelated programs I've referred to.

McCaffrey: Thank you very much, Frank. Now whereas air
pollution was the first regional problem recognized as
requiring handling on a regional basis, one of the most
dramatic matters of current regional concern is the conservation and development of San Francisco Bay. Certainly no subject has received more active expression
of citizen concern. The man who has done a superb job
as the Executive Director of the original commission,
and now of the permanent Bay Conservation and Development Commission is Joe Bodovitz, one of the ablest men
in the entire field of regional management. I've asked
Joe to discuss the Bay and open space as regional functions.

Joseph E. Bodovitz

REGIONAL PRIORITIES AND RESOURCES

In the interests of trying to be brief, I will assume along the lines of Gene Lee's assumptions that all
of you here today agree that the Bay is indeed a matter
of regional concern, and that open space, existing as
it does in many municipalities and counties, is also a
matter of regional concern. I will try instead to go
beyond that and talk more to the general topic before
the panel, which is the governmental job being done in
the Bay Area. I'd like to make two points very briefly
if I may.

Bodovitz, cont'd

A WIDESPREAD CLICHÉ

One is that contrary to the widespread cliché that
we have regional government in the Bay Area, I would
like to suggest that we have nothing that remotely re-
sembles regional self-government.

We have a great deal of regional administration, a
large number of regional agencies--some created by the
state and federal government, some local, some region-
al--all doing things with great efficiency, but if
Thomas Jefferson were to walk on the stage and hear us
describe what we are doing in the Bay Area, it would
not be anything that he would remotely recognize as
self-government as it was envisioned by the founders
of this country 200 years ago. We've really made technology and efficiency our goals, and maybe that's okay,
but we have lost self-government along the way.

STRUCTURES AND DECISIONS

The second point is particularly relevant to what
we are talking about today. It is that the governmental structure we establish affects the kind of decisions we get. This is something I'm sure all of you
in this audience know, but I hope in two brief examples
to dramatize what it can mean.

Take the debate over the southern crossing. Because
of the way we have arranged things in the Bay Area now,
the final decisions on crossing San Francisco Bay are
made by the California Toll Bridge Authority, unless
the Legislature intervenes. How many of you here today, who are perhaps the 300 or 400 most regionally
sophisticated people in the Bay Area, can tell me how
many members there are on the California Toll Bridge
Authority? Can anybody name *one* member of the California Toll Bridge Authority? I see only one lady in
the back.

Bodovitz, cont'd

So as not to leave you hanging, I will tell you.
There are 5: chairman, James M. Hall, secretary of the
Business and Transportation Agency of the State of Cali-
fornia; vice-chairman, Roy E. Demmon, the builder in
Santa Clara; Verne Orr, the state Director of Finance;
James C. Schmidt, vice-president of San Diego Federal
Savings and Loan (not exactly in the Bay Area); and
Floyd Sparks, publisher of the Hayward *Daily Review*.
These are the gentlemen who will decide whether or not
we are going to have another crossing over San Fran-
cisco Bay.

Let me give another example of how the governmental
structure we create affects the kinds of decisions we
make. The federal government primarily and, to a lesser
extent, the state government have preempted the relatively popular income tax, so that local government is
left with the relatively unpopular property tax. This
structure has a great deal to say about the priorities
we then unconsciously go on to set.

For example, those of you in education and recreation are aware that the way we try to finance school
building programs and parks is by passing bond issues
that are usually repaid through the property tax. Unless the Supreme Court holds otherwise, it takes a 2/3
vote to get the money to do this, and our betters are
always telling us that if our case is just we have
nothing to fear--2/3 of the voters will approve our
expenditure and we will have schools and parks.

Now, I would like to suggest that we ought to have
a 5-year reversible financing plan. Every 5 years we
should completely reverse the kinds of expenditures
dependent on each tax base. For example, in year one,
we would finance education, recreation and environmental matters out of the relatively popular income tax
and we would have bond issue votes for such things as
construction of the SST, the space program, and finally,
by a 2/3 vote, small wars in Southeast Asia.

Bodovitz, cont'd

THE REAL JOB

What I mean to suggest, by all this, is that the
real need--the real governmental job for the region--
is setting priorities and allocating resources.   The
need is not just a more efficient transportation plan,
or more efficient plan for environmental matters.   The
two subjects are related.

What *is* our goal in transportation?   Getting the
most cars from here to there at whatever price in environmental destruction?   Or do we want to rank environmental protection higher, even if we must pay a price
in inferior transportation services?   These are the
very tough decisions, and I think we are not at all
governmentally organized to make them.

Suppose we in the Bay Area were to decide that for
the next few years our crucial needs were in the fields
of education and social welfare, and it was in these
areas that we wished to allocate the majority of our
resources.   How, under our existing governmental mechanism, could we do it?   Making that possible is, I
submit, the real governmental job that is needed in the
region, and I look forward to the successive panels
that will tell us how to do it.

McCaffrey: Thank you very much, Joe.   Now our third subject is transportation as a regional function and to
discuss it will be Jack Beckett, who is particularly
well qualified to do so.

John C. Beckett

TRANSPORTATION AS A REGIONAL FUNCTION

Transportation is a service that certainly fits the
definition of a regional function.   Any disagreement on
whether regional transportation matters should be

Beckett, cont'd

controlled or directed by a regional agency centers on
two areas. First, there are those concerned about loss
of local control and those who believe the state is all
the regional government we need. Second, there is a
difference of opinion as to which elements of transportation should be subject to regional planning control.

At the present time we have several regional transportation agencies functioning independently, though
with some degree of voluntary cooperation. These include the Division of Highways of the State of California, District 4, which covers 9 counties--8 in the Bay
Area plus Santa Cruz; the Division of Bay Toll Cross-
ings, a state agency responsible for all Bay bridges
except the Golden Gate Bridge; the Golden Gate Bridge,
Highway, and Transportation District, which includes 6
counties, 4 of which are in the Bay Area; and the Bay
Area Rapid Transit District (BART), which involves 3
Bay counties.

The proposal of Assemblymen Foran, Mulford, and
Knox, AB 363, identified these functional areas of
transportation as those most appropriate for inclusion
in a metropolitan transportation agency: namely, regional highways, both state and interstate, trans-Bay
bridges, and mass transit systems (paragraph 66510).

BART and the Golden Gate Bridge, Highway, and Transportation District were created by the state and operate as independent agencies. Policy for these independent districts is set by appointive boards of directors.
The Division of Highways operates as an intimate part
of the state government and is designed to meet the
regional needs of the Bay Area.

A VARIETY OF NEEDS

During the past two decades we have had two major
studies of our regional transportation requirements.

Beckett, cont'd

The first, by the BART Commission, had as one of its
objectives the broad question of the need for rapid
transit in the Bay Area. Essential to the BART Commission study was a study of the area highway and roads
system. A second and more comprehensive study is the
BATS Commission effort, currently continuing in the form
of a data bank under the auspices of the Regional Transportation Planning Committee of ABAG. The matter of regional transportation planning at an intensive level is
not now being carried on by any group. Needless to say,
it should be, and this is the purpose of AB 363.

Having lived in 4 of the 9 Bay Area counties, I am
aware of the many differences that exist in our Bay
Area cities and neighborhoods. I know there is strong
sentiment to preserve the unique character of local communities and local identity, and that therefore there is
a fear of regional control. In my judgment, variety is
an essential quality of good living in the Bay Area.
However, well-directed regional transportation is a
means of retaining desirable variety while providing
convenient communications between neighborhoods.

On the matter of state government continuing to provide regional service, there is serious doubt as to
whether this is still possible or adequate in view of
the complexity of problems facing the Bay Area as opposed
to the needs of the state as a whole. The needs of the
Bay Area are substantially different from those of
Southern California, for example. Present state practice has been and continues to be a policy to create
new special purpose districts to meet purely regional
needs. There is considerable sentiment that this policy
is outdated, inefficient and harmful to the future of
the Bay Area.

As to what elements of transportation should be
brought under control of a regional transportation agency, this is primarily a political problem. Unfortunately, once independent agencies are created, they are

Beckett, cont'd

reluctant to give up any of their independence to become part of a coordinated and well-directed system of service, such as one proposed for regional transportation. This is particularly true of the Golden Gate Bridge, Highway, and Transportation District and of BART. It is less a factor with District 4 of the state Division of Highways because this group does not now enjoy independent status and is already a part of a larger organization. Further, a regional organization would necessarily have to provide for continued coordination and direction of highways from a state level. However, this is the only area of regional transportation organization where it might be said that a new layer of government is involved. It should be noted that of the independent districts and agencies that already exist, the proposal for metropolitan or regional transportation government merely brings them under unified control.

AMONG THE ADVANTAGES

The main advantage of a metropolitan transportation agency is its potential to plan solutions for those regional needs that involve overlapping authority or lack of authority. As an example of overlapping authority I call your attention to the Marin corridor problem. Here we have two independent agencies sparring for a solution--the Golden Gate Bridge, Highway, and Transportation District, and the Marin Transit District. Adding to the confusion from the sidelines are BART and the Division of Highways. The sparring is sometimes subtle, but nevertheless it is there, and it is delaying a solution.

As an example of lack of authority I direct your attention to the need for rapid transit on the Peninsula. BART by itself does not have authority, and there

Beckett, cont'd

is no regional organization that can bring San Mateo and Santa Clara counties together for planning a solution.

Another point on the agenda is the interrelationship of regional transportation with other regional functions. It is my observation that much of the interest in regional transportation control stems from its potential to effect a practical plan for preservation of open space, better land use, control of future development and the elimination of air pollution. Advocates of these subjects are more articulate than are those who want better transportation for access to jobs, housing and education. The large Mexican-American minority group in Santa Clara County keeps saying, "We need transportation. We need it now." Twenty percent of the people over 16 years of age in Santa Clara County, for example, do not have an automobile available to them. What about transportation for these people?

In relating regional functions, one to another, we may be trying to do too much at once, thereby unnecessarily complicating matters. For this reason I urge support now for AB 363--the Metropolitan Transportation Commission.

McCaffrey: Thank you very much, Jack. The problems we've discussed so far are the ones generally recognized as requiring a regional approach for their management and their solution. However, the areas of housing, jobs and education are not as readily recognized as able to benefit from a regional approach. We are particularly privileged to have with us today John J. Miller, Assemblyman from the 17th District in Berkeley, and Minority Leader of the Assembly, to discuss with us the matter of housing, jobs and education as regional functions.

John J. Miller

FOCUS ON HOUSING, JOBS AND EDUCATION

"No man can live with the terrible knowledge that he is not needed." With this quotation in mind, let me state some ideas of what a regional government should do in the fields of housing, jobs and education.

THE RESPONSIBILITY OF GOVERNMENT

First, some comments on the nature of existing governmental efforts in these fields--if you can call them efforts. In education, the bases of school district support range from the immense, assessed evaluation of $267 thousand behind each high school student in Emeryville (the East Bay's industrial enclave) to $17.5 thousand for each student in Castro Valley. The actual support level per child in Bay Area districts varies from $628 spent in San Lorenzo to $1,600 spent in Berkeley or Emeryville.

Clearly, even when you include compensating and supplemental amounts from state and federal efforts, it is reprehensible that we have not organized our local educational support in a more equitable fashion. A regional effort could correct these disparities.

Next, the issue of housing. The basic problem for government is to change the current philosophy that government's role is limited to serving only the poor in something termed "public housing" or the comfortable with financial programs for private ownership. Just as government in America has acted to supply postal service, at least up until now, education, transportation systems, and, recently, health care, government must act to assure every Bay Area resident adequate shelter. It is an essential need. It is basic to our civilization, to our conduct as human beings, and to the survival of the family. Regional governments must make a greater effort in this area because the economic and

Miller, cont'd

social perspective of local governments has been
plainly shortsighted.

GOVERNMENT AND JOBS

Finally, jobs. Governments should be employers of
the first resort, rather than the last, as some people
urge. There should be a commitment by government to
strike a balance in meeting the demand for labor needed
to accomplish public tasks (building the schools, homes
and hospitals we need), and the employment demands of
private industry.

A job is so basic to a man's life, that we cannot
afford as a society to even think that we have obsolete
men. It's hard to say where government's responsibilities for employment begin, but they have no end, for
without meaningful and challenging work, a man loses
his dignity, his pride, his future and his present.

If regional governments would accept this primary
concept and be able to respond effectively to it, many
of the other problems of our region could be readily
solved.

McCaffrey: We have about ten minutes now for the audience to pose questions to members of our panel.

FROM THE AUDIENCE

Question: Do you think the state government should determine what might be a workable maximum population
density in the Bay Area?

Miller: It would seem to me, since I'm not a "strict
constructionist," that it's essentially within the
purview of government to control the density of population. That's really zoning by another name. It

Miller, cont'd

would seem to be within the health and welfare responsibilities of the government since we can assume now
that such things as the use of open space are proper
governmental functions.

But that's theoretical. Concretely, we have to
change the form of government that we now have in California if we are going to talk in these terms. As it
is, most men elected to public office are elected because they represent the point of view of the majority
of the people in their districts, and I don't believe
that the sophistication that this audience represents
could be found in the general voting population as a
whole. As a matter of fact, some of the things I said
this morning would be considered extremely out of hand
if they were said outside of Berkeley.

I believe your question states the proposition and
reveals what we really ought to be doing. And I think
that if I had more than one vote--or perhaps two, Jack
Knox's included--that we might be able to talk in those
terms. Perhaps we should start thinking anyway, and
some bright day we might be able to move on it.

McCaffrey: Thinking about zoning, as John Miller just
suggested, and then about the subject of open space
that Joe Bodovitz touched upon, it becomes clear that
there isn't any official regional way to initiate this
type of planning in the Bay Area. If you are going to
have zoning in the Bay Area as the way to control population density, you need to have some sort of regional
planning. Joe, would you have any comments on this?

Bodovitz: Well, two brief ones. I think the wording
of the question carried the implication that government
is our master and not us. And yet we still teach our
kids in civics books that we are the government. I
hope your question really is: Shouldn't we be bright
enough to govern ourselves and begin trying to make
some decisions about population density?

Bodovitz, cont'd

That's number one. Number two, I think the planning that would lead up to these decisions really means posing some very difficult questions. We will have to set the priorities ourselves, and the process of doing that is going to mean that all of us are probably not going to agree with each other. We'll win some and lose some; we'll trade one thing off for something else. The problem, I suspect, is that we in the Bay Area have not been willing to face up to these hard decisions, and so they have been made in Sacramento and Washington. Whenever we don't make decisions, somebody in an administrative agency makes them for us. So I think it's up to us to decide whether *we* want to start making the decisions.

McCaffrey: O.K. Frank. A quick comment and one other question.

Stead: The point I want to make is that there are two ways to meet this problem; one is to control the absolute numbers of people, and the other, which has been almost unexplored, is to reduce the per capita environmental impact in our use of energy and resources. It is this latter area that offers you the greatest immediate relief.

McCaffrey: Any other questions?

THE SOUTHERN CROSSING

Question: My prime concern is the Southern Crossing and the fact that although it's a regional problem, the decisions are being made in the state Legislature. How do we go about telling the Legislature to take its hands off that problem and similar problems until regional government gets going?

It seems to me that until the Legislature says to us, or to the Bay Area, "We're not going to solve these

Question, cont'd

problems. We're going to defer them until you do something about regional government, that the problems are
just going to go on being solved elsewhere."

McCaffrey: Perhaps I could quickly comment. Certainly
the state Legislature has authority in this regard. If
it does nothing, the Southern Crossing will proceed as
approved. But the Legislature has the power to take
action to cause it to be deferred or stopped, and the
way you can convey your feelings pro or con is to com-
municate with your representatives--your assemblymen
and senators--especially those who are members of the
committees that are tackling the subject.

POPULATION DENSITY AND TRANSPORTATION

Question: The density of Berkeley and most Bay Area
cities is approximately ¼ that of most European cities.
The question is: Is not a minimum population density
several times that of the Bay Area cities required before you can have a viable public transportation system?

McCaffrey: That's an interesting and involved question.
Jack, do you want to comment?

Beckett: Yes, I do. It's precisely the question that
we are struggling with in Santa Clara County. You talk
about the density in Berkeley. I can assure you that
the density in San Jose or any other city in Santa
Clara County is much less than that of Berkeley, and
it's very difficult to conceive of an efficient econ-
nomical mass transportation system where you have what
is best described as low density. I don't think it's
impossible, but it's difficult.

Now, the BART system is conceived as an interurban,
single-purpose system primarily built to bring people
from the suburban areas into the dense work areas in
downtown San Francisco and Oakland.

Beckett, cont'd

That was a relatively easy thing to see in 1950 when it was basically laid out. But how you would serve a county like Santa Clara, with no physical barriers and low density, is a very tough problem. I think we have to study this mixture, and I don't know that Europe is the best example to help us.

As for our total density: we have 7 thousand square miles in the Bay Area. The total population density will continue to be low, I hope, but there will be special concentrations for efficient transportation purposes.

We have to concentrate our employment areas. Industrial parks have been good in that sense as opposed to the usual helter-skelter location of work centers. And we probably have to concentrate residences, as well. Then we can connect them together with a good transportation system. So long as it's all spread out, a situation the automobile has fostered, then transportation solutions are very difficult.

BILLS AND FUNCTIONS

McCaffrey: Now, one more question.

Question: The speakers this morning mentioned proposals for regional agencies that are either already before the Legislature or are being considered for the future. At the same time some of you talked about a limited function regional government. Are we, on the one hand, creating a general government but, on the other, handing over to single-purpose agencies many of the major functional issues with which we have to deal? Do the proposed bills guarantee that sufficient functions will be given to the regional government if we can set up such a government?

McCaffrey: I'm not sure that I completely understand your question, but I think that it's an appropriate one for the next panel to deal with. Just a very quick answer here: The various regional agencies that exist now are generally single-purpose agencies, such as air pollution, or BART. Several of those mentioned by Assemblyman John Knox are similarly single purpose in nature: The transportation agency proposed by Assemblyman Foran, the Open Spaces Commission proposed by Senator Marks.

However, the major bill to which Assemblyman Knox referred, Assembly Bill No. 2310, would establish a multipurpose regional agency having various regional functions. I don't know if that answers your question, but it at least provides a comment on it. It's really the function of our next panel to talk about organization, powers and representation. Mr. Chairman, I guess that about completes this panel's time.

SUMMING UP

Eugene C. Lee: Let me make a comment or two. We asked the panel not to reinvent the wheel, but to suggest some new ideas to us. This is the challenge Mr. Vella posed in his remarks. I don't know about you, but I have gotten three or four or five ideas in this last hour.

I've heard Frank Stead speak a score of times and each time I've come away with a new idea, a new stimulus. The matrix he laid out for us today of different governmental powers, and the different ways we interact in these jurisdictions, was a brilliant analysis.

From that analysis and from the thread that ran through all of the disscussion, I realized that our main emphasis has been, "What is it that we are taking away from local government?" If the people this morning have driven one thing home to us, it is our ineffectiveness, not in taking away things from local

Lee, cont'd

government, but in dealing with higher levels of
decisionmaking, particularly the federal level. That
is certainly one of the problems that I hope the next
panel will address.

Another question is how to win attention for the
priorities which Joe Bodovitz set for us? It's not
clear from the panel that these priorities will be
followed whether they're set by local or by regional
agencies. It's not clear, as Frank Stead showed, that
they can be determined on a regional level. But what
Joe Bodovitz has made very clear to us is that the region needs to have a greater voice in the setting of
priorities, and that priorities are now being set on
a segmental basis, problem by problem, without any
real coordination from either Sacramento or Washington.

I think Joe's challenge to my use of the cliché
that we've got regional government is very apt. As he
explained, we have a lot of regional administration,
and a lot of regional machinery, but regional govern-
ment--in the sense of public control of priorities--is
exactly what we do not have.

And then John Beckett was quite right--that we need
to start thinking a lot harder now than we have in the
past about the devolution of some state government activities down to the region.

Finally Assemblyman Miller reminded us so graphi-
cally of the inequality of wealth among our Bay Area
school districts. It's one thing to say in the United
States that every kid in the United States should have
an even start in education, and that the assessed
wealth behind a kid in Mississippi should be equalized
to the level of wealth behind a New Yorker or a Cali-
fornian. We have great rhetoric in the nation's capi-
tol about such equalization programs, and yet we
ignore--to our peril--the fact that almost the same
magnitude of inequalities (beginning at a higher level

Lee, cont'd

to be sure) exists in educational financing within our own region. And there is now no regional institution to bring these inequalities even into the area of public debate.

I would like to make just one further comment on education, since we are used to thinking about local decisions being moved upward mainly in the fields of transportation and water. I don't know if you realize that a similar thing is happening in education through the Coordinating Council for Higher Education. The council makes what are in essence regional decisions concerning the kinds of community colleges we should have in this area. I submit to you that here is another place where the opportunity for regional action exists.

In sum, I'm grateful to you all for setting the stage for the hard job the next panel will wrestle with--the really tough political and organizational answers to meet the challenge you've described.

Part Three

Organization, Powers and Representation

Background Paper:

THE REGIONAL JOBS TO BE DONE
AND WAYS OF GETTING THEM ACCOMPLISHED

Stanley Scott

Assistant Director
Institute of Governmental Studies

THE GOVERNMENTAL JOBS: WHO DOES WHAT?

Where We Are Now

Some Tasks Assigned

A number of governmental tasks have been assigned and are being handled by cities, counties, school districts, ad hoc regional agencies, and state and federal agencies. With varying success, these governments attempt both to plan for the future and to deal with day-to-day municipal and county matters, with school administration and with regional, state and national responsibilities in the Bay Area.

Some Big Jobs Not Done

A few big construction, acquisition or operating jobs are not being done at all. Examples include construction of the remainder of a 9-county regional transportation system; development of a comprehensive regional solid waste management program; construction of a regional water pollution control system; planning and implementation of a regional open space acquisition program. (See Table I for various listings of major regional problems.)

TABLE I

TALLY OF REGIONAL PROBLEMS AND REPORT SOURCES

Problems (by frequency of mention)	IGS Bay Area Leadership Survey (1967)	SCR 41 Joint Resolution Creating BARO (1967)	ABAG Goals and Organization Committee (1966)	Governor's Commission on Metropolitan Area Problems (1960)
Mass Transportation		yes	yes	yes
Bay Conservation and Development		a	yes	a
Solid Waste Disposal		yes	yes	–
Air Pollution		yes	yes	yes
Airports		yes	yes	yes
Water Quality Control		yes	yes	yes
Regional Parks and Recreation		yes	yes	yes
Regional Planning		yes	yes	yes
Open Space Conservation		yes	yes	yes
Housing and Urban Development		–	–	yes
Public Health Programs		–	–	–
Social Welfare Planning		–	–	–
Sewage Disposal		–	–	yes
Police Protection		–	–	yes

aBay conservation and development may have been implied in the regional planning and open space functions mentioned by the governor's commission in 1960. It was almost certainly implied in SCR 41, which explicitly mentioned BCDC and the need to consider its prospective recommendations.

Overview Missing

Some essential "overview decisions" are virtually
nonexistent. As a consequence, there is no interweaving
of disparate public policies and programs. This is true
particularly in cases where the programs of independent
agencies need to be coordinated, and where two or more
functional problems have a common "interface." Thus a
lot of governmental machinery adorns the Bay Area's organizational landscape, but a few critical processes of
"fitting the policy pieces together" are operating
poorly or not at all.

This may be the central problem, because establishing goals and policy for the region as a whole is limited by the existing agencies' horizons, which encom-
pass only fragments of the regional system. As the ar-
ray of multiple "limited-horizon" enterprises grows,
the system may become counterproductive. Agency problems increasingly interrelate. Moreover, agency programs offer the potential of mutual support, and of fur-
thering the implementation of the regional goals em-
bodied in accepted plans, such as ABAG's Preliminary
Regional Plan. But narrow horizons and lack of a comprehensive overview function can forestall the implementation of regional plans.

Social and Economic Problems Neglected

Many crucial social and economic problems are not
being dealt with adequately. We generally agree that
organizational inadequacies at the regional level prevent our dealing effectively with a number of Bay Area
physical and environmental problems, although we already have the necessary technology and sufficient financial resources. Organizational inadequacies may be
even more disabling in areas where much more complex
and subtler solutions are required, i.e., problems of
human development and human relations. If we can learn
to improve organization to deal effectively with the
problems of the *environment*, and to build and operate
regional *physical facilities*, perhaps both the lesson

and the new organization can also facilitate greater accomplishments with social problems, which are as critical as the physical ones, and more difficult to deal with.

At the conference of September 14, 1968, to which the April 18, 1970 meeting is the sequel, Assemblyman Willie L. Brown, Jr. suggested that an effective regional government could help with a number of critical "people" problems:

> What is needed is regional government that also addresses the critical questions of housing, jobs, and the inevitable education and manpower retraining. Again, a general-purpose, representative regional government, by integrating the priorities of the rich and poor alike, could make great strides in solving these regional problems. The goals are surely mutual and interdependent. A high level of air pollution is no more deadly than a poisonous social climate which, fostered by poverty, is also regional in scope.[1]

The Next Steps

How much change is needed? We do not need a fundamental or drastic restructuring. A few relatively simple, but crucial, changes will be sufficient. Such changes can (1) help insure optimum performance on the part of existing governmental units, where this has not already been achieved; (2) accommodate any major regional governmental jobs that are now being overlooked;

---

[1] Harriet Nathan and Stanley Scott, eds., *Toward A Bay Area Regional Organization*, (Berkeley: Institute of Governmental Studies, University of California, 1969), p. 88.

and (3) help keep our existing local and regional government from getting in each other's way, and from defeating each other's plans, or those of the region.

TO GET THE JOBS DONE:
ORGANIZATION, POWERS, REPRESENTATION

Alternative Ways of Organizing and Allocating Power

The first alternative would *continue all existing agencies and add a new single-purpose district or authority* as each new regional problem becomes critical. In some ways this would be the simplest and easiest approach. Moreover it has been our historic approach, but it would compound the proliferation of single-purpose regional governments at a time when Bay Area opinion appears strongly to prefer stabilization, or even reduction in the numbers of governments. Moreover, the adding-on approach would fail to meet one of the most important needs: that of providing for an overview function, employing an umbrella agency that is capable of recognizing functional interrelationships and has the power to do something about them.

A second alternative would *continue all existing agencies, but also add an umbrella agency with a planning and overview role.* The umbrella agency could be given one or more powers over existing regional agencies, including authority to: (1) appoint part or all of the membership of the agencies' governing bodies; (2) review regional agencies' plans and require conformance to the umbrella agency's general plan for the region; and (3) approve or veto plans for financing major capital outlays by regional agencies. These powers would also have to apply to important aspects of city and county plans, either directly or through the plans of the separate regional agencies. The umbrella agency's influence probably should also extend to state and federal programs, although it might have to take the form of an advisory review.

A third alternative would consolidate several regional agencies into a few multipurpose regional bodies. For example, it is conceivable that all air and water pollution control and solid waste management functions could be placed under one agency, major transportation functions under a second, open space and regional parks under a third, and so forth. This consolidation would improve functional interrelationships, but only to a limited degree. In the absence of an overall umbrella agency, no arbiter would be provided for disputes among the powerful multipurpose regional agencies.

The fourth alternative would consolidate most or all operations of regional scope into a single multipurpose regional agency. Such a body would be responsible for regional planning and for regional operations. This alternative calls for comprehensive governmental reorganization what would probably be a good deal more drastic than is practical, necessary or even desirable. Many of the existing regional and subregional agencies are functioning reasonably well, at least within the scope of their own enterprises. All that needs to be done is to be sure that (1) they do not get in each other's way, and (2) their plans and programs further the larger interests of the Bay Area and contribute to implementation of the regional plan.

More on the Umbrella Agency Approach

Desirability

The author considers the use of an umbrella agency to be both the most desirable and most feasible alternative. There might also be merit in a combination that consolidates some existing regional agencies into two or more multipurpose bodies under an overall umbrella agency. But the first alternative discussed above (continuation of existing agencies and addition of new districts) is clearly discredited by the troubles we have had with single-purpose agencies. Finally, as was noted above, the fourth alternative (complete consolidation) is unnecessarily drastic.

Powers

The pure umbrella agency would not be responsible for running or administering any function directly. It would, however, be given adequate authority to see that major regional and subregional agencies under the umbrella, as well as local governments, conduct their planning, financing, construction programs and operations within certain guidelines: (1) to promote the larger public interest of the region, and (2) to contribute to the implementation of plans developed for the region.

A Prototype: The Metropolitan Council of the Twin Cities Area

The Metropolitan Council of the Twin Cities Area, established in 1967 by state legislative act, is perhaps the best example of a comprehensive umbrella agency now functioning in the United States. The Metropolitan Council covers a region containing approximately 2 million population, centered on the Twin Cities of Minneapolis and Saint Paul, Minnesota. Indicative of its geographic and governmental scope is the fact that 7 counties, 75 school districts, approximately 200 municipalities and townships, and 21 multiple-jurisdiction special districts are found within the council's area of authority.

The Metropolitan Council's initial assignment, and its central position, were succinctly described in its first biennial report:

> The [1967] law called for studies of air and water pollution, open space acquisition, solid waste disposal, tax structure and assessment practices, storm water . drainage, public services, governmental organization, and development of long-range planning in the Area. It authorized studies on water supply, communication, transportation, population, land use, and government. It established the

> Council as the reviewing agency for
> municipal and special district plans
> and for applications for federal and
> state financing of certain public
> works projects. And it charged that
> the Council prepare a comprehensive
> guide for the social, economic, and
> physical development of the Metro-
> politan Area.[2]

Quite clearly the Metropolitan Council serves as
an umbrella agency in an overseer capacity. It has the
regional planning and research function, which was taken
over, staff and all, from the preexisting Metropolitan
Planning Commission. The council is not an operating
agency, but neither is it "merely" a regional planning
agency, because it has the crucial power to review the
plans of governments within its jurisdiction. It may
disapprove plans of special-purpose districts, particularly those having a regional impact.

In 1969 the Minnesota Legislature conferred important additional powers and responsibilities on the Metropolitan Council and its member governments, strength-
ening the council's ability to insure compliance with
and implementation of its plans for the region. These
new powers include council authority to appoint the members of two service commissions: (1) a Metropolitan
Park Board that will be responsible for a regional park
and open space system, and (2) a Metropolitan Sewer
Board charged with implementing the council's plan for
regional sewage collection, treatment and disposal.

The Metropolitan Council's primary activities have
related to regional physical plant and environmental
matters, but it also has a firm commitment to consider
the social and human needs of the region. This concern

---

[2] Metropolitan Council of the Twin Cities Area, *1967-
1968 Biennial Report to the Minnesota Legislature*
(January 1969), p. 3.

is spelled out in research assignments, and is also ex-
emplified in its coordination of health planning, studies of low-income housing needs, and preparation of a
crime prevention and criminal justice program. In still
other ways the council has demonstrated a sensitivity
to the social needs of the region, and to the importance
of considering such needs when drafting plans to meet
the area's physical, environmental and service requirements. For example, in summarizing a recent staff report on the role of public transit in the region, the
Council's *Newsletter* commented:

> *Social Objectives.*--The Metropolitan
> Area must provide transportation for
> the 46 percent of the bus riders who
> are captives (those riders with low
> income, who have no auto, or who can-
> not drive). The quality of life for
> captive riders would be poor if they
> are completely immobile. The report
> says that the system severely limits
> captive rider mobility, as routes and
> scheduling make social and recrea-
> tional opportunities on evenings and
> weekends practically non-existent.[3]

(Further information about the Twin Cities Metropolitan Council can be found in Appendix V.)

SOME REPRESENTATIONAL ALTERNATIVES FOR A REGIONAL ORGANIZATION

Three representational formulas appear to be the
leading contenders for constituting the governing body
of any new regional organization in the San Francisco
Bay Area: (1) ABAG's constituent-unit formula; (2) direct election from districts; and (3) a combination employing both the ABAG formula and direct election.

The Bay Area has also had a good deal of experience with a fourth formula, namely: (4) a mixture of

---

[3]Metropolitan Council, *Newsletter*, December 1969, p. 1.

constituent-unit selection, ex officio representation, and appointment (the 27-member San Francisco Bay Conservation and Development Commission is based on this mixture).

The BATS Study Group on Organization and Planning, in its report to the Bay Area Transportation Study Commission, recommended still another novel organizational formula to be employed if, instead of a multipurpose regional organization, a transportation district is created. (5) The study group recommended the appointment of 18 members by the State Assemblymen elected from the 18 districts whose combined area virtually coincides with that of the 9 counties. In addition, the Association of Bay Area Governments would appoint 7 members, for a total of 25.[4]

Finally, subsequent to the April 18 conference, the author drafted another proposal for a mixed governing body. (6) The 40-member body would comprise 36 appointees selected from and representing individual county areas and apportioned according to population--the four smallest counties being grouped. Eighteen of the appointees would be chosen by members of the ABAG Executive Committee from each area, and 18 by members of the area's state legislative delegation. The governor would appoint 4 at-large members.[5]

Constituent-Unit Representation (the ABAG Formula)

A proposal supported by the Association of Bay Area Governments would, in effect, reconstitute the ABAG Executive Committee into a 38-member regional legislature, although the general assembly would also be given certain veto and overview powers. Proponents

---

[4] California. Bay Area Transportation Study Commission, *Report--Supplement 1: Organization and Planning: Innovations and Novel Systems* (1969), p. 13.

[5] See Appendix VI for a discussion of this proposal.

point to the Bay Area's long experience with constituent-
unit representation, on which the ABAG formula is based,
as a rationale for employing the principle in setting up
a regional government. (In the last 10 years, varia-
tions in the formula have been employed in the Bay Area
Air Pollution Control District, in BART, and in several
subregional districts.) They also argue that since ABAG
is a live entity and known quantity, with demonstrated
ability to come to grips with regional issues, it should
be used instead of creating a new and untried regional
vehicle. Moreover, a political fact of life in the Bay
Area is the ability of ABAG to muster legislative support. This may mean that any plan failing to win ABAG's
approval will be difficult to enact.

A further argument for the ABAG formula is that all
major regional public functions affect and interrelate
with the local activities and interests of the basic
units of government in the metropolitan area: the cities
and counties. For this reason, close coordination between the cities and counties, on the one hand, and any
regional agencies, on the other, is essential to effective operation. Constituent-unit representation is considered by many to have the advantage of building into
any regional agency's structure a mechanism likely to
insure close coordination with local governments.

Direct Election

Assembly Bill 711, introduced in 1969, called for
the election of a regional governing body consisting of
36 members chosen from equally apportioned districts
for 4-year terms. Moreover, a new position statement
prepared and adopted by the League of Women Voters of
the Bay Area supports..."the establishment of a regional
government for the nine Bay Area counties through legislative action, which includes: (a) representatives
directly elected from newly established, equally apportioned districts...."

The primary rationale behind direct election is:
(1) It is the prevailing method of selecting legislative

bodies that are generally accountable, responsive and vigorous, and that determine policy in general-purpose public agencies, i.e., city councils, county boards of supervisors and state legislatures. (2) A multipurpose government with several important regional functions is, in effect, a general government. (3) Direct election of the regional legislature would achieve the political visibility and accountability that it does for other general governments.

In addition, concern with what they view as some negative aspects of the ABAG formula, or ABAG's performance, undoubtedly motivates some proponents of direct elections. They point out that the ABAG formula involves several rather wide departures from the principle of equal representation, and that the smaller cities and counties are overrepresented. Richmond, for example, with 82 thousand population is equated in the Contra Costa County mayors' conference with Hercules, which has only about 310 people.

Some are critical of ABAG's policy stance--or their interpretation of it--considering it too cautious and not sufficiently innovative and forward looking. They contend, for example, that ABAG had difficulty confronting the Bay fill issue, both initially in 1964-1965, and in the year of the big decision, 1969. Some proponents of direct election also argue that the local government leadership developed through ABAG is too locally oriented, being concerned primarily with the interests of their individual communities. The alleged vulnerability of ABAG representatives to pressures from their home communities is said to conflict with the interests of the region.

Representatives of the Blacks and Mexican-Americans point out that they have little or no representation in ABAG. They argue that direct election from well-apportioned and reasonably sized districts might help insure at least some Black and Mexican-American representation. At the very least, it would insure election of some candidates who are sensitive to the wishes of those communities.

Opponents of direct election express misgivings on several points. In addition to the positive arguments suggested above for the constituent-unit approach, opponents of direct election assert that: (1) It will be much more difficult to obtain legislative and gubernatorial approval of an agency involving a new level of directly elected officials; (2) The demand for a general referendum to approve such an agency may be greater if its governing body is to be directly elected than if it follows the ABAG formula, and this could further delay progress on regional organization, at a time when some regional issues may become critical; (3) Direct elections involve campaigns, and these require money, and thus well-financed special interests could dominate such elections; (4) It is questionable whether adequate public interest can be generated to insure meaningful elections of members of a regional legislature; and finally (5) Minority group representation cannot be assured even by direct election, unless one wishes to specify deliberate racial or ethnic gerrymandering.

A Combination of an ABAG Formula and Direct Election

Assemblyman John Knox has introduced legislation calling for a compromise arrangement, combining direct election with constituent-unit representation. Assembly Bill 2310 (1970) would set up a 40-member regional legislature composed of 20 members elected from equally apportioned districts, and 20 members selected under a constituent-unit formula. The best argument for some form of mixed or compromise formula has been presented by Victor Jones, and is quoted here:

> The Bay Area has two large (or at least vocal) groups, heterogeneous in their make-up, one of which has taken a firm stand in favor of a directly elected regional government, while the other supports the creation of a regional governing body selected by and from elected city and county officials....

As might be expected in a constitutional debate, a Connecticut Compromise has been proposed, but both sides thus far seem to find it uninteresting. I want to argue that, apart from the political realism of a compromise, the proposal to mix the two bases of representation--direct election, and representation of local governments-- deserves consideration on its own merits.

(1) Mayors, city councilmen, and county supervisors should participate in regional policymaking through membership on the governing body, because

    a. They represent tough, ongoing, legitimate local governments with organizational and representational interests in metropolitan affairs;

    b. Cities and counties are more likely to cooperate by willingly carrying out regionally adopted policies, if they participate in the formulation and adoption of regional policies; and

    c. City and county officials can probably defeat any other proposal in a referendum.

(2) It is not true, however, that all interests within a metropolitan region such as the San Francisco Bay Area are represented by mayors, councilmen, and county supervisors. At least it is a matter to be inquired into. Otherwise, one must hold that everyone is virtually represented under whatever system is in effect.

(3) Direct election from districts, as a
means of supplementing mayors, city
councilmen and county supervisors on
the governing body, can increase the
representativeness of the regional
agency. Not only is a combination of
direct election with representation of
local governments a means of obtain-
ing the virtues of both systems, it
is actually likely to increase the
representation of various minority
groups--such as Blacks, Mexican-
Americans, conservationists, and
Democrats.

In any event, the presence of city and
county officials on the regional governing
body would provide formal linkages to city
and county governments. Steps should also
be taken to link state and federal governments into the governance of the metropolitan region. . . . . .

10. *Minority representation may be enhanced
by a mixed system of representation on the
regional governing body.*

A mixed system would provide representation
of groups in the region that might not be
represented among the city and county officials selected to sit on a regional governing body. Suggesting that the ABAG system
of representation needs to be supplemented,
is, however, in no way an admission that it
needs to be replaced.[7]

---

[7] Victor Jones, "Representative Local Government: From
Neighborhood to Region," *Public Affairs Report* (Berkeley:
Institute of Governmental Studies, University of Califor-
nia) vol. 11, no. 2, April 1970. Reproduced in full as
Appendix VIII.

The BCDC Formula

The Bay Conservation and Development Commission has 27 members. Four members are appointed by ABAG to represent cities. Nine more are appointed by the county boards of supervisors--one to a county. The remainder of the commission consists of 2 representatives of the federal government, 4 of state agencies, one from the Regional Water Quality Control Board, and 7 "representatives of the public," 5 of whom are appointed by the governor and one each by the Senate Rules Committee and the speaker of the Assembly. These complicated arrangements apparently were necessary to accommodate the wide range of groups and agencies that are concerned with the Bay and its future.

The primary arguments for this kind of formula are: (1) It is reasonably simple to devise, and can be tailored to fit the function or functions being dealt with; (2) It seems to be a good way to set up an ad hoc agency that is intended to operate for a limited term and must compile a consensus from a number of disparate agencies and groups to accomplish its task; and (3) It has worked extremely well, in the case of BCDC. So far, the commission has measured up to the tough tasks of controlling fill and developing an imaginative plan for the Bay.

The primary arguments against the BCDC formula are the same ones that favor either direct election or the ABAG formula. Proponents of both believe their chosen method would be better for a major, permanent, multipurpose regional organization than a formula like BCDC's.

Appointment by the Bay Area Legislative Delegation

As noted earlier, the BATS Study Group on Organization and Planning made an interesting suggestion for constituting the governing body of a metropolitan transportation agency, i.e., appointment of 18 members by the Assembly delegation from the Bay Area, and appointment of 7 members by the Association of Bay Area Governments. A brief look at the study group's discussion will aid in understanding the reasoning behind the recommendation. Previously the study group had agreed that a directly elected regional government should be established with transportation as one of its functions.

In the event that such a regional government were not created, however, and a limited-purpose regional transportation agency were set up instead, the study group considered direct election undesirable. First, the study group concluded that a transportation agency should be temporary, and that it should be brought under a multipurpose regional government, if and when one were created. Second, because direct election tends to give an agency a sense of immortality and a substantial degree of autonomy, it was judged inappropriate for a limited-purpose, temporary body, whose actions would have profound influences on other agencies and interests in the region. Third, the study group feared that a limited-purpose body would lack the "political visibility" that is essential for meaningful elections.

The study group also did not think that the transportation function should be governed solely by the ABAG formula, or be given directly to ABAG, while the Bay Area's debate over the creation and composition of a regional government remained unresolved.

Instead, the study group sought still another way to (1) represent the electorate, (2) insure public accountability, (3) guard against excessive autonomy, and (4) build in a linkage with ABAG while (5) creating a body that, hopefully, would not resist later reorganization or consolidation by state legislative action.

The suggestion that the Bay Area's legislative delegation constitute the principal appointing authority came from several sources. One was the example of the Twin Cities Metropolitan Council, whose members are appointed by the governor, after consulting with members of the area's state legislative delegation from each council district. All of the available evidence suggested that the Twin Cities umbrella agency was working well.

Moreover, most study group participants believed that appointment of a majority of the members by the Bay Area's state legislative delegation would achieve most of the objectives outlined above. Some study group members argued for appointment of 18 by the assemblymen, and 18 (two each) by the 9 state senators. Other study group members believed that the resulting body--numbering more than 40 members with the ABAG appointments--would be too large. The compromise proposal called for 18 appointments by assemblymen, the theory being that these would be more likely to be representative of minority group interests than appointments from the much larger state Senate districts. The 7 ABAG appointments were added to provide linkages with local government.

LESSONS FROM THE TWIN CITIES

James L. Hetland, Jr.

Chairman, Metropolitan Council of the Twin Cities Area, Minneapolis-St. Paul

My being here today is poetic justice in many respects, since about 3½ years ago we had a very similar conference in Minneapolis and St. Paul, to which we invited representatives from the Bay Area to come and give us words of wisdom.

I must say that we learned. We profited by hearing about some of the difficulties you faced. We also were able to put into perspective the very questions Panel Two will be discussing--that is, the political implications and the decisions that must be made about the kind of structure you want. And if we hadn't gone through that process, I am not sure that we could have politically put our organization together.

I start with the assumption that you know what kind of a region we have--7 counties and 3 thousand square miles, and about 300 taxing units, so basically we have the same kind of government, or fragmentation of government, that you do.

FACTORS TO CONSIDER

Now what were the factors in 1967 that we had to consider in the broad sense of putting together a regional organization? I'm not going to use the word "government" because we really aren't a government in the sense in which the word is generally used. We are a metropolitan council as I'll explain in a minute.

Let's start first with business, as it is politically rather difficult to ignore the metropolitan business community when we start to put together any kind of
a regional group.

In 1967 our business community for the first time
was waking up to the fact that Minneapolis could no
longer attract new industry and no longer could be the
dog for which the rest of the area was the tail. All
of a sudden both Minneapolis and St. Paul realized that
it was rather silly for the business communities of
Minneapolis and St. Paul to go on separate business-
soliciting excursions, with the St. Paul people selling
the attributes of St. Paul and the Minneapolis people
selling the attributes of Minneapolis. And when outside
businesses visited our area most of the business development committees were trying to convince them that one or
the other city was better, with the result that we either
would not get the new business or commercial industrial
concern, or it would go to a suburban location. The net
effect was that the business community recognized that
it was losing business and, more importantly, it was
losing development potential.

So the business community started with the core of
an economic recognition that it represented a single
economic unit that was competing with other single economic units around the United States.

Second, the business community came to recognize
that what it had to sell in our area is a healthy business climate and an attractive environment. And if it
were going to remain healthy as a business community,
it had to make sure that those they wished to bring into
the community would have a quality of life that instills
a desire to stay. We do not have the climatic advantages that Californians have. Therefore, we had to have
something else to bring this about. And that meant
basically that we would have to preserve the quality of
our waterways, our forests and air.

MUNICIPAL CONCERNS

The next areas of concern were the municipalities. The municipalities in 1967 were just beginning to feel the tremendous pressures for service. The delivery of municipal and school district-type services was becoming impossible in an economic sense. And the municipalities became informed through their metro section--we have a state League of Municipalities and a metro section of the league which represents the municipalities in the metropolitan area.

The metro section took the leadership in convincing its member communities that if strong municipal government were to survive, municipal government must rethink its service functions and get rid of those functions that it can no longer adequately perform.

If you just think about it for a minute, this becomes a highly critical question. It is the municipalities that are going broke, in effect, trying to balance a budget that includes services they can no longer perform economically, such as the treatment of sewage or the building of a transportation system. The one thing they can do is to eliminate their responsibility for that function. And by so doing, they can retain those functions that are more critical to them, such as the location of the local parks, the way in which local police, fire, rubbish and waste are handled. Those kinds of things can be a lot more critical to local government.

With this view in mind, the metro section of the league can now look upon the creation of a council as a matter of saving strong municipalities.

There is also another factor operating. Municipalities, frankly, did not trust the counties. The experience over a number of years led them to believe that they could not look to the counties to become the recipients of the power or the functions they wanted to be relieved of. They thought that they could do better by creating a regional agency. Counties, fortunately or

unfortunately, at this point in time were not a major
factor. They were simply not a strong unit of government. They were a service unit to perform state-
directed services and as such they had not developed a
strong general form. They had defaulted 20 years ago
from the basic social problems and had continued to de-
fault ever since.

THE POLITICAL DIRECTION

Next, the political parties: Both political parties in 1967 came to the recognition that the name of
the political game was change. The true issue, based
on winning elections in our state, was going to be solving the environmental problems in the urban area sur-
rounding the Twin Cities of Minneapolis and St. Paul.

And it was a fact of life that whichever party
undertook the leadership, resolving those problems, and
was recognized by the voting populace as having had the
best approach, would most likely be the majority party
in the state for the next 10 to 15 years. So this was
a purely pragmatic decision on the part of the political
parties. Fortunately at that point in time, with some
differences in detail, they both resolved that one of
the things needed was a regional agency capable of coordinating the overall development of the 7-county area.
Thus, the political parties were moving in the same
direction.

THE VIEW OF CIVIC GROUPS

The civic organizations for years had been concerned primarily about the lack of coordination. We had
many regional functions being performed by independent
service districts, the same as you have here. Those districts were truly independent and truly hidden forms of
government. There was no way in which those functions
could be coordinated, and the civic organizations felt
strongly that there had to be coordination.

Moreover, we had a metropolitan planning commission that had been in existence for 10 years. It had a good staff. It was a good planning commission, but lacked power. The general consensus was that it was staff-dominated, namely, that all the decisions made by the planning commission were made by the staff and that the members of the commission were rubber-stamping, and I'm afraid there was a degree of truth to this.

Now it didn't matter so much who drew the overall plan so long as there was no real change about to be implemented. But once implementation became possible, then you had to concern yourself with what kinds of plans they were. And the federal government, in designating a planning agency for federal funding review on an area basis, all of a sudden cast upon that agency some very effective powers--namely, the right to determine whether a given function would or would not be consistent with the overall development of the 7-county region.

In 1967 the civic organizations said: "Those decisions must be made by a group more representative than the technical professionals who are members and staff of the planning commission." So there was a desire to get the public voice into the development decisions from the civic point of view. Those were the factors, and they were all leading, of course, towards some form of regionalism. The issue became not whether there should be an effective regional agency, but what kind of agency it should be.

Additionally, in Minnesota we had to concern ourselves with the relationship of the Twin City Metropolitan Area to the state. And in this, you are in a somewhat different situation. But in our state the metropolitan area has at the present time, more than 50 percent of the population of the state; it also has 2/3 of the economic wealth. Therefore, it becomes very critical not to cut the metropolitan area away from the state of Minnesota, because otherwise we would have an effective separation of the state into two states.

THE REPRESENTATION QUESTION

Now this factor was played out in a very practical political game. It turned on the question of whether we were going to have an elected or an appointed council. Once the decisions had been made that we needed a regional organization to coordinate the overall development, the question of elective or appointive representation became critical. It became particularly critical to the state Legislature because it involved a choice between creating a government or having an administrative agency of the state, in effect, perform the main functions. Those descriptions are not entirely apt, but in many respects they tend to put into focus the two bills that were the alternatives proposed.

We had gone through the process, by the way, of talking about a COG [council of governments], and we had talked about total governmental mergers. We had talked about limited function and total governmental function. We had a major city mayor who wanted to consolidate all the counties and cities in the 7-county area into a single metro-operating government. So both ends of the spectrum had been debated by political figures.

The real pressures in the legislative session of 1967 boiled down to two bills. One was for an appointed council with limited powers. The second was for an elective council with broader powers, primarily the power to determine the priority and the use of the metro tax dollars for regional functions.

And that power, I think, was the critical question. With somewhat vague legislative definition of the discretionary areas, we were talking about a council to whom the Legislature could give general directions and provide funds, or take funds away. The regional agency would have discretion in the way the funds would be managed, but there was no way in which it could shift funds from, say, sewer treatment plans over to open-space needs, if the regional agency thought open space

needed more money at a particular time. It was that
kind of a question.

In '67 it was debated hot and heavy. Strangely
enough, the metropolitan legislators were all for the
elected council, almost to a man. The rural, upstate
legislators, to a man, were for the appointed council.
In the state Senate the question came, after great debate, to the floor, and it went to a tie vote, broken
then, of course, by the lieutenant governor of the
state. The result is that we adopted an appointed
council. It was that close.

The issue will come up again in the 1971 legislative session. Our metro section of the League of Minnesota municipalities has just adopted a program looking
toward the 1971 session, giving to the council substantial additional powers, but ending up by saying that
these powers should be granted only if the decision is
made to make the council elective. So the issue is not
resolved.

THE WAY IT WORKS

Let me explain the council's structure. We created
a council composed of 15 members. Fourteen are appointed
by the governor from election districts. (We roughly
combined two state Senate districts to make a single
council district.) They have a constituency of about
125 thousand people per district and they serve a 6-year
term. The initial appointments were for 2, 4 and 6
years, so we turn over 1/3 of the council every 2 years.

A council appointment is a part-time job. The appointments by the governor are to be confirmed by the
state Senate. The fifteenth member of the council is
the chairman. He serves at large; serves at the plea-
sure of the governor; and his is also a part-time job.

When the initial appointments were made, the governor, in my opinion, exercised a great deal of political

wisdom--not in his selection of the chairman, but in the way in which he resolved the appointment of the district members. The person appointed from each district is of the same partisan political persuasion as the majority of the state legislators from that district. Just that fact alone has helped us immeasurably in avoiding partisan allegations by a political party with regard to decisions by the council.

How does it work? In the first place, we've had very excellent attendance and energy. We run at about 90 percent attendance. The council members have to spend between 10 and 20 hours per week. They are quite responsive, frankly, to their constituents, but surprisingly they are much more responsive to the municipalities and the governmental units in their districts than they are to what you think of as the voter electorate.

Second, the council, by virtue of the fact that members are not elected, is not a visible public agency. In that sense I do not think we are truly a governmental-type forum. We do not have a voting constituency that requires you to look around and see what the 51 percent factor is.

Now this is both good and bad. If you know where the 51 percent factor is, sometimes you can be more courageous if the 51 percent are with you. On the other hand, if you want to be more courageous and you don't have to worry about the 51 percent, this can also be very helpful. We had the fortitude, for instance, to suspend the location of a new major commercial airport in the 7-county area in the middle of the last legislative session. This was a highly controversial decision. I'm not sure an elective body could have made that type of decision--but maybe it could.

In addition, we have basically the power to suspend capital planning of the independent and special service districts, and the regional single-purpose districts. This has worked well. But it has two primary difficulties:

(1) Negative powers can mean that you never really get to know the alternatives. It's very difficult to try to get the special service districts not to treat you as just another one of their many adversaries. They will make a decision on what they want to do, but you cannot effectively get from them the background information, staff work, and all the rest of the things you need to make a good decision. It's like pulling teeth for us to get information from our metropolitan airports commission, which is still a single-purpose district. It shouldn't be that way.

(2) Negative powers cannot lead to affirmative action. In spite of the fact that we have passed a very excellent piece of legislation dealing with protection of the environmental concerns having to do with a new major airport, the metropolitan airports commission has not yet presented to the council, for our review and decision, the question of a new major airport since over a year ago. Until the airports commission decides it wishes to move, the council is, in effect, helpless in regard to the new airport. Meanwhile the question of noise pollutants over our major residential areas with the existing airport is getting worse day by day. We know that the big answer here is to build a new airport. It's the kind of thing where a year's delay is very frustrating.

So as I see it, these are the two major difficulties with negative power. An advantage was that the Legislature in effect staged the development of the metropolitan council. In '69 we took a second step, and we did benefit by the fact that we knew that this kind of a loose relationship was not going to work effectively. So we can get some benefits just by virtue of experience.

DESTROYING THE OCTOPUS

The second major thing that happened with this negative review, is that we relieved the anxiety of all of those who were concerned about the octopus, the big government, the reaching out, the strangling, the usurpation, and all the other color words that tend to put the regional government in a bad light to the voting populace. We did tend to alleviate those attitudes. In that sense, it was successful.

We have, in addition to the suspension power, and the review power, A-95 review, which by the way is a very effective thing to keep the highway departments under control--extremely effective.

We have a right to review municipal plans. This power is a 60-day stop power, and on paper it's about the most worthless power imaginable. In practice it has turned out to be a highly effective tool. The municipalities, when they change a plan or adopt a new comprehensive plan, have to submit it to the council, and the council is required to inform the neighboring municipalities about the plan, so that they may then object, or raise questions, or bring the public spotlight to bear on these matters. Municipalities and elective municipal councils are as sensitive to the opinions of their neighbors and their own constituents as any politician is, and as a result if there's a big hue and cry, chances are pretty good that they'll change their action. The net result is that we have had a very considerable success with stopping some undesirable border-type changes, the bad location decisions with regard to mobile homes, those kinds of things that are within the municipal zoning areas.

In addition to the powers that I mentioned, the Legislature in 1967 said, "Come back to us with recommendations on how to solve those regional functions that are not presently being undertaken, including sewage, air, solid waste, open space, and the rest of the laundry list." Well, we decided we couldn't take the entire list, but we would take 6 of the items.

We created 5 citizens' advisory committees--25-member committees--to really permit the council to

increase its manpower and in doing so, we created 25
very effective lobbyists. I note that the conference
background material says that the Legislature of Minnesota takes the recommendations of the metropolitan council and adopts them without question. This isn't so.
We speak by and large with a metro voice, and this is
extremely helpful and highly desirable. But never down-
grade the effect of those 25 persons who spent 6 to 9
months studying a given broad area to understand how it
should be resolved functionally. When they have come to
their conclusion, they're difficult to stop in the legislative stream. So a part of the success of the 1969
legislative program has to be the existence of those
very effective persons on our advisory committees.

A KEY TO MATURITY

We also knew that disposal of our sewer effluent
in the Twin City metropolitan area was looked upon as a
key to the maturity of the metropolitan council. Four
legislative sessions had gone by in which this had been
a primary issue, but it still had not been resolved.
We are an area of high water table, so that the way in
which you dispose of your sewer effluent is highly critical. You cannot effectively use drain fields and sep-
tic tanks. You can grind your heel on the ground in
certain places and find water--it's that kind of water
table. Also we are an area that is highly dedicated to
the preservation of our water resources, our lakes and
streams and rivers, so that where you put the sewer effluent was highly critical.

The council decided to proceed this way: because we
knew we had to make a decision on the sewer effluent
matter, we decided that issue would also be the vehicle
for talking about the way to properly structure an operating agency under the auspices of the council. We went
through the question of whether we would recommend creation of another autonomous, independent district again,
or whether we should have an operating department as a
part of the council, or whether we should do something

different. We decided to do something different. We
created a quasi-independent board. We did this because
we feel strongly that the metropolitan council must be
the generalist. It must have the capacity to worry
about, think about and resolve the overall development
questions. And it cannot do this if it has to spend 90
percent of its time worrying about the price of chlorine,
and employee wages and this kind of thing. So therefore, another type of board to handle the operating detail was needed.

The three keys, as far as we were concerned, for
the relationship between the sewer board and the council
were these: First, budgetary control: pocket-book
control. We issue the bonds, and pass on the capital
budget and the operating budget, with a right to add and
to subtract. We require the sewer board to submit 5-
year capital budgets. Next is the adoption of the master
sewer plan by the council. The sewer board must abide
by that plan, and this controls the way in which we are
going to sewer the 7-county area, and where we're going
to dispose of sewer effluent. The engineering plan, the
building and the ownership all reside in the sewer board.
Third, and I don't think this is nearly as critical, we
appoint the 7 members to the sewer board. This gives
us at least the right to be listened to. I'm not sure
that it carries much more connotation than that.

So this was the way in which we divided the powers,
and we adopted the same basic format for our regional
open space planning, open space board, and a slightly
different format for solid waste management.

The council created and has already adopted plans
for solid waste disposal and eventual land-fill location
in the 7-county area. Our problem is not that we lack
land-fill area locations, it's that our big municipalities do not have those locations within their corporate
boundaries. Therefore we had to make them available to
municipalities throughout the 7-county area. Representatives of the counties are the governing body rather
than a new regional solid waste board, as we're again

trying to carry out a thesis that you don't create government if you don't need to. If there's a government
capable of performing a function, let it do so. The
primary concern is two-fold: to make sure it's done;
and to make sure it's coordinated.

LESSONS AND OBSERVATIONS

And here we are in 1970. One observation: I do
not think that if we had to put all those functions under
the council in 1967 we would have been able to get them
done. Don't underestimate the time and difficulty of
putting together a governmental form--and in coordinating and bringing under your wing existing governmental units. It's an extremely difficult and time-
consuming problem. Communication is at best difficult.
I started out with the thesis that I would literally
visit every one of the city councils and governing units.
And if you just take one working night for each, with
300 taxing units, you see, I had to take more than a
year. It is extremely difficult, and I say, "Please
don't discount it."

Another observation: I would not claim, nor should
anyone ever claim, that the council is a completed form,
or that it's an ultimate form, or that you can make it
work in every region. At best it is a start. It works
for us and it has the potential of working in most other
areas. I've observed in my recent visits to metropolitan areas in the United States that the problems--
economic, political, social--are quite similar. And I
have a feeling that this can work if you're willing to
do a step-process, getting the powers and the functions
resolved first, and letting the rest of it evolve. I
think it can work.

A few quick observations: First, I think that however you decide to appoint or elect members, make sure
they come from election districts that do not coincide
with any given units of government. That is critical,
so that there is no concept of delegate representatives
from another sub-unit of government.

Second, make sure the regional agency has its own tax base. We have our own operating funds, we tax for it; the counties actually collect the tax, but we levy it.

Third, make sure that you have terms of office for your members. Fourth, I would assume that at least initially it can't be a full-time job even though it should be.

Fifth, I think on the elective-appointive debate, it must revolve around powers--it can't just be an emotional consideration.

On the concept of coordinating existing government functions, don't call it a new government. That word carries very little actual significance but has great emotional significance. The critical thing is being able to effectively coordinate the overall development.

By the way, did you notice that the first three pieces of things we tried to put together were open space, sewers and transportation? Given those three, you can do quite effective overall community planning as far as spread development is concerned, and begin pulling that development into tighter patterns that make some sense for your total environment.

A few more observations: Make sure you do not overload the regional agency with detailed decisions. Give it time to make the big ones. Establish in the minds of your citizenry the need for a change. There has to be some particularly focal issue around which the need to coordinate develops. I don't know what it is here--in our area it was the need to control the use of our river valleys and lakes, and to dispose of our sewer effluent. That is many respects was the key to the creation of the council.

Again, in our area, and I assume in most areas of the United States, you don't use the word "government" unless you truly mean it. You scare people. Talk about regional functions. Talk about the fact that these functions are already being performed, and more of them are going to be performed, and we need to know how to effectively coordinate them to make sure, for example, that you don't build airports in areas that have a high water table and that you protect areas that should be preserved as natural open space--because the airports commissions aren't going to worry about that. And yet we have to have some effective way of putting those needs together and making them balance.

I think planning for development is highly desirable if you work that out. It depends on how far you wish to go and how sophisticated your citizenry really is. Protection of the municipal base is, I think, essential to any regional concept. You must make sure that your municipalities are in agreement that the functions are truly regional. This may sound difficult, but it really isn't. Once you begin talking about certain things and begin subdividing, to a large degree your municipal officials are highly realistic about what is going to improve their overall environment and, therefore, reduce their political problems. I think you'll find them quite happy to stay with you if you go at it properly.

PARTICIPATION OF MINORITIES

Now about the minorities. One of the big arguments always is that regional organization is a device by the power structure to avoid the political strengths that have now devolved upon minorities and low-income people. We do not have in the Twin City area a large minority problem, but I think that all persons should recognize that the regional structure cannot be a device to avoid minority participation in the decision-making process. It can only be a device to give them representation in the decision-making process.

These regional functions are going to be performed. The question is how, and in what kind of governmental

structure? It does our minorities little good to have
a voice in city functions if the city is no longer functioning. If the city is not making the big decisions,
the quality of life decisions, then it seems to me what
we have done is to try to fool our minority citizens.
And obviously this is not desirable.

In our area, for instance, the question of low- and
medium-income housing is critical, not from a racial
point of view, but from an economic point of view. Our
suburban communities do not wish to pay to educate children, because it's expensive unless you have a big tax
base. Therefore to balance our tax base, we put restrictions on residential construction and building requirements. Thus we make sure that the older citizen or the
affluent citizen comes into the suburbs, but not the
low- and medium-income citizen with small children to
be educated.

Now, when you put that together with the fact that
the jobs--the industrial jobs--are also located in the
suburbs, the choice of residence becomes critical in
two senses. One, everyone recognizes the need for variety of choice. But two, we place an unnecessary
burden on our entire transportation system--rapid transit, public transportation and highways--when we force
the decision and make it mandatory that persons not live
close to where they work.

That's really what we're doing now. We're taking
the lower-scale, lower-economic group people, and saying,
"You find core-city houses." Then we create the jobs
out in the suburbs, and then tell the people they have
to get out there.

Now we can go through the inordinately expensive
process of building up transportation, but there's no
guarantee that you're ever really going to solve the
problem with that kind of process. Maybe it's easier
to build some houses out there, to give people a decent
choice of whether they want to live near where they work,
and to encourage them to do so.

PLANNING AND THE LOCAL TAX BASE

We're in the process of trying to resolve what we call our economic disparities problem--the have and have-not communities--and the fight centers on our tax base, the industrial-commercial tax base to be located within a given municipality, or a given school district, or a given service area.

The planning decisions--all the hard and important decisions--realistically aren't going to be made if local officials must rely upon the real estate tax base located within their municipal boundaries to provide all the municipal services.

By moving functions up, you have alleviated some of the problems on the regional level, but you still have not solved the basic ones. You have to find a method for distributing the tax base so that there is no longer this total necessity to sacrifice all of the environmental questions to get in a new industry, or a new commercial location, or a new shopping center, with all that may be involved in doing so.

We've located steel mills on some of our lakes, as an example. We give no thought to the question of whether to put an electrical power plant in one of our prime river valley areas, because that community needs a tax base. The question of where to locate our new major airport is environmental in one sense, but it's tax base in a real sense. Communities in the northern sector of our area want that airport for the economic benefits it will bring, not because they love jet noise.

So I say at some stage make sure that your regional agency undertakes to do something about the way in which you distribute back your tax base--particularly your real estate tax base, so that you're not constantly in chains of bondage on development questions to the real estate tax. I don't know if we're ever going to resolve that or not. But we feel that we have to try and I hope we can.

And then, lastly, let me wish you all sorts of success. What you're doing here is tremendous. Profit by our mistakes. I look forward to inviting some of you out to tell us how to do it a year from now! And I thank you very much for inviting me here.

ORGANIZATION, POWERS, AND REPRESENTATION

Moderator: Ira Michael Heyman, *Professor of Law and City Planning, U.C.*

Panel: T. J. Kent, Jr., *Professor of City Planning, U.C.*

Don Fazackerley, *Vice Chairman of the Board, Commonwealth National Bank; Chairman, Committee on Governing Regional Functions, Bay Area Council*

Mary W. Henderson, *Councilman, Redwood City; Member, ABAG Committee on Home Rule*

Joseph P. Bort, *Supervisor, Alameda County; Chairman, ABAG Committees on Home Rule and Finance*

Donald P. McCullum, *Attorney; President, NAACP, Oakland*

Ira Michael Heyman

ALTERNATIVES FOR ORGANIZING AND ALLOCATING POWER

Before we begin, I want to try to set the stage. To do this I am relying heavily on the background paper, "The Regional Jobs to be Done..." prepared by Stanley Scott. For those of you who haven't had time to read it yet, I want to briefly outline the alternatives he poses for organizing and allocating power, as I believe they are crucial to our discussion. For we aren't only going to be discussing the alternative regional organizations that are practical, feasible

Heyman, cont'd

and desirable; we are also going to question the political feasibility of their creation.

How would they relate, for instance, to existing state and federal entities? What would their constituencies be? What legislative powers would they wield--the big regional legislature? the big regional council? the big board of regional supervisors? How would members be selected? These are important problems for us, and they can be looked at from many points of view.

A CHOICE OF FOUR

With respect to the alternatives, Stan Scott sets forth four. The first isn't actually an alternative to regional government. It is the continuation of single-purpose agencies, of taking each new problem that comes up and trying to address it with a single-purpose district. I don't believe we'd be here if that's the solution that we think is viable.

A second alternative is to consolidate some of our existing regional agencies so that they handle more of the problem. For instance, we heard today about a bill relating to BART, relating to the Highway Division and relating to the bridges. That would be a form of consolidating a number of existing agencies around some functional issue like transportation.

Another alternative--probably the most drastic one--would set up a single regional government agency to take on all of the regional functions.

And the fourth alternative--which is really the one that Stan Scott stresses, although we don't have a party line--is the notion of an umbrella agency. That would be the continuation of existing agencies and the creation of an umbrella agency with a planning and overview role. It might have the power to appoint some

Heyman, cont'd

of its members to existing regional agencies; it might
have the power to review the plans of existing regional
agencies for conformance to a set of priorities and
allocations determined by the Legislature; it might
and ought to have the power to approve or veto plans
for major capital outlays by regional agencies; and it
ought to have some powers with respect to city and
county decisionmaking.

POWER AND REPRESENTATION

With respect to powers, we talked this morning about
the major functional areas for regional government:
transportation, solid wastes, air pollution, water
quality. And we talked about the social problems faced,
such as jobs, housing, health and racial and economic
segregation.

I want to stress very briefly, however, another way
of cutting the power lines. There are different kinds
of functions. There are regulatory kinds of functions,
reviewing kinds of functions, and operating kinds of
functions--or powers, if you will, and others yet to
be considered. It is the mix of these functions in
the framework of the kinds of alternative organizations
that Stan Scott listed that must be considered in the
determinations we make.

And, lastly, there is the question of representation. After we choose the alternative we wish, how
will representation be determined? Ought it to be the
constituent-unit formula, such as now is used in ABAG,
in which representatives of existing governments in
the Bay Area are persons who become the legislators in
the regional government? Or should we do it by direct
election? Or by some combination of direct election
and constituent-unit selection? Or as we have done
up to now, with a combination of constituent-unit selection, plus some representatives appointed by the

126

governor or President or somebody else? And then
there's the interesting idea recently proposed where
the men in the regional legislature would be chosen by
the assemblymen from the 18 Assembly districts within
our area, plus some persons chosen by ABAG. As we see,
there is again a wide range of avenues to consider.

Moreover, what would be the difference in terms of
the policies pursued if one or the other were chosen?
What interest groups and what individuals within the
region would be favored or disfavored if the legislative body was composed one or another way? That is the
kind of topic that we are going to be talking about.

Our first panel member is Jack Kent, who is going
to address himself in part to the questions of alternatives and representation. And all of us on the
panel obviously are going to be going back and forth
in discussing alternatives, power and representation
since they are all really part of a whole.

T. J. Kent, Jr.

REGIONAL FUNCTIONS AND THE UMBRELLA CONCEPT

I wish to preface my remarks by stating some of my
underlying beliefs for those who don't know what they
might be. I believe in municipal home rule. I am a
strong believer in local self-government. And I am
consciously working to bring about some kind of an effective regional government that would be limited to
those regional problems that do exist, that need attention if we are to continue to have strong local municipal governments. If that sounds complicated and confusing, wait till you hear the rest.

On the question of organization, my own experience
leads me to believe that it would be best if we could
find a way to agree on how to create a unified, but

Kent, cont'd

limited-function regional government for the Bay Area. That was referred to by our chairman in quoting Mr. Scott's background paper as the most drastic solution, but I think of it as the most conventional, the most reasonable, the most controllable solution. In effect, we would be thinking about creating a government for the metropolis and the 9-county region, limited to those regional functions that need attention and that can't be well cared for locally. Since it would be unified and have control over the operating agencies, you would know who was in charge.

However, I am getting impatient over the years, waiting for something constructive to happen. I am willing to accept a compromise. And to me the notion of an umbrella agency is, in effect, a compromise on the organizational level.

It may not seem to be quite as much a compromise, however, if the real functions of the governing body of the umbrella agency are as complete as those indicated by Professor Heyman. If, in fact, the umbrella agency is going to set priorities, and control budgets, and say "yea" or "nay" on capital improvements, and authorize programs outside the physical development fields that are now functions of the state government, then it really is going to be an influential and powerful governing body. Moreover, the notion that the umbrella agency might continue to have as part of its organization the existing special districts, and their staffs and their governing bodies makes a lot of sense. I think it would be workable.

Now as to powers, I have two points to make. First, we all are assuming that the several existing regional programs are needed and will continue. We are also assuming that there will be additional regional needs that will be acknowledged by the Legislature and the citizens. My own concern, going back to my conviction about the vital importance of strong municipal

Kent, cont'd

self-government, is that before we create any kind of
government at the regional level, we should realisti-
cally find a way to limit the powers of the government
so created.

POWER AND VETO POWER

My hope is that as a part of the actual legislation
creating the government, provisions can be written in
to require any extension of the powers of the regional
government to be thoroughly debated and thoroughly reviewed. In fact, those powers should be subject to a
veto by local governments for a period of time sufficient to make absolutely certain we were not creating
another distant and remote government that is going to
expand rapidly and get out of control. I think a government of that sort could create physical and social
programs that would be harmful to local communities
and minority groups within the region, as well as to
the environment as a whole.

So my number one notion on powers is to make sure
that they are limited, and that city and county governments and their legislators have an effective role in
guiding the enlargement of the functions that will
eventually have to be given to a limited regional government.

Second, once those provisions have been worked out,
I think that the government we create must have real
power to do the jobs given to it. It must not be a
paper tiger. And it must be recognized that in dealing
with problems where other programs already exist, such
as air pollution, more controls will be required. With
respect to those programs that have not yet been authorized, such as the one concerning regional open space,
new and painful controls are going to be necessary.

Kent, cont'd

FOR DIRECT ELECTIONS

Finally, concerning representation on the governing board of either an umbrella regional agency or a unified limited-function regional government: For many years I have taken it for granted that direct election is the most conventional, conservative, natural way for Americans to organize a committee of their fellow citizens to exercise vast powers over their affairs. That is what we do for the general-purpose governments that are cities and for the general-purpose governments that are counties. Stanley Scott in his background paper states the reasons very clearly and I don't think I should take time to elaborate on them. I would just remind you that I call for a directly elected governing body because that is the normal way to entrust citizens with the power to exercise authority over their fellow citizens. I think it is also necessary to have direct elections to bring about more direct representation by minority groups of all kinds, racial, economic and other, and I think territorial democracy does that better than any other system that I know of. There can be no real question that the person elected to serve on the Sonoma County Board of Supervisors from a definite territorial district or a person elected to serve on the Berkeley City Council has his first loyalty as an elected representative to the people who elected him and the government he serves.

The limited regional government of the future, whether unified or an umbrella agency, will have very large duties and controversial issues to cope with. As citizens of the Bay Area we want a chance to carefully consider candidates within each electoral district, so we can know if they are pro-conservation, pro-overdevelopment, or in the middle. We want to know they are clear-cut in their positions during the debates on their election. I don't see any way to know that about regional issues unless you have the old-fashioned, typical American secret ballot campaign.

Kent, cont'd

THE VIRTUES OF COMPETITION

Finally, it is my view that to maintain a relationship of citizen exchange (I don't mean citizen control—I am for representatives who use their own judgment and don't take a poll every time they vote), we must realize that we made democracy work in big affairs, at the federal and state level, by using a system of organized political competition based on two or three or four political parties. I think competition is inevitable. I think it is healthy. And I think it is necessary that regional affairs be conducted on a partisan basis.

I don't think big decisions made by nonpartisan bodies provide follow-through and continuity. One of the great weaknesses of our current city and county governments, in my opinion, is that we inherited a tradition that says in local affairs you elect good fellows who then get together once in a while and vote on things. I think that's one of the reasons our local governments are not as strong as they ought to be, especially on racial issues, on poverty issues and on environmental issues. So when we go to the regional level, I hope we can change tradition.

Heyman: Thank you, Jack Kent. Our second panel member is Don Fazackerley.

Don Fazackerley

A BUSINESS PERSPECTIVE ON REGIONAL GOVERNMENT

One of the more interesting aspects of this seminar today is that it has brought together two groups of people frequently believed to be at loggerheads.

I refer to the business community and the conservationists. Conservationists, rightly or wrongly, tend to regard the word "business" with some mistrust; many

Fazackerley, cont'd

businessmen, by the same token, regard conservationists
as obstacles to progress, obstructionists, impractical
idealists. The fact that some businessmen are indeed
despoilers of the landscape and some conservationists
are indeed narrow-minded has tended to overshadow the
basic fact that their interests coincide in many matters.

The need for regional government is one of those
matters. In order to serve their separate purposes,
both business and conservation need a regional structure. If there are any differences to be settled, let
them be settled within the regional framework, in the
interests of efficiency, economy and speed.

How long it has taken us to arrive at the stage of
a permanent Bay Conservation and Development Commission.
How much better a job of saving the Bay might have been
done if this regional mechanism had existed 10 years
ago. How much easier it would have been for businessmen to plan their developments if the regional regulations had been laid down 20 years ago. What a lot of
waste motion and time and energy have been expended to
get where we are today.

The Bay Area Council is a business organization,
made up of business leaders. But what do we mean by
business? Are we talking only about the people who
run business--the presidents of the corporations? Certainly not. Business is people: the people who work
to produce goods, the people who work to market them,
the people who buy them. Business in this sense is
what makes the Bay Area a functioning reality.

There isn't an organization in the Bay Area that
has studied our regional problems more intensively than
have the business corporations that form the San Francisco Bay Area Council. As a matter of fact, it was
the urgent need for a regional approach in the Bay Area,

Fazackerley, cont'd

a need that wasn't being met at all on the political
level, that led to the formation of the Bay Area Council
in 1945.

REGIONAL BUSINESS

Business must operate on a regional basis. It
serves a region, not a community or several communities.
Business operates on a regional basis because it's more
efficient and productive to do it that way. It provides
better service for customers--and customers are everywhere, without regard to county lines or municipalities.

Business is going to go on operating regionally,
whatever political structure may exist in the region.
But it makes the greatest common sense, from the business point of view and from almost every point of view,
to organize the Bay Area on a political basis that cor-
responds to the economic reality. Of course, that's the
way every community was originally formed. The tragedy
is that the political form tends to harden and obso-
lesce, while the economic form changes and grows to serve
the changing, growing population. After a while the
political, governmental structure is out of date; it
doesn't meet the needs of the time. The strongest proof
that it is out of date is that the business community
wants to bring it up to date. That's what's happened
here.

To demonstrate at least one reason that business
favors the regional approach to regional problems, let
me take the example of the United Bay Area Crusade. It
has eliminated to a considerable degree the piecemeal
approach to the use of charity to solve social problems.
Since business organizations are among the chief donors
to charitable drives, the regional United Crusade was
a welcome innovation. The problems of the poor and the
handicapped are everywhere; they are problems of the
region; and business is well served by the regional

Fazackerley, cont'd

approach that permits the charitable contribution to
be made in one lump, with the assurance that it will be
efficiently distributed to demonstrably worthy recipients.

Business favors the regional approach to regional
problems, while it wants that approach to be efficient
and economical. The proliferation of single-purpose
agencies with which we have hitherto met each regional
problem as it arose is neither efficient nor economical. While it is sometimes politically dangerous and
inexact to compare efficiency in business to efficiency
in government, certainly it would not be common sense
for a business to solve each of its problems or deal
with each of its customers, with an autonomous, separate department and with no overall coordination.

Nor is it common sense in government to treat each
regional problem as if it were isolated and insulated
from every other. Certainly in the field of ecology
we are suffering from this fallacious approach every
day. To pretend that air pollution and water pollution are two separate and unrelated things, or that
solid waste disposal and Bay fill have nothing to do
with one another, or that transportation by bridges
and highways is distinct from transportation by rapid
transit--to act as if each problem were complete in itself, and its solution complete in itself--is nonsense.

Nobody disagrees with this, I think. Everybody is
ready to admit that ecology and development and transportation are all so closely interwoven that they must
be dealt with collectively. Everybody admits it. Yet
we still don't have the mechanism that will permit us
to handle these matters collectively, except by the
roundabout route through the smoke-filled rooms of
Sacramento, and the logrolling exchanges between our
senators and assemblymen and those of Southern California.

Fazackerley, cont'd

Now what I am saying is that we must make decisions that are regionwide, and if we don't, they'll be made for us in Sacramento or Washington or by the forces of nature. I submit that we need to set up this regional mechanism by which we can express our regional will right away. We need regional home rule.

VOTING FOR THE REGION

I submit further that the only true way to make those regional decisions is as regional citizens, which means that we must make them by electing regional representatives. When we vote for councilmen or supervisors we vote for people to deal with local problems, and we want them to devote their attention to these local problems. But when we vote for somebody to make regional decisions we want people who will devote themselves to the region's best interests.

If the owners of an office supply manufacturing company give a man a job as manager of a plant to produce pencils, they want him to do the best job he can to produce the best pencils he can. And they want the manager of their paper mill to produce the best paper he can. But they don't ask these two men to quit making pencils and paper for one or two days a month and make the big decisions about whether the company should go into the business of producing copying machines or typewriters, or should refinance itself with debentures, or should set up a profit-sharing plan.

Those are companywide decisions, and while the local plant managers certainly have every right to add their voices and their viewpoints and their data, a different set of executives are needed to work on the companywide basis.

The analogy is not exact in every detail, but the viewpoint is precisely applicable. We want the best

Fazackerley, cont'd

possible representation of our interests at the local
level. We want the best possible representation of our
interests at the county level. And we want the best
possible representation of our interests at the regional
level.

This, I submit, means a directly elected regional
organization. At the present time I feel that the
route offered by Assemblyman Knox's bill to make BCDC
elective, with added environmental control functions,
is far and away the most promising. The Bay Area Council will support it I am sure, and so will many non-
business groups, such as the LWV (League of Women
Voters) and the AAUW (American Association of University Women).

I'd like to digress here for a moment to discuss a
phenomenon that we might call "philosophical parochialism." We all know the geographical parochialism that
impedes the move to regional organization because of
local jealousies and fears about possible impairment
of home rule. But recently we have encountered a point
of view among some of the friends of conservationism
that can be just as obstructionist and divisive. This
is the point of view that legislative efforts to expand
BCDC, and make it elective, might lose for us the gains
achieved in last year's BCDC victory. In other words,
don't rock the boat.

Those who think that merely preserving the Bay's
shorelines is an end sufficient in itself are just as
shortsighted as the mayor or supervisor who is afraid
his wings will be clipped if a regional organization
is set up. What, indeed, is the value of saving the
Bay as a mere matter of map-making convenience if the
Bay we save is simply a cesspool because the air above
it is foul? The only real security for BCDC lies in
the extension of its powers to include the other environmental functions that also affect the Bay: such
as air pollution, water quality control, open space,
transportation and airports.

Fazackerley, cont'd

Conservationists would best serve their own cause
if they join the drive for total ecological control
through a regional mechanism directly elected and thus
directly controlled by the citizens of the Bay Area.
This is precisely what the Bay Area Council and the
business community are prepared to advocate.

Heyman: Mr. Fazackerley proposes a unified regional
government, building on existing agencies. As for the
Bay Conservation and Development Commission, he would
change the form of choosing the legislative power in
that agency from the present selection method to direct
representation. Moreover, in addition to regulation of
the Bay and the shoreline strip that BCDC now controls,
he would expand its functions at the regional level to
water quality, air pollution, transportation, airports
and solid waste disposal. I think later on we will
perhaps want to talk in terms of whether all of these
are operating or regulatory functions, and how they
would mesh with functions being carried out by other
governments. But first I think it would be best to
hear from our third panelist, so I'm going to intro-
duce Mary W. Henderson, a councilman from Redwood City,
who has just been overwhelmingly reelected and who has
been on the ABAG Committee on Home Rule.

Mary W. Henderson

LOCAL ATTITUDES AND REGIONAL REPRESENTATION

After hearing some of the comments of the previous
panel, I'm not sure whether we came here to praise
Caesar, to bury ABAG, or perhaps to plug baseball.

But I will start out where somebody else ended.
The background paper prepared by Victor Jones [See
Appendix VIII] concludes with this statement: "Clearly
many features of local government and politics are
being evaluated without reference to each other or to

Henderson, cont'd

the system as a whole. In the meantime local government as we have known it may actually be withering
away." I would like to report to you as a city coun-
cilman--and therefore the lowest form of local government life present among you today--that I refute this
suggestion that local government is withering away.
It's not the case. The truth is we simply look that
way on Saturday mornings.

In the discussion of organizations, powers and representation that we are participating in right now, I
have to add one other point that I feel is of tremendous significance: attitudes in my opinion are the key
to the potential for the success of regional government.

LESSONS FROM ABAG

I have been directed towards certain questions, as
have the other members of the panel. And just to give
you a framework for what I'm going to say, I would like
to read some of these questions to you: What are the
specific lessons we have learned over the years about
constituent-unit representation, the ABAG plan? Are
the lessons of the past, when ABAG was largely an advisory and voluntary discussion forum, applicable to a
nonvoluntary organization with enforcement powers?
What kinds of changes could be anticipated? What political and special-interest groups would gain or lose
position or advantage under the ABAG approach or under
the direct-election approach?

Obviously each question in reality is linked to the
others. But on the first question of what lessons we
have learned from constituent-unit representation, I
think Charlie Brown, one of my favorite philosophers,
would say that ABAG as a regional government is the
crabgrass in the lawn of local government. In local
government we think we can do things better than anyone else, and that we must protect ourselves from

Henderson, cont'd

sinister outside agencies that may try to change what
we are trying to do. Sometimes it is said that we in
government are lonely up at the pinnacle, but if we
are lonely, it is interesting that we rarely venture
down. We just wait to see what comes up before we have
something to say. This has been much the case in communications between regional and local governments.

Certainly there are lessons from ABAG's past experience that can be applied to the potential for a new
regional government. All lessons are always applicable,
even if only to show what not to do. In fact, in the
early days, ABAG was something to which, in a substantial number of cases at any rate, many city council
members, supervisors, and mayors were assigned by their
local governments because it seemed a safe and harmless
and out-of-the-way place to put them. I've always nur-
tured a sneaking suspicion that that is why so many
women were assigned to represent their governments on
ABAG. I think the lesson in this is that regional organization was not taken seriously, representation was
not taken seriously, and the net result was that we
lost much time in realizing the importance of our attitudes, and of our involvement in the problems that we
preferred not to recognize.

Fortunately, ABAG had some excellent individuals
involved in its activities from its inception, who were
able to overcome some of the shortsightedness that local governments displayed. And so it became suddenly
noticeable to others in local government that something was going on in the outside world, and that we
had better pay more attention to ABAG and to its critical concerns before something came along to rock our
boats.

REGIONAL REPRESENTATION

The current question about representation in a new
regional government is something that concerns me

Henderson, cont'd

tremendously. If we were to use the constituent-unit
form of representation--in other words, a regional government that has powers, but whose members are chosen
by the local governments, as is the case now with ABAG--
I think we would see quite a different attitude forth-
coming about who gets the assignments from local governments. I'm not sure that the reason for this change
in attitude would be the one most beneficial to the
general public. In solving the problems of the region,
there may be some who like the idea because you can get
paid for it. Unfortunately, this is not what we need.
It is one of the things that particularly concern me
when it comes to considering whether constituent-unit
representation is the way the governing body of a regional government should be chosen.

I believe that we have to have regional government,
and I believe that this is the case because local government has proved itself incapable of widescreen
vision. Local governments are constantly making decisions without considering the side-effects of those
decisions, and if this continues when we suddenly come
together as a regional government, we may discover what
everybody's been doing to us. We may all sit down, and
say: "Of course we need to have a regional approach.
But the problem is on your side of the Bay, not on my
side." And we could find ourselves making sure that
whatever we propose won't affect anything on our side,
but will take care of the problems emanating from the
other side of the Bay.

When we consider constituent-unit representation,
the question has to be how those individuals who join
the regional government are chosen by their local governments. I have already expressed to you my concern
that the method might not be the most directly beneficial for the general public good. But I would find
myself similarly concerned with direct election of representatives, unless the regional government has a sufficiently large number of representatives to allow

Henderson, cont'd

specific special-interest groups--whether these are minority groups, conservation groups, business groups,
small town groups, or large city groups--to have truly
effective representation within a directly elected regional group.

And therefore, I would advocate that regional government be directed by a body of substantial size. I
think I can subscribe to the proposal we heard discussed
for an umbrella type of government. With this in mind,
I recall the remark of Joe Bodovitz that what we have
now in our area is not regional government, but regional
administration. I think he was saying that although we
have a competent, professional administrative capacity,
we lack the policy-making body to guide the administrative body. And that in my opinion is what the local
elected government ought to be doing. Personally, I
think that the idea of requiring local government to
work with directly elected regional government representatives might work.

In concluding my comments, I would just say that if
local governments are, as Professor Jones says, possibly
withering away, then, for heavens sake, don't let the
withered set the patterns for the programs that we need
on the regional basis.

BUT WHAT IS THE REAL DIFFERENCE?

Lee: This panel has given us a good start, but what I
challenge the panel and the audience to think about is
whether Jack Kent's belief in a kind of perfect democracy is adequate to the needs of the 1970's or whether
there could be a more complicated situation today than
Jack will admit.

For example, let me pose to you two questions: What
is really so different about a local city representative elected by voters in a city of 100 thousand people,

serving on a regional body, and a local representative
from a district of 100 thousand especially elected to
represent that district? Why is one any more parochial
or likely to misconstrue the general purpose of the region than the other? I suspect there are some differences, but the panel hasn't suggested them to us yet.

I don't want to see this discussion get caught up
with the whole issue of partisanship, but Jack poses
the role of the political party at a time when political scientists are worried about the eroding of the
party as a national institution. It behooves us not to
just say that parties insure competition when we are in
fact concerned about the quality of that competition.
Similarly, I suggest that those who want to consider
constituent-unit representation must also consider the
quality of the representation of the local unit.

I suspect, on the issue of sufficient representation of minority groups, that it would make a great
deal of difference if the governmental representation
in some of our largest cities was, in fact, more nearly
adequate for the minorities. In other words, the structure of the regional unit cannot be divorced from the
kinds of politics we already have in Oakland or San
Francisco or San Jose. They are inextricably inter-
twined.

BEYOND THE GENERALITIES

We've only got 50 more minutes to wrestle with this
subject and what we really need to do is get off of the
generalities and onto the hard questions of what kinds
of politics we are going to have in a direct election
system. Who's going to put up the dough to run in campaigns? What risks do we run in direct-election systems, what risks in constituent-unit systems--in the
ABAG system, if you will? What interests are advan-
taged and disadvantaged by different forms of government?

Lee, cont'd

I'll recall for you the remarks of Assemblyman Willie Brown, Jr. at our conference 18 months ago. Assemblyman Brown said: "We should have districts that are racially gerrymandered." We should not just set up districts; we ought to have as a goal that these districts be politically contrived, to guarantee minority representation. What would those districts look like? How small would our districts have to be to guarantee widespread representation?

And then Assemblyman Brown went on to say something else very interesting: namely that there should also be indirect representation on a regional body. Why? Because this would give minority political groups an added incentive to control their local units of government. And because, by controlling their local units of government, they would have an extra added voice on any regional agency that would come before us.

Just one final point, Mr. Chairman, and I'll turn this back to you. I think this group cannot avoid the question that has been posed to us by every speaker before this panel: That we face monumental problems and that the real need is for a regional lever on state and federal decisions. So the question I want to pose to you is: What kind of political unit will increase regional leverage on state and national government? How do we involve state and national decisionmakers, directly or indirectly? How do we influence them? What different strategies do we have that will influence Washington and Sacramento?

Heyman: And now our next speaker is Joe Bort.

Joseph P. Bort

THE ABAG PRESENCE

First of all, I support the ABAG approach to representation, and I'll tell you why. In doing so, I'll

Bort, cont'd

involve not only theory but to some extent the practical aspects of political life.

One, it is a going organization. Unfortunately it doesn't have the tools to do the job it would like to do. It is a voluntary organization. It is an attempt to provide better government, rather than more government, for the area. It has, for instance, developed a general plan, including open space, transportation, housing, liquid waste disposal in a broad sense, and as far as I know, except perhaps for the Twin City area, it has gone further than any other region in developing a plan. But it doesn't have the power and the authority to implement that plan at this time.

There's an old joke that I've often used. It goes this way: A fellow was lost in the hills. He was trying to get to Atlanta, and finally he ran across one of the men who lived in the area, and he asked, "How do I get to Atlanta? I'm lost." The man started to respond with rather complex and confusing directions, but after a while he stopped and said, "Mister, if I was going to Atlanta, I wouldn't start from here."

Now, I wish we weren't where we are. But there's no doubt about it, we are here, and we have to accept that fact. We have all these special districts, all these cities, all these counties, and, in many instances, all these organizations that are operating well. We have to make use of them.

A LOCAL HERITAGE

The other reason I support the ABAG proposal is this: Not only do we have a heritage of beauty of nature in California that we must preserve, but we also have a heritage of local home rule and participation that I think is absolutely necessary if 100 years from now we're still going to have real citizen participation in the democratic process of government.

Bort, cont'd

In our area we have about 91 cities and 9 counties.
There are some 500 elected city councilmen, members of
boards of supervisors and mayors. I make a prediction
that if we had a directly elected regional body of 18
or 36 or 42--whatever it might work out to be--that
after a period of time they would be the government,
and the local government would not have a significant
job to do.

I noticed that even when Mr. Hetland was defining
and eliminating what was regional in the Twin Cities
and what was left to the local government to do, that
his list of local functions was rather weak.

Certainly there's been a good deal of criticism of
local government. It hasn't done the job. If I live
in Berkeley, and there is a question of filling the
Bay or not filling the Bay, I may well vote yes, if
I can't vote against San Rafael or Fremont or San Leandro or Sausalito or San Francisco's filling the Bay.
But if I'm in a position to preserve the Bay, to vote
against those people who also can vote against me, I
will have as much a regional approach as anybody who
is directly elected.

ABAG is a group that can be given the power to do
the job by merely a turn of the pen. You don't have
to create another agency. We could follow the Twin
City project of using the going organizations in a sense
as a committee relating to a council. But whether this
be the East Bay Water or the A/C Transit or the Bay
Area Rapid Transit, or now BCDC, as Mr. Hetland pointed
out, one of the worst things that could happen is to
have equally balanced organizations where neither one
has control, or has at best only a negative control
over the other. When that happens, you can't get positive action; you can't really determine the alternatives.

And yet virtually everybody that I know of agrees
that we should not have a multiplicity of independent,

Bort, cont'd

single-purpose, regional agencies. If you look at the
history of the legislation in this area over the last
few years, however, you find we've been running down
this road pretty nearly as hard as possible, particularly if the bills that are before the Legislature today are implemented without any coordinating or
umbrella-like agency whatsoever. There is no doubt
that the public will eventually demand that there be a
regional government or agency that will have the ability
to set priorities for the regional monies that are
available.

I think we ought to get going on this basis, because
I would rather have it done, even on a direct-election
basis, than to sit here and have the state or the federal government doing it for us. We're the people who
live here, and if we run into a problem that's larger
than the region, like air pollution from automobiles,
then we should be perfectly happy to accept the higher
authority beyond that.

THE PRICE OF SUCCESS

Now, what would happen if you have a direct election? Well I've run in a couple of elections, and one
estimate is that the regional districts be about 125
thousand people each. My guess is that it would cost
today about $30 thousand to $60 thousand to win an
election or to contest an election, in a district of
this size. It might well be higher than that in a
highly competitive district, or with a little larger
population and inflation in the future.

This basically means that the people who are going
to be elected will be those who have the backing of
pressure groups. What could these be? They could be
political parties. And while Jack Kent and I go hand
in hand down the lane when we're talking about preserving open space, we are back to back when he talks

Bort, cont'd

about partisan politics on the local level, because I
don't believe in it, and he does.

Or the pressure group could be big business. Or,
it could be the conservation groups. Or, it could be
labor. Whichever the case, I don't believe that the
pressure groups electing an 18 or a 36 or whatever-it-
may-be governing body in this area would provide us
with good government in the long run, where the people--
just the people--would have the real voice.

Heyman: Well, Joe, I'm glad your viewpoint has been
expressed. I'm going to give Jack Kent, after Don Mc-
Cullum's through, an opportunity to rebut if he wishes,
because I would like to get a little debate going on
some of the factors we're talking about. It seems to
me that's the only way we're going to get down into
some of the very real practicalities with respect to
how the devil one gets a bill through the state Legislature creating a regional organization that will evolve
in the right directions.

But before we turn to debate on those kinds of
issues, I want to present to you Donald McCullum.

Donald P. McCullum

MINORITIES AND SURVIVAL

One of our initial concerns is the question of priorities. Everyone here assumes--I assume--that everyone here is for regional government. And probably
everyone here *is* for regional government. But everyone
who is not here--and look around, look to your right
and look to your left--may not be for regional government.

Now I hate to attack motherhood, because motherhood
is the basis on which all of us float, but today we're

McCullum, cont'd

meeting at a regional conference on regional planning
and regional government, and we look around us and the
visible minority--Blacks--are in very, very, very small
attendance, if present at all. The high probability is
that other identifiable minorities are not here either.
The high probability is that those whose economic level
is lower than those who are present are also not here.
But they too comprise this thing called the 9-county
Bay Area.

On the program you have outlined things like open
space, environmental quality, transportation, housing,
jobs and education, as subjects for discussion. I would
suggest to you that minorities--the Blacks and the
poor--are not concerned at this time with open space,
the quality of the water, or the air. That is because
their concerns right now are survival concerns. I
talked at great length, on March 1, 1968, as I usually
do, around these issues. And I'm going to reach back
off the dusty shelves to go back to what I said, as a
starting point.

WHAT MINORITIES FEAR

One of the greatest fears, speaking of minorities,
is that in cities such as Oakland, some form of regional government will decree from on high that it is
wise, healthy, and in the "public interest" to build a
strip through the heartland of the city from over the
hills in order to provide the suburban residents access
to the sea. They further fear that the progressive development of the shoreline of, say, Oakland by such
agencies as the Port of Oakland will be usurped by a
regional complex for the exclusive use and benefit of
citizens who are not residents of the central city.

Whether it is fact or fancy, real or imagined, myth
or doctrine, the prevailing attitude of the residents
of the central city is that the regional concept of

McCullum, cont'd

organization is nothing more than a veiled attempt to
reestablish political control of the heartland of our
cities under the guise of regional government. The
same people who used to support local control and responsibility are now the supporters of regional government, meaning the people who have moved to suburbia.
These are now the people who are the identifiable conservationists, who are interested in the quality of
life, who say ecology is now the thing. In the meantime, the issues that I'm going to talk about are being
treated with benign neglect, as some astute people have
suggested.

But in a very real sense, if you have any idea of
establishing a viable governmental agency that will
concern itself with the needs of its constituencies,
then you must reorient what we're talking about. We've
got to talk about jobs, education, and housing in that
order. It does not matter to the Black and other minorities who live in the central city whether the Bay
really is covered over with blacktop and made into a
parking lot, although I know this probably hurts all
of you to the quick.

But they are concerned with the everyday needs of
survival, while you want to concern yourselves with the
ecological needs of the 70's. Unless you deal initially with the person-to-person problems that exist
within our local communities, and in our society in
general, you can't really talk about transportation
and air pollution and water pollution and waste disposal and so forth.

So you see, I don't know why I always get invited
to come back to participate in these things, because
really, as an individual, as a spokesman, and as an
identifiable leader of minorities and of Blacks within
the Bay Area, I'm not interested in whether we should
or should not have regional government. I'm not interested because that's number 10 on my Hit Parade.

McCullum, cont'd

And when I say my Hit Parade, I'm talking about Blacks, the poor and minorities.

THE ANOINTMENT-APPOINTMENT PROCESS

Someone asked here, "What's the difference between 100 thousand people voting for a city councilman who then sits on ABAG, or 100 thousand people voting in a direct election for a representative on regional government?"

One of the differences is this: The historical experience in a community like Oakland, where the anointment-appointment process has been refined to its highest degree, indicates that no person ever runs for city council--he is anointed and appointed. And then he is blessed with being elected the next time around. Members of the school board in Oakland, the one that gives us so much difficulty on educational issues, were also, with the exception of only two persons, anointed and appointed. And then they were able to run as incumbents. So this is one difference.

Secondly, there is the whole question of ABAG. There is a cute phrase that they use in the streets about ABAG: ABAG is a bag. Minorities know nothing about it. We have no inputs into it, even though Oakland has 9 city councilmen, and there are 5 members on the county board of supervisors, and we have somewhere between 20 to 55 percent of the population, minority or Black, depending upon who's taking the census. And still we have no representation.

Now, what does this do? We can mouth phrases all we want to about the democratic process, and about viable response, and responsible elected representatives, and the like, but the fact is, in the City of Oakland, on the one hand, and the County of Alameda, on the other (save Mr. Bort, only because he's here),

McCullum, cont'd

government is unresponsive to the needs of the poor and
the Blacks in that community.

A STRUGGLE FOR POWER

So we are engaged in a struggle for power. And
this reminds me of another cute phrase, something we
call the "P-P Syndrome." Our problem is a paucity of
power. Their problem is a preponderance of power. And
what we are working for is a parity of power.

On the question of how members of a regional agency
should be selected, I would rest easier with the 18
assemblymen, whosoever they may be, making direct appointments to any regional organization, because this
is the only area where we have made significant inroads
into representation in the democratic process. No matter how good democracy is, democracy has no meaning to
me, unless it's able to respond to my needs, as I per-
ceive them, and not as you define them.

In short, what I'm suggesting is that this conference ought not to take place. And if it must take
place, then you ought to have another agenda, and the
agenda should be: "What are the needs of the 9-county
Bay Region as defined by the inhabitants of that region?"

There are a number of things I might comment on,
but, really, it's only because of my own masochistic
tendencies that I am here. It should be important to
you that there are no Black people here. It should be
important to you that there are no poor people here.
It should be important to you, if you are concerned
about the quality of life, that an organization such as
this has something to say directly and immediately about
the economic needs of the people within this area.

One final closing thought: They talk about local
control, they talk about big government. There is

McCullum, cont'd

nothing sacrosanct about home rule. If I've got to
have the type of home rule that I have in Oakland, I
would be better off without any rule. I would be better off with benign neglect from the administration in
Washington than the type of attention that we get in a
place like Oakland. We set up all of these shibboleths
of what our needs are, and how we're going to trade off
with ABAG for this if we get that. But really all
you're talking about is power, and what we're looking
for is the orderly transfer of power. And I'm not
talking about power as they have it in the agenda, but
power as it relates to either getting things done or
not allowing things to happen. This is what you've
got to talk about. You've got to talk about whether or
not you're going to share power, or whether or not
there's going to be any type of orderly transfer of
power, from those who have more than their needs dic-
tate to some of those who have less than their needs
require, or who have none.

And unless you want to talk about it in that context then my purpose is better served two blocks away,
saying, "Right on" to the rebelling Berkeley youngsters
who are all white and affluent. Because the interesting thing about what goes on here in Berkeley in an
all-white situation is that it creates all sorts of
ambivalent problems about where you are. See? You
can talk about how disorderly, irresponsible, and mili-
tant Black people may be, but when young, affluent,
middle-class white youngsters at the University go up
against the wall, then you've got problems that you
have to deal with. I don't have to deal with them.
From the day I was born, I knew I had a problem, but
the recognition of the reality of your problem is now
coming home to you.

Heyman: I think I'll throw the floor open for questions, but before I do, Assemblyman Knox thought it
might be a good idea if he did a little bit of summarizing, with respect to the range of questions we've

Heyman, cont'd

been seeking to address right at this point, rather than waiting until the end of the conference.

SUMMING UP

Knox: I must say, Mr. Chairman, that I thought my mind was made up more firmly than it is now after listening to some of the comments today. I'm very intrigued with the presentation with respect to the problem of direct election. I listened again, as I have before, to my friend Joe Bort defend the ABAG view. But I still feel that we need a fresh organization, Joe.

However, I think we can take advantage of the great work done by ABAG, and I think that ABAG can be involved in the new organization as it is in the present proposal before the Legislature, which I think will pass the Assembly and maybe also pass the Senate this year.

The Minneapolis-St. Paul experience is extremely intriguing to me. I didn't know much about it before I heard from Mr. Hetland, and I hope to be able to go there sometime and take a look at what they are doing. But it also reinforces my view that regional organizations have to be tailor-made for the particular area involved. What works here, I don't think would work in Los Angeles, for example, and I suspect it wouldn't work in Minneapolis-St. Paul, either.

With respect to Mr. McCullum's comments, I think that we're all sympathetic with his view. But let me give you an idea of how the solution of ecological problems can also be of great assistance in the problems that Mr. McCullum mentioned: If we are able to get ourselves organized to build the proper sewer treatment facilities for the clearing up of water pollution, we will be spending about $1.5 billion over a five-year period for the purpose of giving people jobs to build those facilities. That's true of practically

Knox, cont'd

every other ecological problem--you have to do some
building, you have to do some construction, you have
to put people to work in order to solve the problems.
So I think that we may be able to attack the problems
in different directions.

PROS AND CONS

Vella: It is very odd to find that the one person who
seems to have fathomed what I was talking about this
morning is Mr. McCullum. I mean that very sincerely,
and I doubt very much that he listened to me. I think
he had trouble finding a parking place and got in late.

McCullum: Right on!

Vella: But I do believe that power is one of the things
we had better talk about; it isn't a superficiality.
That's the first point on which I have to agree with
him.

The second point is that I come from what I like to
call an "emergent cow-town county," that contains about
2 percent of the Bay Area's population and has, by the
grace of God and the way ABAG is set up, a little less
than 2 percent of the representation on the executive
committee. And we suffer in our county from exactly
the same syndrome Mr. McCullum suffers from, namely the
fact that our own progress is in great danger--and not
all progress is bad--because you want us to be your
suburban open space.

Just to take one of the situations: I have four
children, and I feel, rightly or wrongly, that they
have the right to as good an education as children in
Berkeley have for the $1623 that you spend. My school
tax rate continues to go up, as does yours, except if
you relegate me to permanent open space then I will
have no chance to increase my tax base. Therefore the
quality of education will suffer.

Vella, cont'd

The nitty-gritty of this will be possibly brought
up in the next panel, which is a panel dedicated to
"How do we finance all these high-faluting ideas?"
So I'll end with a verse from Kipling in Gunga Din,
where he says,

> You can talk of gin and beer,
> When you're quartered safe in here,
> And you've set the penny pipes in
> Aldershot.

That was the Fort Ord of Britain.

> But when it really comes to slaughter,
> You will do your work on water,
> And you'll kiss the bloomin' boots
> of him that's got.

When it really comes to the nitty-gritty of this
thing--to the financing of it--that's when we're going
to kiss the boots of them that's got. When you show
me then, how we are going to do these things, I will
feel that the position of the presidency of ABAG into
which I was thrust somewhat against my will is worth
something besides the title on a piece of paper.

Henderson: I have the feeling that I'm going to be one
of those who also may not be invited back, Mr. McCullum.
I want to disagree left and right, very quickly, on a
couple of points.

PROVINCIAL LOCAL GOVERNMENTS

I disagree, first, with Professor Lee's contention
that the concern is with state and federal government.
I really feel that the provincial decisions of local
government are what created the need for a regional
approach. I disagree even while recognizing that I'm
a part of what I disagree with, namely ABAG. I'm an
advocate of ABAG, I'm damn glad we have it; we wouldn't

be where we are even now in considering some of our
problems without the voluntary association that we have;
we are a going organization. The trouble is I'm not
quite sure that we're going anyplace.

Then there is the point about local government not
having any significant jobs to do. It's my own conviction that there are many jobs that local government
could do better, if local government were not also acting as regional government.

This is why I can separate myself from the issue of
constituent-unit representation vs. direct election.
As a member of ABAG I believe that ABAG needs to present the alternative of constituent-unit representation,
because it must be examined before you choose another
method. But as an individual I believe in the need for
direct election of representatives to regional government.

Local government can do a much better job than it
is doing on many things, including the social concerns
that Mr. McCullum has so clearly pointed out to us, if
local government were to devote its energies more specifically to them. This is one of the benefits that I
think could come from separating who would be serving
which government.

I also feel that if you're to have directly elected
regional government, it's going to have to include a
lot of people, not just a few. We heard in Mr. Hetland's interesting description of what goes on in another area about a small council that has 5 advisory
boards with 25 members each. The possibility of
electing 125 people and having them serve in council
capacities within their election district might provide an alternative that would give representation
through direct election to smaller groups, and yet provide an escape from some of the horrors of large direct elections, where the evils of financing or

Henderson, cont'd

partisan politics or pressure politics or special-
interest politics are involved.

FROM THE AUDIENCE

Heyman: I think I'll turn to the audience.

Question: I have several questions that I want to ask.
Number one: What kind of research has been done to
define the effect that regional government would have
on potential Black political power within urban areas?
If there has not been that research, I want to know
why. If there has been research, I want to know what
the findings are.

The final question: Since there is a widely held
suspicion among Blacks that the notion of regional government is an attempt by the white Establishment to
continue carving themselves out as the majority, what
has been done to counter that attitude within the
Black community?

Heyman: I'm going to ask Professor Lee to answer, because I think he's probably the most knowledgeable of
all of us on those questions.

Lee: I can't take a piece of paper with a complete
answer out of my pocket. But it's well within the
limited skills that political scientists have, to answer your question in considerable detail once we have
a set of assumptions. In other words, we could answer
questions such as: "What kind of district pattern
would maximize minority political participation? How
small would those districts have to be? How would they
be carved out? What kind of an indirect constituent-
unit ABAG approach would produce minority representatives if Oakland or San Francisco happened to be themselves districted in different ways?" These are questions that can be answered, as a matter of fact, in
fairly short order, once you have a set of assumptions.

Lee, cont'd

We know when we draw up the central city districts what the outcome is in terms of minority representation. We know that if you district it in different ways you have different forms of representation.

Question: Has the research been done?

Lee: Yes.

Question: Well, what are the findings?

Lee: Quite a bit of research has been done by our conference committee. It's available, and if you'll give me your name I'll send you the information we have. But let me say this: just ask yourself this question. What influence do the minority people of the Bay Area have on the solution of regional problems now? The answer to that question is almost none--if not absolutely none. Under the system of direct election that has been proposed, there would be directly elected representatives from the minority community, who would have to be from that community, under the rules as established in the bill before the Legislature.

The thing to remember is that minorities have no influence whatsoever in their present status. There's no minority influence on the Bay Area Air Pollution Control District, or on the Bay Area Rapid Transit District, or on ABAG, or on any of the regional programs that I know of. If there is some, it's of a very minor nature. We are proposing that there be some. And that's what our research disclosed. If you keep the situation the way it is now, then people in minority areas will continue to have no influence on the solution of regional problems.

Question: Well, okay. Let me say this, my visit to the ABAG office didn't indicate any type of Black representation. And what you call direct election doesn't promise more, since the whole election procedure was

Question, cont'd

set up to maintain the power of the white establishment.

Now I'm saying that the regional government is moving in the same direction. I've been to the ABAG office, and they said they hadn't done any research on
that; you say some research has been done. I want to
know who has done the research and what was found?

Heyman: The citizens of Berkeley have done a little
research on that. We have three Blacks regularly
elected to the Berkeley City Council because of a
citywide coalition of liberal Democrats, over the last
15 years. If you'll see me right after the meeting...

Questioner: I can't stay. I've got to go home.

Lee: As a matter of fact, there are research reports
of the Institute of Governmental Studies that indicate
the present racial makeup of all the regional agencies
and of the legislative delegation. I think that's as
far as we can go to answer your question.

Heyman: Could I make just a brief comment on where we
are right now as a comparison? We obviously are going
to have to make changes to get larger minority representation. John, I think there are 18 Assembly districts in the Bay Area, aren't there? As far as I know
there's one Black--that's John Miller who is basically
from Berkeley. Oh yes, Willie Brown, too--excuse me.
There are 2 then, out of 18.

Audience: March Fong. She represents me.

Heyman: I'm talking about Blacks specifically. You
know the largest minority in this state, I guess, is
the Mexican-American.

Henderson: As far as ABAG is concerned, I'm active because I chose to be active, really. I was willing to

Henderson, cont'd

be active, and so my board appointed me. You have Mr. Livingston, who is the mayor of Richmond, and Terry Francois, who is chairman of one of our committees, whom we have urged to come on the Executive Committee. All they'd have to do is find the time to show up, and maybe they can't; there's no criticism meant. There's a Black member on the Oakland city council and, if he would show up he would be on the Executive Committee as Oakland's representative. Mrs. May represents Berkeley--there are three Blacks on the council there. And if one of them wanted to come, I know Mrs. May-- she'd step aside.

Very frankly, either through direct election or the ABAG formula, the representation is rather small. That's why I think Gene Lee brought up the subject that Willie Brown talked about last year, "Do you want to gerrymander so that you absolutely know that there will be a larger group?" This could be done on a city level as well as on a regional level.

Heyman: I'm sorry, but I'm going to have to break this off. It's time for the next panel to begin. I think one thing I've learned, at least in the last half hour, is that there's a lot of agreement around here in terms of generalities, but once we start to go beyond those generalities and discuss what functions are needed and how to select the people who will serve on the regional legislature, there's much less consensus than one might suspect otherwise.

Part Four:

Financing the Jobs that Need to be Done: Who Pays and for What?

Background Paper:

FINANCING A REGIONAL ORGANIZATION IN THE BAY AREA: A WAY OF THINKING ABOUT THE PROBLEM

Leslie E. Carbert

Tax Economist
Pacific Gas and Electric Company
and
President
Associated Regional Citizens

History written in 1980 about the San Francisco Bay Area will surely record the fact that the idea of a regional structure had been well developed by early 1970. Both written and oral argument, the record will show, were in large supply and of a quality to demonstrate the infinite variety of the human mind. Problems crying for solution by governmental agencies had been identified, measured and dramatized. Yet the technological skills of the day were grossly underutilized in the pursuit of social goals. The inability of existing political institutions to cope with regional problems had been amply demonstrated by the realities of the environment and clearly articulated by many participants in the discussion, including elected or appointed officials with a high sensitivity to the frustrations that come from energetic but idle acts. Indeed, from the perspective of 1980 it will no doubt appear incredible that it took intelligent men so long to construct the governmental machinery to provide intelligent solutions.

Hopefully, by 1980, it will be possible to look retrospectively upon an operating regional entity assigned a variety of interwoven and blended functions, properly representative of the will of the people of the region, and with adequate fiscal support to solve present problems and to plan for the solution of future problems. No doubt such an agency will be surrounded by appropriate limitations to protect the proper functions of traditional institutions of local government, for the issue concerns a regional solution of regional problems and not a regional solution of local problems.

But from all of these hopeful speculations one clear certainty emerges: If such a regional enterprise is eventually created it will find its principal reason for existence in what might be called the "fiscal imperative." Given the complex political forces that shape our regional destiny, it is clearly impossible to demonstrate the need for new governmental forms unless it is possible to demonstrate a fiscal advantage that will flow from such an innovation. Not only is the argument politically necessary, it is, I suppose, a fair and reasonable condition to impose upon all of the participants in the debate.

THE PROBLEM OF REGIONAL EXPENDITURES

The Straw Man

Unfortunately, while the principle of the fiscal imperative has been frequently recognized, most recently in the hearings and reports of the Joint Legislative Committee on Bay Area Regional Organization, the issue has been a captive of other controversies and other slogans. The atmosphere of fiscal crisis (whether real or feigned), that has pervaded the California scene in recent years, has inevitably led to the notion that no change of present governmental machinery is admissible unless it can be expected to produce significant savings in taxes and expenditures.

One must admit that this simple argument is a legitimate statement of basic economic and fiscal policy. Indeed, to argue the contrary would be to assume the

indefensible posture of arguing for inefficiency and
social profligacy. But crucial to the judgment is the
manner in which comparisons are stated or, more often,
implied. Naturally we should be able to show that an
altered governmental structure carries monetary benefits, whether we can measure them with precision or not.
Naturally we should be able to show greater efficiency
and economy in expenditure programs. But the real issue
turns on the nature of the comparison.

From a policy point of view it is, I think, improper
to formulate the comparison purely in terms of a reduction of present tax burdens. It is highly unrealistic
to expect any regional government, total or limited, to
reduce taxes or expenditures below present levels. Attempts to sell regional government on this promise must
be judged to be, at best, simple-minded and, at worst,
dishonest. Inflationary forces alone would make charla-
tans out of any who held up such enticing fruit. Further, anticipated population growth would add to the un-
reality of this simple comparison.

The Hypothetical Case

There is, of course, a conceptual way of looking
at the cost comparison in static terms--of assuming all
variables to remain the same except the form of governmental organization in the Bay Area. Presumably this
would involve a transfer of a limited number of functions now being performed by local agencies and by regional single-purpose agencies. But the level of services would have to be the same after the transfer as
before. We would then have conceptually isolated the
question of whether greater economies are possible under
a regional structure than under the present fractionated
structure.

Although these assumptions are obviously unrealistic and probably do not lend themselves to quantitative
analysis, they still present some interesting opportunities for speculation. The first search would undoubtedly focus on those functions that lend themselves to

economies of scale. It might well be that the larger
and more integrated the operation the lower would be
the costs of providing individual units of service.
Such economies might be identified as opportunities to
mechanize many administrative techniques, to consolidate information systems, to institute large-scale pur-
chasing and to achieve economies in large-scale capital
financing.

Yet this search for economies of scale should not
be so structured that each present function is examined
for such economies in its own presently narrow definition. It might be, for example, that significant economies could be realized by unifying the total transportation system or by developing closer relationships between solid waste disposal and air quality control. If
a regional solution of one problem leads to the solution
of another, surely economies are inevitable. Regret-
tably, much of the present thinking has focused on a
search for economies of scale by keeping these and other
regional functions in their existing but unreasonable
little boxes, predefined by earlier standards of convenience and necessity.

The search for economies, under the artificial con-
straints of our assumptions, might proceed to the possibilities that arise from the elimination of overlapping
and duplicative activities. I have a feeling that this
is an extremely fruitful area of analysis, although we
clearly should not build the whole case on these conclusions. Much of the regional advantage will be in
the reduction of administrative personnel, although I
am rather less sanguine than many about these possibilities. Any regional agency will obviously need to provide for some administrative decentralization, although
substantial reductions might still be possible. There
are also obvious duplications in capital facilities.
One would guess that this might be the case of solid
waste disposal systems and sewage treatment plants,
among others.

In much the same sense, greater efficiencies might
be expected to flow from increasing specialization within

the region. Such functions as port and airport development suggest themselves. So too does the increasing tendency to provide institutional specialization in the field of hospital care. Imaginative thinking would undoubtedly turn up many more.

The Need for Improved Services

The most relevent cost comparison is, of course, one that starts with a clear statement of those presently unmet regional needs that might best be assigned to a regional, multipurpose agency for satisfaction. It is then proper to ask whether these services could be more efficiently and economically performed under a regional structure or under our present form of local and regional mix.

Needless to say, this appropriate question is not as easily answered as the inappropriate one. In addition to the need for predicting population changes in terms of total size, distribution within the region, economic and social characteristics, and age composition, and in addition to the need for predicting price changes for the things Bay Area governments buy, it is necessary to predict the costs of needed services not yet being performed. Even the costs of capital construction projects already designed are difficult to estimate with precision, as the experience of the Bay Area Rapid Transit District would suggest. But in spite of these difficulties of measurable cost comparison between regional and fractionated government, the same opportunities as those discussed above in the hypothetical case for economic advantage on the expenditure side would seem to lie with a regional treatment of regional problems.

The Negative Argument

It is argued by some that service levels of Bay Area governments are already adequate. Of course, some arguments go even further; to some extent this is a philosophical statement and need not concern us here.

But the argument has an economic content that makes it
a legitimate part of the financing question for Bay
Area governments.

   In answering the argument we must broaden the concept of costs to include the external and sometimes subtle costs of not increasing the level of government services. Assuredly there are very real economic costs to
business and the general public of not providing adequate transportation services. There are health costs,
and therefore economic costs, of not solving problems
of air and water pollution; and there are dozens of
identifiable economic costs to society of not rational-
izing our port and airport complexes. These costs are
paid for in a thousand ways in the market place, but
they are properly described as the costs of nongovern-
ment or inadequate government. Perhaps they represent
the most basic element of an extensive mythology that
surrounds the fiscal issue of regional enterprise. It
is too easily assumed that governmental services are the
fringe on the garment, when the broadest concepts of
economic costs and resource allocation tell us that they
form part of the basic fabric. It follows that if regional services can be provided only by a regional entity, these external costs must be built into the cal-
culation.

THE PROBLEM OF REGIONAL REVENUES

   But enough of the expenditure side of the financial
question. An equal body of mythology exists on the taxation side.

   Much has been said about the inability of local
governments to finance local services. The rhetoric
has most frequently, but by no means exclusively, focused on the fiscal problems of the central cities. In
slightly different terms, the problem has been identified as the inadequacy of the property tax to serve as
the major financial foundation of local government.
Aside from the regional question, the search for solution

has been in two directions: the search for new sources of local revenue, and the search for support by higher levels of government. Both have approached desperation.

Support From Higher Levels

The search for support by higher levels of government has brought many frustrations, as countless officials of local government will testify. Most of these frustrations have stemmed from two sources: the great competition for scarce funds, and the unwanted controls imposed upon local governments over expenditure programs. These issues are relevant but of secondary importance to the present discussion.

New Local Sources and Community Competition

By far the greater set of frustrations arises from the search for new sources of local revenue in a closely knit regional setting. Here too the issue is one of competition for scarce resources, but the issue is more complex. It also involves a much more intense form of economic competition, for the bodies in the dispute are much closer together; share many of the same development desires and, more importantly, demonstrate many of the same economic attractions. They are able, through common communications media, to observe the machinations of their competitors.

This kind of competition frequently takes the form of a desire to increase the tax base by attracting industrial, commercial or expensive residential development. This result is accomplished, it is felt, by keeping tax burdens lower than those of regional competitors. In this sense, local tax resources are sparse partly because of competition for tax base. Thus, local revenue scarcity is frequently self imposed within the regional context. Results often include uneconomical land use policies, the destruction of necessary open spaces and a lack of adequate governmental services.

While the effects of these local competitive pressures can easily be observed at the local level as being

destructive, the impact on the whole region is immense.
And, for our purposes, the lessons it teaches for regional finance are most significant.

It might be possible to find examples of magnanimity
among local agencies in financing regional needs, but
the environmental evidence suggests that, if purely local tax levies are involved, such magnanimity is soon
dissipated. The realities of local politics are such
that expectations of voluntary local levies for regional
purposes appear unrealistic. In all fairness, however,
it must be said that many officials of local government
in the Bay Area have shown remarkable sensitivity to the
need for a unified fiscal base.

Evidence of competitive pressures in the search for
new tax sources has been most apparent in the San Francisco proposal to institute a payroll tax that would
have the effect of exporting some burdens to the residents of other jurisdictions. The response was loud and
immediate, but not unexpected. Most recently, attempts
have been made to achieve a kind of cooperative payroll
tax by several Bay Area communities. In addition, it
should be noted that the Association of Bay Area Governments has been active in searching for a unified tax
base.

A Poor Solution: Regional Conformity for Local Purposes

But we should not be deluded by these attempts.
For, with some exceptions in the ABAG deliberations, the
proposals have been designed to develop regional conformity for local purposes and not for regional purposes.
It is not only probable that voluntary conformity will
be spotty and temporary, it is also probable that few
regional purposes will be served in the process.

Nevertheless, there is an important lesson to be
learned from these attempts at fiscal conformity. They
demonstrate that (1) competitive fiscal pressures are
severe, and that (2) they call for more drastic solutions than voluntary agreements by existing jurisdictions.

It would seem from past history (some of it recent) that it is virtually impossible to create a regional tax base without also creating a regional governmental entity with a separate life and full governmental powers within a specified range of functions.

Some Guiding Principles

But what then? Are there principles to which we can appeal in order to develop a reasonable regional tax structure for regional purposes? Four such principles are of particular relevance to the regional issue, although other common principles of public finance are certainly germane.

Adequacy of Support. The total amount of money to be raised by the regional tax system will obviously depend upon the functions assigned to the regional agency and on future growth within the geographical boundaries of the region. But it can be stated as a general conclusion that a unified and noncompetitive tax system will provide an easier road to adequate support than will the present system. Problems will still exist, of course, for the region itself is by no means a closed economy. But the size of the problems should be much less terrifying with the above-mentioned system.

Economic Effects. Again, the unification of the tax base should minimize the disruptions of the present competitive system. The problem, however, is bigger than this, for it suggests the importance of choosing with some care the types of taxes to be used for regional support. Before such selection is made in final form there is need for some clear planning statement as to the desirable characteristics of the Bay Area that a regional tax system might play some role in promoting. The relationship between development and conservation, the characteristics and distribution of housing, the patterns of employment opportunity, and the particular mix of industrial and commercial activities are proper subjects of concern in this design process.

All things considered, there is some advantage to selecting types of taxes of general application rather than those that impose burdens on specific activities or specific enterprises; but this conclusion does not rule out specific levies if they are justified within the context of overall planning goals. Some activities might be discouraged (air and water pollution) by taxes levied on these activities. Other activities might be encouraged (use of mass rapid transit systems) by judicious use of taxes or user charges for rationing purposes. But these special levies are likely to perform more of a planning function than a revenue function. They are nevertheless important and useful for the economic effects they might produce.

The Equity Issue. Certainly one of the elements of judgment of any tax system is the fairness of its application. To be sure, standards of judgment are rather weak, particularly within the range of opportunities open to regional government, but nevertheless, the issue must be squarely posed. It is doubtful, for example, that a set of services available principally to the relatively affluent should be supported by a tax system whose weight is borne principally by the relatively poor. Perhaps the use of the property tax should be limited, even though it is a much less onerous levy at the regional level than at the local level.

We can, of course, note considerable variety of economic conditions among the many separate communities of the Bay Area. A fiscal blending of these communities through a unified tax base will help to eradicate the impact of these differences. This result will occur, however, only if a nonregressive package is designed for regional use.

Administrative Issues. Finally, the options for developing new tax forms are greatly increased by the appearance of a regional entity. Taxes that could not possibly be effectively administered at a narrow local level become possible at a regional level. The often-discussed payroll tax would seem to be one of these.

Even a system of personal net income taxation would become marginally possible on administrative grounds, although the corporate equivalent would still present some difficulties of income allocation.

CONCLUSIONS

It seems clear from this brief and consciously suggestive examination that on both the expenditure and revenue sides of the question the advantage must be assigned to a regional organization for the pursuit of regional problems. Final conclusions are few, but the logic seems inescapable. If we wait for final conclusions before we develop the fiscal elements of a regional constitution, we will, most assuredly, never have a regional constitution.

FINANCING THE JOBS THAT NEED TO BE DONE:
WHO PAYS AND FOR WHAT?

Moderator: William L. C. Wheaton, *Dean, College of Environmental Design, U.C.*

Panel: Ralph Andersen, *Principal Assistant to the Director, League of California Cities*

Leslie E. Carbert, *Tax Economist, PG & E; President, Associated Regional Citizens; and former State Planning Officer*

Earl R. Rolph, *Professor of Economics, U.C.*

William L. C. Wheaton

I do not propose to make any long-winded introduction, nor do the members of this panel propose to make individual statements. Instead we're going to try to have a discussion of selected issues.

The state Council on Intergovernmental Relations attempted to estimate what the budgetary deficiencies of local governments were in 1969. To operate our present package of government services conducted by municipalities and counties, we estimated we then needed $300 million a year for each category of government. And that would be without any improvement in the quality of services or without any additional services, which we all recognize we desperately need.

174

Wheaton, cont'd

If you push that estimate forward a few years, local
government is going to be $1 billion a year short in
this state, and I suppose that means about $300 million
short in the Bay region. Part of the reason local government is not as responsive as Don McCullum would like
it to be lies there.

Indeed the members of this panel have agreed that
a regional agency lacking the resources to overcome
some of the very large fiscal inadequacies in our present tax system won't have very much power and certainly
won't have enough resources to grapple with all the
problems that require attention today.

Therefore, the panel has agreed to concentrate on
the issues revolving around how much resources such
an agency might raise, how it would do so, what would
be the benefits, and what would be some of the costs.
We will leave aside the question of whether the regional agency need necessarily spend those resources
itself.

THE REGIONAL BUDGET

The first issue is raised by the regional budget
on the pink sheet that you have been given [See Appendix VII], which reveals the very interesting fact that
the federal government spends more in this region than
both the state and local governments do. So the first
question I'm going to ask the panel is: Why is this
the case and what influence might a regional agency
have on the sources of funds in the future? Why don't
you try to lead off, Ralph Andersen?

Ralph Andersen

I think that your opening comments about the revenue gap faced by local government in this state--a

176

gap that exists if we merely continue to provide services at current levels--is illustrated dramatically
by the Bay Area "Regional Budget" that we received.
If you look at that budget, and if you understand that
many of the dollars that are set next to local government actually come from state government, then one of
the things that the budget indicates is simply that
the federal and state governments have control over the
major sources of revenue that are capable of producing
the amounts of money needed to solve the problems we
face here in the Bay Area and in the state. So I think
that the first thing the Bay Area budget shows you is
who has the sources--the federal government, basically,
and the state government.

I think the figures also indicate that all levels
of government are now assuming some responsibility for
the solution of regional problems in the Bay Area.
Each level is spending a fair amount of dollars for the
solution of these problems in the 9-county Bay Area.
What this emphasizes, really, and what the budget de-
monstrates pretty rapidly, is that, in conjunction
with the debate on regional organization, there is an
equal need to look at the allocation of service responsibilities, and to reach a consensus on which levels
of government should provide which services. This is
as much a part of the discussion on how to solve regional problems as is the funding issue, which I consider to be the basic problem.

Leslie E. Carbert

It seems to me that when we're talking about the
distribution of costs among types of government, we
should be careful not to think of this as demonstrating
any inherent abilities to collect revenues. We don't
really have a solid regional organization, so we should
not be surprised that it has a low budget, or that a
collection of separate regional entities also have
relatively low budgets.

Nevertheless we might think of some of the functions that these institutions are now performing that are clearly regional in character, and ask ourselves the important question for subsequent discussion: Could these functions be more efficiently and effectively performed if they were brought under a unified organization and if opportunities to consolidate were recognized?

THE FEDERAL MONSTER

Earl R. Rolph

The budget sheet shows that the federal government is a monster, which is what we all know already. And so, one question is, what to do about it? Students of federal operation and finance are very much concerned about the difficulties the federal government is having in coming up with anything that makes very much sense in its own operations.

Perhaps some of you heard the lectures given by George Schultz, former director of the federal Bureau of the Budget, here at Berkeley about a year ago. He was so concerned about the inefficient organization of the federal government that he was proposing that the government decentralize itself into regions for purposes of administration. So if you look at it from that point of view, a very strong case can be made for having a structure of government that would be more relevant to the needs of the public than the present one. That's point number one.

My second point has to do with what Mr. McCullum was talking about. I think a major function of the federal government ought to be, and already is in part, the redistribution function. And, as you know, President Nixon has a negative income tax plan. (It wasn't his plan; it was actually started in HEW [Department of Health, Education, and Welfare] under President Johnson, by the way. Alice Rivlin was the one who

Rolph, cont'd

prepared that.) That proposal looks as if it may see
the light of day. If it does, this is going to change
fundamentally the problems of local governments in this
country, because it will take a very large chunk of
welfare expenditures off the backs of local governments,
particularly county governments.

Also, under the new plan, the vocational migration
effects of the present welfare system would be under-
mined. In all likelihood the concentration of poor
people in the core cities would be reduced.

UNCLE SUGAR AND THE LOCAL PROBLEM

Wheaton: I'd like to come back and comment on the budget again. If you look behind it, and realize that
about half of local government expenditures are by that
special district government called school districts,
and about 20 percent each by cities and counties, and
10 percent by other special districts, it becomes apparent that there really are no local governments in
the United States, or in this region. There isn't a
local government. There are layer upon layer of local
governments, each of which has only a very small piece
of the action.

Second, there's a story that a college president
was asked what would happen when the federal government
cut back on National Science Foundation and other programs that have supported university research programs
and graduate students so heavily in recent years. The
president replied, "Well, first there will be this loud
sucking noise." The illusion that somehow Uncle Sugar
is going to cut a melon and declare a $2.5 billion
dividend so that all of our financial problems in local
government will go away is probably just that: an illusion. Uncle Sugar may cut a melon; I suspect it'll
be a relatively small one, not likely to pry loose very
much of that $2.5 billion or so.

Wheaton, cont'd

And this leads me to the second question, which is:
What kinds of revenue-raising capabilities might we expect from an effective regional organization? What
kinds of taxes might it levy to resolve the resource
shortage problem? And at what kinds of rates? Earl,
do you want to tackle that, first?

GETTING MONEY WITHOUT STRINGS

Rolph: Well, let me make a general statement first.
Speaking regionally, the wealthy areas of the United
States are the metropolitan regions, and the rest of
the county (I might have trouble documenting this to
the last penny) would, on balance, be a net drain on
the metropolitan regions. The rural areas certainly
are already. So we're talking about economically viable
areas when we talk about metropolitan regions, and
they're only going to grow in one direction, and that's
up, even if the population should ever stabilize.
That's a basic fact of life.

As far as getting money is concerned, there is one
critical problem. Assuming you had some sort of regional agency, would it or would it not be entitled to
the kind of money that is now being spent by the state
Division of Highways in the Bay Area? And if the answer is that it would be entitled to the money, would
there be any strings attached? Would the regional
agency get that number of hundreds of millions per year
without having to spend it on highways--which is a very
radical idea, but not so radical as it used to be--and
be able to spend it for whatever the regional agency
saw fit?

Now if you take all the various programs that are
presently performed by the state, and the federal programs that are performed federally, and then look at
those that could be treated regionally, try to answer
these questions: Will the federal government pay the

Rolph, cont'd

region to perform the service, if it's a federal activity? Will the state government do likewise? Or, alternatively, will they grant to the municipal government the money that the other level otherwise would spend? Will they put any strings on money paid to the region or not?

These questions are absolutely critical. Because, in effect, if the federal government just took away the money from the existing regional agencies, that would mean that the federal government would stay swollen and the drain on metropolitan areas would be even greater than it presently is.

That's one question. I don't know the answer to it, and I don't know anybody who does at this stage. But, in any case, it's a fundamental issue.

There are lots of tax devices that a metropolitan area can use, just as local governments can. One, for example, is the property tax. If you take the amount of commotion going on in Sacramento, I think it's evident that our elected representatives believe that this is the most unpopular tax in the whole tax picture. Otherwise, I don't understand their behavior.

However, without going into great detail, I think one can show that owners of residential property don't even pay their way, once you compare the property tax with the benefits they receive. This really is a class type of argument in the sense that it is the middle and higher income groups who are asking for relief. I personally can't buy that argument.

But to get back to the main point: I think extension of the property tax to a regional government is perfectly feasible. There are a lot of other things that can be done as well.

One could be the much more scientific use of prices by agencies that are now performing services on a

Rolph, cont'd

regional basis, such as the provision of bridges. I
would guess that if you scientifically price the service of the Bay Bridge, the profits would be so large
that the group in power would be embarrassed to be
known as a nonprofit agency. I simply assert this, but
I think it can be shown.

My point is that if you take bridges--and you don't
need to restrict yourself to them--you can, in fact,
raise huge amounts of money. There was a study made
of the Los Angeles region by a former student of mine,
Jack Stockfish, and he found that if the city of Los
Angeles priced services in a sensible way, it could
raise as much revenue by doing that as it presently is
raising by 40 percent of its tax base. I simply mention this as a very important potential source of revenue for a metropolitan region.

A MIX OF TAXES

Carbert: Going back to the first question, I'm not as
concerned about the size of that federal figure as
other people might be. I'm perhaps a little disturbed
by the sensitivity level at which it's spent, but nevertheless it seems to be perfectly appropriate that a
fairly substantial volume of funds comes from the federal government for a variety of programs in which the
federal government has demonstrated an interest, and for
which the local base is inadequate.

I would anticipate, as Earl Rolph suggested, that
that figure would increase with any developing regional
institution, because I would hope that such an institution would receive fairly large grants from the federal government to perform regional functions in which
the federal government has taken an interest. The
major form of current grants to regional agencies is
of course that of the planning grant that goes to ABAG,
which is not very large.

Carbert, cont'd

I also think that there are important opportunities that arise at the local level or at the regional level, that develop from the unification process itself. Earl talked about the use of the property tax at the regional level, and I think this is indeed a possibility. In fact it's a greater possibility than exists for increasing the local property tax under the present fractionated structure, if only because one city is reluctant to increase its tax rate if the adjacent city is not about to also do so. They're both in competition for certain kinds of tax bases. I've seen this reluctance demonstrated many times in a concentrated, compact metropolitan area. What it tends to do is create a false sense of inadequacy. It may well be that the property tax could yield a good deal more in total than it yields now because of the competitive elements that exist among our present communities.

I think also, that it's true that other kinds of taxes can be more adequately administered by a single unified agency than by a variety of small agencies. I've suggested the marginal possibilities of even thinking about a net income tax that is larger than life in terms of its comparison with the so-called payroll tax.

And I still anticipate many collections being made at the state level, under locally and regionally imposed taxes. I would perhaps also anticipate--except that this is more and more being preempted by the state--an increase in the sales tax for these purposes.

All of these taxes are subject to their own standards of desirability, and we might want to get into that a little later. Earl touched on it when he was talking about equity levels and equity characteristics. And, of course, this exists not only in the field of taxation, and the particular mix of taxes that you use for regional purposes, but also in the kinds of functions that you assign to the regional agency for its expenditures. For these, too, can have either a progressive or regressive or redistributive effect.

THE IDEAL TAX

Andersen: The whole question of what kinds of taxes
might be appropriate for a regional agency reminds me
of the story that Houston Flournoy, the state controller, told many times when he was in charge of the governor's task force on tax reform. He said that his
commission's responsibility was really a very simple
one. All it had to do was find one source of revenue
that would meet the needs of state and local government, resolve the inequities, be adequate from the
standpoint of the dollars needed, and be paid for totally by visitors to the state. And that's about how
easy our question is to answer.

Nevertheless, the funding question: What types of
revenue sources might be made available to an organization designed to cope with regional problems?--is
probably the most important one. Obviously it doesn't
make any difference how much authority you have if you
don't have the dollars to support that authority.

An unavoidable question, however, is: What do you
want the regional organization to do? Solely plan, and
put forth guidelines? Or do you want it, in addition
to planning, to have something to do with the implementation of those plans?

If you're talking about the latter, and if the proposals are going to be packaged as regional home-rule
proposals, then I think this question needs to be
looked at: Can you in fact have regional home rule
when you are dependent solely or primarily on the federal government for your revenues? Obviously so long
as the federal government has control over the principal sources of revenue, that's where a good part of
your monies will come from.

THE THREE PRIME SOURCES OF TAX REVENUE

But on the assumption that it would be desirable
to really give meaning to the regional home rule

Andersen, cont'd

concept by providing the regional agency with its own
local sources of revenue, then I think you have to look
at one of the three sources that are capable of producing large amounts of money--property taxes, sales
taxes and income taxes. User fees are substantial
too, but basically, if you're talking about tax
sources, you're talking about property, sales or income.

I think also that if you're talking about a funding
program for a regional agency, and if you are going to
expect the regional agency to do its job, then you have
to provide that regional agency not only with the ability to raise funds, but with the ability to do it without a lot of restrictions attached. If you're going
to give them the responsibility, then give them the
tools to do the job.

In developing this regional association, I think
you also must provide, as most have urged, an on-going
and meaningful relationship for the existing units of
local government that are in the Bay Area today. As
Assemblyman Knox has indicated, if you're going to
draw your regional government in a way that fits the
circumstances of the Bay Area today, then the funding
program that you design for the regional agency should
be sure to protect and preserve the integrity of those
existing units of local government. You can't take all
the property and all the sales and all the income taxes
away from cities and counties and expect them to continue to do the job that they will have to do under the
regional framework.

And, finally, the funding program ought to, in my
opinion, take into account this question of equalization, because there is no question, as Les Carbert has
indicated, but that there are better ways to levy
taxes. Since the broader the tax base, the more equalization you generally get, you do have an opportunity
to equalize with a regional tax base. Equalization
alone will not solve the funding problem or the revenue

Andersen, cont'd

gap problem, but it can go a long way toward providing
that minimum level of service that all are entitled to.

HOW MUCH AND FROM WHOM?

Carbert: I don't think we should be deluded by the title
on the budget sheet that suggests that it's a regional
budget. If you look at the regional districts and agencies on the next page, and go down the list, I'm sure
you can all identify some that are performing their
services fairly, others that are performing them poorly,
others that are performing them abysmally, and others
that probably shouldn't even exist.

Given this situation, I think we should not be
deluded into thinking that $62,650,000 is the absolute
amount of money we're trying to raise. On the contrary,
I think we must consider that one of the reasons for
regional government is the opportunity to increase
those service levels; and increase them partly through
efficiencies but partly, and admittedly, through new
sources of revenue. Or, if the services are not new
in style, at least new in level.

I don't think we should delude ourselves that we
can expect significant reductions in total tax expenditures by the invention of a local governmental entity.
I just don't think that's going to happen, and I for
one, don't want it to happen, because I want to see
our problems solved. That's one of the reasons I'm
interested in having a regional institution.

Having said that, I don't think there really are
any absolutes. How much money can we raise? I think
we must first spell out the problems that are to be
solved. And then we should ask ourselves: Can we
raise this much money without destroying the body poli-
tic? That is the fundamental question.

Carbert, cont'd

Next we start asking: Where can we get it? We go to Washington, and we go to Sacramento, and we look inwardly to see how much we can raise ourselves. Then we look to the visitors, Ralph [Andersen].

But I think if you start assuming that there is an absolute amount of money that can be raised, and then asking what problems we can solve with this absolute amount of money, the whole political issue is reversed. You see, there's an inborn tendency for existing political jurisdictions to do precisely that--and justify it as budgeting. Well, let's not saddle a new agency with the same illogic. It will get there fast enough.

A REGIONAL INCOME TAX

Wheaton: Let me clarify one point. It always seemed to me that a regional agency could, in fact, levy an income tax at a level and in a way that no municipal or county agency could, because of displacement effects. The same thing would be pretty much true of the sales tax. Therefore, the two basic tax sources that have enabled the federal and state governments to command most of the tax resources, and that are not available to municipal and county government, do become available to a metropolitan government. Is that correct? Do you agree?

Carbert: I do, and I think Earl does too.

Rolph: Yes.

Wheaton: In that case, for financing purposes, we might very well be able to leave our existing local government structure pretty much as it is, perhaps relieving it of some responsibilities, while we create a new level of taxing ability that simply doesn't exist for local government today. I think that's a very important consideration. Several of you have referred to the problem

Wheaton, cont'd

of equity. I wonder in what respects regional revenue--
and by revenue I include taxation and service charges
or user charges--might really markedly improve the
equity in our present local tax system?

EQUALIZING THE TAX BASE

Carbert: Well, for one thing it would permit some of
the people of Atherton to help pay to solve the problems of the people of East Oakland.

Wheaton: Are you trying to get votes out there in
Piedmont?

Carbert: No, it's just a fact that when you equalize
the tax base, you equalize the tendency to locate in
communities of different economic levels. Depending
on the specific taxes that you use, of course, you can
also reverse the whole thing. But an equal tax base
tends to equalize the differences between communities,
as well as between individuals.

Wheaton: I wonder whether any member of the panel or
the audience can quickly apply his slide rule to find
what it would cost in income tax terms to equalize educational expenditures up to that $1,600 level cited
in an earlier panel.

Rolph: Well, before somebody gets his slide rule, may
I make a suggestion? Education is a particularly
critical type of public service; there's a great deal
of disagreement about how it should be financed. There
is more or less agreement that the present way of financing education is not very satisfactory; I think
that's about all you could get agreement on.

Now my own thinking about this has led me to a
fairly radical conclusion, which you may or may not
want to buy. I don't suggest that you buy it off-hand,

Rolph, cont'd

because I didn't buy it myself very quickly. But I'm convinced that in the poorer regions of the cities, as matters presently stand, the probability of radical improvement in the quality of educational service being delivered to these people is very small. Moreover, I'm not impressed by the quality of public schools as I see them, not only in this area and state but elsewhere, even in those schools that cater to high-income children.

All this has led me to the notion that perhaps we should adopt the Friedman scheme, which I hate to agree with, but nevertheless I think I do. That plan, as far as education is concerned, would give parents a genuine choice; it would break the monopoly of the local school district and of the local school.

It is sometimes called the "voucher system," but in any case the essentials are that there would be federal financing of the education of each child, and that he and his parents would be entitled to spend the value of that voucher, which would be a substantial sum, for either private or public educational service of acceptable quality. There would have to be standards for this. If this sort of thing were done, the problem that you mentioned would not exist. It seems to me that this would be a highly desirable, really necessary type of step to take if we're serious about trying to improve the quality of education of our children.

Carbert: Did you notice the sucking sound already?

THE COST OF CHANGE

Andersen: I think, Mr. Chairman, that in addition to the fact that a regional tax levy would provide improved opportunity of sharing the wealth within the region, the other point that needs to be stressed is the one the panel began on. That is, that there exists

Andersen, cont'd

today a very serious revenue gap that needs to be closed just to permit government to continue providing existing services at existing levels.

Now if you're talking about regional problems as they're generally defined, when you're talking about transportation, you're not talking about local streets and roads as much as mass-transit systems. When you're talking about open space, you're largely talking about the preservation of open space through acquisition. When you're talking about solid waste, you're talking about the acquisition of adequate sites that are large enough for an area to use that will continue to be sufficient over a period of time. When you're talking about water quality, you're largely talking about sewage treatment facilities.

These are major cost items and the equity question is not going to resolve that problem. You could reallocate every revenue source that's levied today, and still not solve the basic funding dilemma that a regional agency is going to face in terms of solving its problems.

In the general tax reform discussions that have gone on in Sacramento, it's often been suggested that with respect to city government, for example, you should reallocate the sales tax so that those cities that don't levy a property tax will be forced to levy one. Now, that's an issue. But there are only some 29 cities in the state (representing only about 5 percent of the population) that don't levy a property tax. Even if you took every dime that those cities received, and reallocated it, you wouldn't begin to get the kinds of revenue necessary to meet the real funding problems that a regional agency will face.

Wheaton: Does anybody want to estimate what kind of rates of either property or sales or income tax we might be talking about if we're talking about a $300 million gap?

Rolph: I forgot to bring my slide rule. But may I say something about this gap business? The words crisis, gap, efficiency, what-have-you, have been and continue to be used about local governments. In fact, if you read the literature you would think that we were living in a country that was about 5 percent richer than India. If you listen to mayors and their moaning, you would think that the wealth in the city is very small.

But as we all know, this is a bunch of baloney, except for certain cities in the United States that are in real trouble. When a politician says there's a gap, what he's really saying is, "What'll happen to me politically if I support measures that will have the effect of upping the property tax by so much?" And everybody knows what's going to happen to him if he does that. He's going to get kicked out of office.

So the constraint is not economic. It isn't true that the city of San Francisco is poor, by any stretch of anybody's imagination. It is a mere fact of life that Mayor Alioto knows that his political career turns on talking this way. He does not believe it any more than I do.

Wheaton: But it *is* a fact that Joseph Alioto as a mayor today could not levy a one percent progressive income tax, whereas as a member of a metropolitan regional agency he could do so and it would not have serious displacement effects. Isn't that correct?

Carbert: It gives you a much better economic mix of tax types, if you can use a variety of taxes for equity purposes. A mix of taxes--some of which are progressive, some of which are relatively neutral, and others that are perhaps even slightly regressive in the manner in which they're administered--creates a little easier impact on the political institution that uses them.

But you don't have this opportunity, really, in our largest cities. The City of New York tried to do this and did develop a kind of income tax, but it's rather a

weird sort of institution. Why? Because the City of
New York is in competition with its own suburbs, and
it's in competition with New Jersey, Pennsylvania and
Connecticut. And so it not only has the usual political hurdle, but it has an economic hurdle in resolving
what the politicians seek in terms of economic development.

The panel has emphasized fully and carefully the
possibility of a greater equity with a regional tax
base and the redistributive opportunities that could
exist. But if we take Don McCullum's principal
problems--housing, education, and jobs, and translate
the job problem partly at least into transportation--I
would only see one of these problems as being directly
the responsibility of the regional government. And
that's transportation.

That means that if the redistribution is going to
be meaningful, some of the money is going to have to be
turned back to local governments to spend for these
other purposes, or the purposes are going to have to be
taken away from local government and given to the regional government. I'm wondering what the panel members think about this question. Which way do they think
it might go? If it's going to result in cash payments
from the metropolitan government to local governments,
how will that be worked out?

A MATTER OF PRIORITY

Wheaton: Let me answer that question in one way, and
that is that to a slight degree ABAG is already beginning to perform a reallocation function with respect to
that federal money. Under A-95, ABAG must clear every
application to the federal government from a local government in the region. ABAG has no authority whatsoever to say, "No, you can't have the federal money if
you can get it out of the feds." But it must say, "It

Wheaton, cont'd

is in conformity with our plan, or it is not in conformity with our plan." And it must comment.

I think it's pretty evident that as federal control over federal grants-in-aid becomes more serious, as there are efforts to make those dollars work more efficiently and to make them respond more closely to regional needs, ABAG, or any regional government agency performing this federal review function, will ultimately be setting some priorities. Confronted with 5 applications for sewer improvement from 5 different counties, the feds are very likely to say, "Which is the most important, or which performs the prior function in eventually establishing a regional system?" So it seems to me the probability is very great that a regional agency will get its hands on a big chunk of that $3 billion flow in the long run, and do so as it begins to establish priorities.

Now I come back to an earlier question. If you look at housing and education and jobs, federal government now has a fairly substantial stake in the housing and job functions. It seems to me that much could be done at the regional level to allocate those funds to areas of greater relative need. Our present system probably tends, as many of our grant-in-aid systems do, to further reward the areas that are better off and to further penalize the areas that are worse off.

Would you like to respond, Mr. Vella?

Vella: Mr. Wheaton, I would like to reply to a point you made about the A-95 review. There are people here who were in Atlanta with me at the Council of Governments' Convocation, where we were told by quite a few that the interpretation of A-95 was going to be considerably different. If you wish to consider it a settled issue--and that's what I consider it to be at the moment--we at ABAG are going to get to review all 5 of those applications, but we are not going to set the

Vella, cont'd

priorities on them. We're going to bundle them up, and
we're going to send them up to Sacramento, and the state
is going to assign those priorities. You know who's
going to get the blame? ABAG's going to get the blame,
but the state is going to assign the priorities.

With administrative edicts, it is not the written
word that is the important thing, it is the administrative interpretation, and that is the administrative
interpretation that HUD is going to put upon A-95. It
has already begun; my own county in an application for
a general plan on an innovative 701B wound up number
three on the list--not on ABAG's list, but on the
state's list. I believe I wound up in the third place
not simply because the plan wasn't innovative enough,
but because, very frankly speaking, I was the third
largest of the constituencies that applied, the other
two being Contra Costa and San Mateo counties.

A CHOICE OF METHODS

Wheaton: There's one final question I would like the
panel to address itself to: If we accept the notion
that a regional government will have important responsibilities in raising new revenues from new regional
sources, and important responsibilities in achieving
greater equity in the raising of revenues and in the
distribution of these rather massive public funds that
we've been talking about, what kind of institutional
organization of regional government is most likely to
serve those revenue-raising and equity-achieving functions?

Is it the umbrella-type institution, which was the
first option; is it the central operating agency, at
the regional level; is it a combination of consolidated
special districts? And then, is it one that is governed
by a directly elected board? Or one that is a federal
system representing local governments? Or the kind of
mixed ruling body that Jack Knox spoke of earlier?

Wheaton, cont'd

Do any of the panel members want to step into that one?

Andersen: Well, let me just try a couple of considerations on for size. I think there are several considerations, and it's a very important question.

If you're talking about cities continuing to play a meaningful role in the provision of regional services, then the funding proposals for the region, as I've indicated, must be developed with this in mind: Individual units of local government are going to continue to be meaningful partners in the solution of problems facing the region.

With this in mind again, there are only three sources of revenue, basically, that are capable of providing the kinds of money that will be necessary. What I'm suggesting is that the governmental structure must allocate these sources in a way that will permit all of the participants to meet their responsibilities effectively.

I think a second consideration that is equally important is the relationship between representation and funding. During the tax reform discussions that have been going on in Sacramento, many have tried to place the emphasis on the total tax structure of state and local government, rather than looking at tax reform in a piecemeal way. They have emphasized the importance of looking at the total structure and seeing how it affects the individual taxpayer.

And in the Bay Area, where we're concerned with priorities and the best allocation of resources that are available, representation of existing governmental units becomes exceedingly important, it seems to me, since they are going to continue to be spending and raising a portion of the dollars that are going to go into the solution of the problems facing the region.

Andersen, cont'd

So if you are looking for a unit of representation, or a system of representation, that will encourage the broadest look at spending and revenue-raising, then it seems important to me to involve existing city and county officials in some way in the representation process, because they certainly are going to be playing an important part in that area.

THE NEED FOR LOCAL CONSENSUS

Another consideration--a very practical one: It seems to me that whatever proposal for regional organization in the Bay Area is made, if that proposal is going to be successfully implemented, it's got to have the consensus of the people in the region. And the easiest way to get that consensus is to have your existing units of local government--your leaders in your local communities now--playing a meaningful part in that proposal and having a role that they will continue to play so that they will support it locally. Their support will not only help to get that consensus for the proposal, but will be essential to implement it.

Carbert: I don't see that as a justification for a relationship at all, Ralph. After all, the State of California goes about developing its fiscal structure without direct representation by cities and counties, except by such fine advocates as you. I see no justification for changing the representation on the regional body just because they have a stake in the total revenues of the region. It seems to me that there has to be a constant dialogue, obviously, since we all live in the same place. But I don't see that as a justification for connecting the system of representation and the style of the tax system in the Bay Area. Do you see my point?

Wheaton: Les, which kind of representative body do you think is most likely to have the guts to levy an

Wheaton, cont'd

adequate level of reasonably equitable taxes--a federal or a directly elected body?

Carbert: I think a directly elected one, if it's given careful and adequate instructions from the state Legislature, as to what its functions are.

Wheaton: Earl, do you want to comment?

Rolph: Let me comment on this in a way to get at a problem that you raised earlier. The reason some people are advocating a regional system is that certain parts of the region are providing particular benefits to these people. The open space advocates, as a case in point, are all gung-ho for open space, although they may be living in apartments in San Francisco. So the cow-county type of local government, or local government in a cow-county--or an emerging cow-county, finds itself with a low tax base. Now the proper solution to this, economically, is for the people who love open space to compensate--pay for--the commodity they like--open space--which means paying the people who own that space.

You don't in this world get anything for nothing, ordinarily. What you can do, of course, is to pass a law saying, "This area shall remain open space," and then that just means that the people who live around that area pay higher taxes or get lower services, or both, likely both. Whereas the people who like and demand that service ought to be the people who pay for it. So if you extend the price system much more generally than is the case now, you can get rid of most of these nasty problems that otherwise exist.

Vella: You're talking in another context, but that's just exactly what Sonoma County would like!

Carbert: It seems to me that in that statement you're forgetting all of the externalities. There really are

Carbert, cont'd

virtues to open space that go beyond sitting in a park.
There are many virtues to open space in a regional setting. The benefits are widely diffused and consist of
much more than plucking posies; they really are terribly
significant for the intelligent development of a region.
Now if you act as if everybody wants to become San Francisco, and do nothing, then I think we ought to face up
to the fact that that is the kind of society that we're
going to have.

Call it the cost of doing nothing, and see how expensive it is, socially. We don't add these external
costs into so many of our considerations, because
they're vague and diffuse, and not capable of direct
quantification, but they're there. Now I'm not picking
on Sonoma County.

Wheaton: Supervisor Vella's problem reminds me of a
crack made on the radio last year. It went like this,
"Fewer people are visiting Los Angeles this year. They
know that Los Angeles will shortly move to them. So
watch for Los Angeles in your neighborhood! We'll soon
be with you." That's what I'm afraid of.

But now our time has run out. And in closing this
panel, I want to come back to the issue that was framed
for us at the beginning of the day: It is evident that
local government in the Bay region lacks the resources
and the government structure necessary to provide many
of the services that the citizens of the region increasingly recognize that they must have.

It will be expensive to provide them. There will
be economies of scale and of efficiency that might be
made possible in selected areas, but basically we are
looking toward a new level of taxation, and a new capacity to tax, to enable us to pay for the joint services
that we need so badly.

I hope that in his concluding remarks, Jack Knox
will comment on the differences in the ability to

Wheaton, cont'd

grapple with these financial problems that would be
generated by different legislative representational
formulas.

I want to thank the members of the panel for their
share in these proceedings, Mr. Andersen, Mr. Carbert,
and Mr. Rolph.

Part Five

Summary and Commentary

SUMMARY AND COMMENTARY

Eugene C. Lee
John T. Knox
Ignazio A. Vella

Lee: To conclude our session, I'm going to ask Supervisor Vella and Assemblyman Knox to return to the stage with me for just a few minutes to see what we can make out of today's discussion.

As they walk up, let me tell you briefly what I make of it. I take from our few hours of discussion these conclusions: There seems to be an increased recognition, from what we have heard today, of the need for increased coordination of the existing agencies.

If there was a feeling that we could continue the status quo approach, that we could go up the single-purpose route into the future and rely upon other levels to coordinate these functions for us, some of the remarks today have certainly put that notion to rest, at least to a considerable degree. Secondly, there is certainly a continued uncertainty over the consequences of various patterns of representation.

QUESTIONS AND CONCERNS

We heard comments that raised questions and concerns about the campaign costs and the role of special interest groups and parties, in the creation of a new and explicit type of regional politics involved in direct elections.

On the other hand, the concerns over ABAG's type of constituent-unit representation go long and deep.

Lee, cont'd

They particularly include the failures of the local government units to be adequately representative of different groups within the community and the way these failures reflect upon the regional organization itself. They go to the real problems of adapting one form of local election system--basically the system we know so well where you vote for 3 out of 5 and so on--adapting that form of local politics and local elections for regional purposes.

Mary Henderson believes that as we consider this problem, we have to think quite differently about the kind of local agency--the kind of local legislative body--we're talking about. She suggests that maybe we should look to a far larger legislative body (either mixed or directly elected) than we have been considering.

I'm interested that we seem to be confined in our discussion to these two patterns of representation; we are apparently not interested in other alternative patterns, such as different methods of appointment, either by the governor or the Legislature. At least from today's discussion, we seem to be confining our attention largely to either direct election or the constituent-unit system.

ARE WE WILLING TO CHANGE?

Moreover, it's not clear to me from our discussion today whether the citizens represented in this room are so convinced of the need for coordinated regional action that they're willing to compromise on forms of representation.

I got throughout the meeting a clear view that the momentum for the moment seems to be running with state agencies. They are the ones that increasingly are making the critical decisions facing the region. I believe

Lee, cont'd

only the major land-use decisions are now being made
by county governments.

And finally out of our last panel came the fundamental point that the deck seems stacked against
change--against effective regional organization--because
of our seeming inability to consider new alternatives
of taxation. It's a paradox that the wealthiest regions
in the world cannot finance their own needs. Apparently
these are political and organizational questions, not
simply economic ones.

I conclude from this that perhaps one of the
political reasons for the creation of a regional government or regional organization is to make new kinds
of revenue practical and possible. For only by region-
alizing can adequate revenue be made available for the
various public programs we need.

I've asked both Jack Knox and Supervisor Vella to
help us conclude this meeting with some final comments.
Let me first turn to Assemblyman Knox.

Knox: Thank you very much, Gene. Somebody at lunch
suggested we take a couple of straw votes--not that our
audience constitutes a scientific sampling, or anything
of that nature, but the people who are here should at
least get a chance to express their views. Before I
ask you to raise your hands on just a couple of issues,
I'd like to indicate as strongly as I can that we propose this year to try to obtain a regional organization
for the San Francisco Bay Region. The bill that I hope
will become the vehicle for it is AB 2310.

This bill constitutes a number of compromises based
on the research we've made and on the assistance that
many of you have given us over the past few years.
We're prepared if necessary to compromise further--to
find other solutions--but at some point the buck has to
stop, and some of us in the Legislature are going to
have to be the arbiters of the situation.

Knox, cont'd

I would only hope that if the bill isn't exactly the way you'd like to have it, you will have in mind that we're trying to please millions of people and that's very difficult to do. But we will naturally try to have this bill reflect as comfortable a situation, as effective a situation, as it possibly can for the region, as well as to make it workable.

But I do want to indicate that we are going to push this bill this year, just as hard as we can. What is it old George Miller used to say? "That bill will pass over my dead body!" But, of course, there are a lot of dead bodies in Sacramento. I would hope that this bill will pass, and will become an effective vehicle. And also after it passes, and after it goes into effect, don't forget that the Legislature meets every year, and if we've made some horrible mistake--which has never occurred up to now--we stand ready to attempt to alleviate it.

THE AUDIENCE VOTES

Now for the audience vote. I am first going to ask about representation. I will give three alternatives. Please vote for the method you'd most prefer of these three: direct election; a combination of both a directly elected legislative body and a constituent-selected body; or everyone under the ABAG constituent system.

[Ed. note: By the time the straw vote was taken at the end of the afternoon, part of the audience had left. Voting was by show of hands to indicate general preferences. Since no actual vote count was made, observers' estimates on results are included in square brackets after each vote.]

I'll start with the last one first: Who here prefers the pure ABAG system? [few] Now how many prefer

Knox, cont'd

a combination of the two? [more] And how many prefer
solely direct election? [most]

Now this next question is a little more difficult
to answer, but we'll do the best we can. Of the various forms that Stan Scott suggested, I'm only going to
mention two: Do you (1) most prefer a regional organization that will take over all of the functions presently operated by regional agencies and then add to
that the additional functions that aren't being performed by anybody at the present time, or (2) do you
prefer the type of umbrella agency that is in the proposal now in Sacramento? First, how many prefer the
umbrella agency approach? [fewer] Then how many prefer taking over all of the functions of a regional
nature? [more]

Now the last question: In our current bill there
is a provision that after the Legislature finishes
setting this matter up, the whole question of whether
it will be established will then be put to a vote of
the people--a referendum. How many think that a referendum is important and necessary? [fewer] And how
many feel that the state Legislature should just establish this and not put it to a vote of the people?
[more] Okay. Thank you very much for a very interesting day.

Vella: It was very interesting to note Mr. Carbert's
comment on taxes. It reminded me of a budget session
at the Board of Supervisors' level. We can get 350
people out for a discussion on mobile homes; we can get
550 or 600 out on the Jenner question; but we get a
half dozen out when we discuss the budget.

However, all these things are related to the budget, so I agree with Mr. Carbert. I would also commend to him that he read AB 1846 (1969), which was our
version of John Knox's AB 711 a year ago, and he may
also find some of it amended into AB 2310 this year.

206

Vella, cont'd

In regard to Professor Rolph's views on educational
financing, I wonder if it would hurt to go back to the
original concept in 1935 when the sales tax was put in.
It was put in, you remember, with the idea that 50 percent of it was supposed to go to education. It was supposed to give to education a growing tax, one that
would grow with the population and supposedly with its
needs. And all the Mickey Mouse financing that's gone
in between has been an attempt to justify why that
sales tax has been diverted away from education, at
least in great part, to the point where in my county
the state share only represents 38 percent and the rest
is ours. (Mayor Alioto has said that he's down to 12
percent--I don't know about that, because I don't live
in San Francisco, but that's what he told me.) I think
maybe if we went back to 50-50 a lot of our school financing would become an awful lot easier.

Now I'm going to say something that is my own opinion but was reinforced by my trip to Atlanta. And that
is that there is in the Department of Housing and Urban
Development right now--and I referred to it from the
floor in A-95 procedures--a very definite chance that
everything involving procedures that put teeth in the
review of grant applications is going to be referred
to the state and then *up to* the federal government.
Secretary George Romney has this idea--I heard him and
his own man expound it--and I feel that this is one of
the ways that there is going to be an increasing amount
of federalism included under the state and local aegis.
I think we have enough already. Mr. Knox agrees we
have enough, too. I commend this extension of federalism to your watchfulness, because I think we ought
to oppose it. They're worried about it in Atlanta,
which has, like San Francisco, a regional agency for
HUD (Department of Housing and Urban Development.)

Another thing I commend to your attention is a
provision in the 1966 Demonstration Cities Act that
people seem to have totally overlooked. There is a

Vella, cont'd

provision in that act that says: "If someone, i.e., state or local government, does not act, the federal government can mandate the state Legislature to take action." And while John Knox and I may disagree about many things, we will never come to so bitter a disagreement that I would rather have the federal government write the provisions of regional government than I would John Knox's committee.

This is why I consider that no matter how odious a regional government bill may be, if it gets a dialogue started, it is a very great thing for the people of the Bay Area. Because if we don't do it, ladies and gentlemen, somebody else is going to do it for us. The HUD regulations are there to do it, the Demonstration Cities Act is there to do it, all that remains is for us to do nothing.

"THE OWL AND THE PANTHER"

Now to end on two notes. One is that I notice that the public servant of today still has need of those virtues celebrated in the New Testament, the virtues of the compleat gentleman, and that's spelled c-o-m-p-l-e-a-t.

The second is to remind you of the poem about "The Owl and the Panther."

I passed by his garden, and marked with one eye
How the Owl and the Panther were sharing a pie,
The Panther took piecrust, and gravy, and meat
While the Owl had the dish as its share of the
   treat.
When the pie was all finished, the Owl as a boon
Was kindly permitted to pocket the spoon,
While the Panther received knife and fork with
   a growl
And concluded the banquet by eating the Owl.

Vella, cont'd

As a local government official, it's very nice to know that there are so many worried owls in the world outside.

Lee: In closing let me thank all the panelists and moderators. Our goal has not been to reach decisions or conclusions, but to increase our information, so that we can be better prepared to move ahead and to influence our local and state legislators. We hope that we have in some fashion achieved that goal. Thank you so much for coming.

Appendices

Appendix I

COMPARATIVE ANALYSIS OF THREE STATE LEGISLATIVE PROPOSALS FOR BAY AREA REGIONAL ORGANIZATION

Ora Huth

LEGISLATIVE PROPOSAL	AB 1846 (BAGLEY) 1969	AB 711 (KNOX) 1969	AB 2310 (KNOX) 1970
REGIONAL AGENCY	BAY AREA HOME RULE AGENCY	REGIONAL GOVERNMENT OF THE BAY AREA	CONSERVATION AND DEVELOPMENT AGENCY OF THE BAY AREA
ORGANIZATION:			
I AREA	The 9 Bay Area counties: Alameda, Contra Costa, Marin, Napa, San Francisco, San Mateo, Santa Clara, Solano and Sonoma.	Same as the area under the San Francisco Bay Area Regional Water Quality Control Board. Includes San Francisco and most of the area in the 8 other Bay Area counties.	The 9 Bay Area counties.
II ESTABLISHMENT	Created by the legislation.	Established by referendum in the region as authorized by the Legislature.	Same as AB 711
III GOVERNING BODY A. Composition	*Executive Committee*--38 members and alternates: the president and vice president; 32 members appointed to 2-year terms by local elected officials from their governing bodies; and 4 members appointed by the U.S. President,	36-member board directly elected from substantially equal districts to 4-year staggered terms.	40-member board directly elected from substantially equal districts to 4-year staggered terms.

LEGISLATIVE PROPOSAL	AB 1846 (BAGLEY) 1969	AB 711 (KNOX) 1969	AB 2310 (KNOX) 1970
REGIONAL AGENCY	BAY AREA HOME RULE AGENCY	REGIONAL GOVERNMENT OF THE BAY AREA	CONSERVATION AND DEVELOPMENT AGENCY OF THE BAY AREA

ORGANIZATION:

	AB 1846 (BAGLEY) 1969	AB 711 (KNOX) 1969	AB 2310 (KNOX) 1970
A. Composition, cont'd	the California governor, and Bay Area assemblymen and senators from federal and state officials. *General Assembly*--1 representative and alternate from each Bay Area city and county governing body. Federal and state appointees serve as nonvoting members. The president and vice president vote to break a tie.		
B. Executive Committee	Executive committee as the principal governing body. The general assembly responsible for the annual budget, proposals adding to agency functions and authority, and appeal matters from the executive committee.	6- to 10-member executive committee appointed by the board responsible for duties delegated by the board. Decisions would be subject to amendment or repeal by the agency board.	No provisions.
C. Compensation	Executive Committee: $50 per diem payment not to exceed $200 per month and official expenses reimbursement. Additional pay for president, vice presi-	Board: $6 thousand salary paid in equal monthly installments and per diem set by the board not exceeding an assemblyman's compensation.	Board: $2400 salary paid in equal monthly installments.

executive committee.		year. Executive committee: Added pay not to exceed $2 thousand per year.	Same as AB 711.
D. Vacancies	Filled by appointing power. Executive committee vacancies filled immediately; general assembly representatives serve until successors are appointed. Members serve so long as they hold qualifying office.	Over one year remaining: filled by election called within 30 days. Less than one year remaining: filled by appointment by the board.	Same as AB 711.
IV OFFICERS: PRESIDENT AND VICE PRESIDENT	Any qualified elector eligible on nomination by petition signed by 15 local elected officials. Election for 2-year terms by secret ballot of all local elected officials in the Bay Area. Presiding officer of general assembly, ex officio chairman of executive committee. Vacancy: Vice president becomes president and executive committee appoints new vice president.	Selected by the board from among the members. President given a second vote for tie-breaking purposes. Presiding officer of the regional board and the executive committee. In the absence of the president, the vice president serves.	No provision for selection. AB 2310 specifies various duties for the president and, in his absence, the vice president, including provision for a second vote for tie-breaking purposes.
V PERMANENT COMMITTEES	Executive committee and a 6-member finance subcommittee appointed by the president.	Executive committee and 5 standing committees for Bay, transportation, environment, parks and open space, and utility elements.	4 standing committees for Bay, transportation, environment, and parks and open space elements.

LEGISLATIVE PROPOSAL	AB 1846 (BAGLEY) 1969	AB 711 (KNOX) 1969	AB 2310 (KNOX) 1970
ORGANIZATION:			
VI STAFF	Executive director, legal counsel and finance officer appointed by the executive committee; nominees of the executive director approved by the executive committee; other employees appointed by the executive director.	Administrative officer, attorney, clerk, auditor and other officers appointed by the board; appointees of the administrative officer including the treasurer, planning director and other authorized officers.	Same as AB 711.
VII CIVIL SERVICE	No provisions.	Board authorized to establish a civil service system.	Same as AB 711.
VIII RETIREMENT BENEFITS	No provisions.	Retirement system authorized.	Same as AB 711.
IX ADVISORS AND ADVISORY COMMITTEES	Advisory committees required for each function (initially 9) to be appointed by the president from Bay Area residents on approval of the executive committee. Commission and committee members for BCDC, BATS and the Bay-Delta Program to be retained for 2 years as advisory committee members. Other special technical and advisory committees are authorized.	Advisory and technical advisory committees are authorized. Could include officers and employees of the agency. Compensation for necessary and reasonable expenses provided.	Same as AB 711.
X INITIATIVE, REFER-	No provisions.	Subject to standard pro-	Same as AB 711.

I FUNCTIONS	Required planning elements are: (1) Comprehensive regional planning, including housing, (2) solid waste, (3) open space and parks, (4) airports, (5) Bay conservation and development, (6) transportation, (7) sewage and waste water treatment and disposal, (8) air pollution, and (9) criminal justice planning and supplementary law enforcement programs. The agency would: assume the functions of BCDC, BATS and the Bay-Delta Program; be responsible for the federal and state grant review function; and be authorized to make joint powers agreements. New functions could be authorized by the general assembly. Agency planning would be advisory to local governments.	Required planning elements are: (1) Bay conservation and development, (2) transportation, (3) environmental quality, (4) parks and open space, and (5) public service facilities. The agency would: assume the functions of BCDC, BATS, the Bay-Delta Program, and operation and maintenance of regional parks and open space; be responsible for the federal and state grant review function; provide a clearinghouse for job training and job placement programs; and be authorized to make joint powers agreements. New functions would be authorized only by the Legislature. Standards and criteria for planning would be binding on local governments.	Preparation of a regional resources plan is required with elements for: (1) Bay conservation and development, (2) transportation, (3) environmental quality, and (4) parks and open space. The agency would: be responsible for the federal and state grant review function, and be authorized to make joint powers agreements. Agency rules and regulations for planning would be binding on local governments. New functions would be authorized only by the Legislature.
II REGIONAL SERVICE AREAS	Regional service areas are authorized to administer programs not applicable to the region as a whole. For this purpose the agency could acquire and operate facilities, furnish services, cooperate for joint	Regional service areas are authorized to administer programs not applicable to the region as a whole. For this purpose the agency could provide for: flexible boundaries, special bonds, special	No provisions.

LEGISLATIVE PROPOSAL	AB 1846 (BAGLEY) 1969	AB 711 (KNOX) 1969	AB2310 (KNOX) 1970
POWERS AND DUTIES:			
II REGIONAL SERVICE AREAS, cont'd	programs, issue special bonds and collect service charges and special taxes (on voter approval). The special area could be initiated by the agency, any local agency or voters.	property taxes, service charges, and contracts. The special areas could be initiated by the agency, any local agency, or by petition by voters or landowners.	
III RESPONSIBILITY FOR REGIONAL PLANNING			
A. Regional Plan Preparation	Responsible for preparation of a plan for each of the mandatory elements. Specific plans are authorized.	Responsible for preparation of a plan for each of the mandatory elements within 5 years. Must consider: population characteristics, business activities, housing, facilities including transportation, land uses and blighted areas, important sites and structures, and natural resources. Could include plans for matters usually of local agency concern without conforming to local plans. If reasonable, would consider proposed public actions over a 5-year period after plan adoption, anticipated programs, future public land acquisition, future facili-	Responsible for preparation of a plan for each of the mandatory elements within 3 years. Must consider population characteristics, business activities, housing, facilities including transportation, land uses, blighted areas, important sites and structures, and natural resources. If reasonable, would consider: proposed public actions over a 5-year period after plan adoption, anticipated programs, future public land acquisition, future facilities, people displacement, future development needs and controls, plus public funding available, and social and economic consequences of public actions. Specific and interim plans

			and controls, plus public funding available, and social and economic consequences of public actions. Specific and interim plans are authorized.
B. Regional Plan Adoption	Following hearings on the plan, adoption is authorized by majority vote in the general assembly, tabulated separately for city and county representatives. Adoption of specific plans is authorized.	Following hearings on the plan, adoption is required within 5 years, with at least 1 element to be adopted each year. Adoption of specific and interim plans is authorized. Adoption of an interim general plan is required within 30 to 270 days, including the BCDC, BATS and Bay-Delta plans.	Following hearings on the plan, adoption is required within 3 years, with at least 1 element to be adopted each year. Adoption of specific plans and interim plans is authorized. Adoption of an interim resources plan is required within 30 to 270 days, including the BCDC plan.
C. Regional Plan Alteration	Following adoption, changes could be made in the same manner provided for adoption of the Regional General Plan.	Following adoption, changes could be made at any time under procedures requiring notification to cities, counties and interested persons regarding proposed changes and hearing dates. Adoption of changes would be in the same manner provided for the regional general plan. Continuous plan review is required.	Same as AB 711.
D. Regional Plan Implementation	The regional plan would be advisory only. The agency	implement and administer	Local agencies could be required to use agency data in
		Authority is given: to	

LEGISLATIVE PROPOSAL	AB 1846 (BAGLEY) 1969	AB 711 (KNOX) 1969	AB 2310 (KNOX) 1970
POWERS AND DUTIES:			
D. Regional Plan Implementation, cont'd	is authorized to conduct conferences to develop special plan elements to contain implementing policies and standards. These would be followed by: conferences to explore means of implementing the plan elements; a staff proposal for implementation; submittal of an implementation program to the general assembly by the executive committee, to include a finding that the problem is regional and outlining area of benefit; and a vote on the element by the general assembly under the same procedures required for adoption of the regional plan. The agency could not make and enforce local zoning regulations. Following adoption of a special plan element the agency could undertake implementation.	a Bay plan enforced by ordinances setting permit, variance, and hearing procedures covering Bay waters and immediately adjacent land; to adopt ordinances prescribing standards and criteria for the other mandatory elements, with conformity and compliance required in the plans of local agencies; and to recommend model ordinances to local agencies to implement discretionary elements. Local agencies are required to supply requested data and carry out comprehensive local planning. Authority is given for: water quality control and management, including power to require sewage connections; regional parks and open space, including power to own and operate parks and buy land for these purposes; and the regional highway system,	preparing local plans and to supply requested data. Local planning and development action having a direct effect on matters covered by agency plans must comply with agency rules and regulations for mandatory planning elements. Agency planning could not preclude adoption of any local plans, ordinances or regulations affecting these elements.

E. Property Acquisition and Facilities Operation	Eminent domain power is authorized for acquisitions declared in the public interest and necessity. Consent of local agencies required for acquisitions necessary for plan execution before real property can be acquired by any means. Exceptions are acquisitions relating to regional plans mandatory elements for which local consent is denied. For these, the agency must give 90 days notice and obtain general assembly approval by a 60 percent majority vote, tallied separately for cities and counties, and representing 60 percent of the population. Fair compensation is required. Facilities operation and property improvement could be carried out by contracts or by use of agency employees.	The agency could acquire real property by purchase, gift, condemnation, or otherwise. Eminent domain power would be implemented by 2/3 vote of agency board members and payment of fair compensation. The agency could make contracts to develop or maintain the acquisition.	No provisions.
F. Intergovernmental Relations	Authority is given to: accept money, labor, materials, and facilities construction and operation	Authority is given to: accept money, labor, materials, and facilities construction and	Authority is given to: accept money, labor, materials and facilities construction and operation from public or

LEGISLATIVE PROPOSAL	AB 1846 (BAGLEY) 1969	AB 711 (KNOX) 1969	AB 2310 (KNOX) 1970
POWERS AND DUTIES:			
F. Intergovernmental Relations, cont'd	from public or private sources; cooperate with other public agencies for the joint exercise of powers and joint sharing of property, facilities, data, and information; give assistance with grant applications; make regional studies and recommendations; and give regional special districts representation on standing advisory committees.	operation from public or private sources; cooperate with other public agencies for the joint exercise of powers and joint sharing of property, facilities, data, and information; give assistance with grant applications; make regional studies and recommendations; and collect and give out information on job placement and training matters not being handled elsewhere.	private sources; cooperate with other public agencies for the joint exercise of powers and joint sharing of property, facilities, data, and information; give assistance with grant applications; and make regional studies and recommendations.
G. Review Over Other Agency Action	The agency is given authority similar to county local agency formation commissions' powers and duties for boundary changes for existing or proposed multicounty agencies and could cooperate with these commissions for making studies and recommendations. Responsible for review of other agency's plans and action in matters affecting the general plan, including: multicounty districts, state agencies, federal agencies, and cities and counties in the Bay Area.	Agency planning and policy decisions are to coordinate planning and related activities of all public and private agencies when they affect planning and development in the Bay Area. Local agency plans are required to conform to mandatory elements of the general plan and local agencies' planning activities must conform to agency standards and criteria, the exception being planning affecting only discretionary elements.	Agency planning and policy decisions are to coordinate planning and related activity of all public and private agencies when they affect planning and development in the Bay Area. Local agency plans are required to be consistent with the mandatory elements of the resources plan and local agencies planning activity having a bearing on the resources plan must conform to agency rules and regulations.

... federal assistance grant
review required under
state and federal statutes
and regulations.

FINANCING:

I TAXING AUTHORITY	Operations are financed by a business privilege tax and a regional income surtax at a rate set by the general assembly, not to exceed ½ of 1 percent and based on the ratio of the state income tax to the bank and corporation franchise taxes and corporation income taxes.	Operations are financed by a business privilege tax and regional income surtax: the income tax to be in multiples of 1 percent and not to exceed 1 percent of state income taxes; the business privilege tax to be imposed at the same level in multiples of 1/100th of 1 percent of regional gross receipts. Public and charitable agencies would be exempt. These taxes are to be based on the ratio of state income tax to the bank and corporation franchise taxes and corporation income taxes. Property taxes could be imposed for debt service on bonds or other agency indebtedness.	Operations are financed by a business privilege tax set at a rate not to exceed ¼ of 1 percent of the personal income taxes assessed in the region. The tax is to be in multiples of 1/100th of 1 percent of regional gross receipts, and be based on the ratio of the state income tax to the bank and corporation franchise taxes and corporation income taxes.
II INDEBTEDNESS	Authority is given for issuing general obligation bonds for implementation of plan elements on approval by the general assembly	Authority is given to issue general obligation bonds subject to majority voter approval in the region under a debt limit	The agency would be authorized to borrow money and issue notes in anticipation of receipts during the first 2 fiscal years.

LEGISLATIVE PROPOSAL	AB 1846 (BAGLEY) 1969	AB 711 (KNOX) 1969	AB 2310 (KNOX) 1970
FINANCING:			
II INDEBTEDNESS, cont'd	and the electorate in elections as specified in the Public Utilities Code. The agency could issue revenue bonds and acquire and improve property by special assessment.	of 20 percent of assessed value of taxable property to be paid by a property tax levy. The agency could issue revenue bonds, acquire and improve property by special assessment, and borrow money and issue notes in anticipation of income during the first 2 years.	
III OTHER REVENUE	Authority is given to impose service charges to cover the costs of performing authorized functions.	Authority is given: to impose service charges to cover the costs of performing authorized functions; to impose and collect environmental quality fees, Bay fill fees, water quality fees, and air quality fees; and to contract with public or private sources to pay for regional studies and research.	No provisions.
IV SUBVENTIONS TO LOCAL AGENCIES	No provisions.	Surplus money, in excess of an amount equal to 20 cents multiplied by the total regional population, must be subvened and distributed to Bay Area local governments. This include all available	No provisions.

Excluded are: general reserve funds; money earmarked for prior obligations, for debt service on bonds, to pay debts in regional service areas, and other earmarked funds; and gifts for special purposes.

Appendix II

TO CREATE A BAY AREA HOME RULE AGENCY
1969 PROPOSAL: AB 1846

Ora Huth

*Introduced by Assemblyman William Bagley on April 7,
1969. Sent to the Assembly Committee on Local Government for interim study by the 1969 Legislature. 38 pages.*

ORGANIZATION OF THE AGENCY

I AREA
  A. Agency jurisdiction would include the 9 Bay Area
     counties with borders touching San Francisco Bay:
     Alameda, Contra Costa, Marin, Napa, San Francisco,
     San Mateo, Santa Clara, Solano, and Sonoma counties.
  B. The agency would be authorized to provide service
     to subregions in the 9-county area.

II ESTABLISHMENT
   The agency would be established by the legislation.

III GOVERNING BODY
   A. Composition
      1. *Executive Committee*
         a. The 38-member executive committee would be
            the principal governing body of the agency.
            The general assembly would decide on any pro-
            posals adding to its authority and functions.
            Executive committee decisions would be sub-
            ject to review by the general assembly on
            appeal backed by petition of 15 official rep-
            resentatives to the general assembly.

Acquisitions of property could be appealed to the general assembly by the affected city or county.

b. 32 of the 38 members or their alternates would be selected by the mayors, city councilmen and county supervisors of the Bay Area from their councils or boards, as follows: *Alameda County--7 representatives*: 2 by the board of supervisors, 2 by the conference of mayors, and 3 by the Oakland City Council. *Santa Clara County--6 representatives*: 2 by the board of supervisors, 2 by the conference of mayors, and 2 by the San Jose City Council. *San Francisco City and County--5 representatives*: 2 by the board of supervisors, 2 including the mayor and one other elected or appointed officer selected by the mayor, and one representative to be appointed alternately by the mayor and the board of supervisors. *Contra Costa and San Mateo counties--3 representatives each*: one by the board of supervisors, one by the mayors' conference, and one appointed alternately by the board of supervisors and the mayors' conference. *Marin, Napa, Solano and Sonoma counties--2 representatives each:* one by the board of supervisors and one by the mayors' conference.

c. The executive committee would include 6 other voting members or their alternates: (1) the agency president and vice president; (2) one appointee of the President of the United States from relevant federal administrative agencies; (3) one appointee of the Governor of California from among the heads of relevant state administrative agencies; (4) one appointee by and from the Bay Area state Assembly delegation; and (5) one appointee by and from the Bay Area state Senate delegation. The agency president would have a second vote for tie-breaking purposes.

2. *General Assembly*
   a. The general assembly would make the final
      determination for adding to the authority or
      functions of the agency, approving the annual
      budget, establishing the regional tax rate,
      and would rule on executive committee action
      brought to it on appeal.
   b. The general assembly would be constituted as
      follows:
      (1) Each county board of supervisors and city
          council would appoint one representative
          and an alternate from among their chair-
          men, mayors or members. San Francisco
          would be considered as both a city and a
          county for purposes of representation:
          the mayor as the city representative could
          appoint his alternate from elected or
          appointed city officers.
      (2) The agency president, vice president and
          the members of the executive committee
          appointed by the President of the United
          States, the Governor of California, and
          the Bay Area state legislative delega-
          tions would be nonvoting members of the
          general assembly. A tie vote among ei-
          ther the city or county representatives
          could be broken by a vote of the presi-
          dent.
      (3) Each representative or alternate would
          have one vote. Votes would be tabulated
          separately for county and city represen-
          tatives, with affirmative votes of a
          majority of a quorum of each required for
          action on nonlegislative items.
      (4) Proposals to increase functions, and ap-
          peals from a local agency involving ac-
          quisition of property or facilities,
          would require favorable votes by at least
          60 percent of the city and 60 percent of
          county representatives in attendance.
          Each of the two groups of representatives
          must represent 60 percent of the total

population of the cities or counties in
the region.
(5) On all other legislative items a favorable vote of at least 50 percent of the
membership, plus one, would be required.

B. Executive Committee

The executive committee would be the principal
governing body of the agency.

C. Compensation

1. Members of the executive committee or their alternates would receive a per diem payment of
$50, not to exceed $200 per month, while on official agency business. Reimbursement of official expenses would follow rules set by the executive committee.

2. The executive committee would fix the compensation of the president, vice president and members of standing advisory commissions. Officers,
executive committee and standing advisory commission members would be entitled to compensation for transportation and reasonable travel
expenses while on official agency business.

D. Vacancies

City and county officials would serve on the
executive committee and as representatives to
the general assembly so long as they continue
to hold the offices that qualified them for the
agency positions. Executive committee vacancies
are to be filled immediately by the appointing
authority. Official representatives and alternates continue to serve in the general assembly
until their successors are appointed and qualify.

IV OFFICERS: PRESIDENT AND VICE PRESIDENT

A. Any qualified elector residing within the region
would be eligible for election as president or vice
president. Nominations for these offices would be
by petition of at least 15 mayors, councilmen or
supervisors. Election would be by secret ballot of
all supervisors, mayors and city councilmen within
the region. Terms of office would be 2 years.

   1. Special provisions would apply for the election
      of the first president and vice president who
      would serve only until the end of the first gen-
      eral assembly meeting.
   2. The president and vice president would serve as
      president and vice president of the general as-
      sembly and as ex officio chairman and vice chair-
      man, respectively, of the executive committee.
      In the absence of the president, the vice presi-
      dent would act in his place.
   3. A vacancy in the office of president would be
      filled by the vice president. The executive
      committee would then appoint a replacement for
      the vice president.

V PERMANENT COMMITTEES
   The executive committee and a 6-member finance subcommittee appointed by the agency president would
   be permanent committees.
   Three of the finance subcommittee members would
   represent cities and the other 3 would represent
   counties. Their appointment would be subject to
   executive committee approval.

VI STAFF
   A. The staff would include an executive director, a
      legal counsel, and a finance officer to be appointed
      by a majority of the executive committee, and depu-
      ties of the executive director as nominated by him
      and confirmed by the executive committee.
   B. The executive director would appoint and remove all
      other employees of the agency, subject to applicable
      personnel regulations.

VII CIVIL SERVICE (No provisions in the bill)

VIII RETIREMENT BENEFITS (No provisions in the bill)

IX ADVISORS AND ADVISORY COMMITTEES
   A. Standing advisory committees or commissions would
      be required for each originally specified function
      and for each additional function assumed later.

Specified regional functions requiring such committees would be: (1) comprehensive planning, including
housing; (2) solid waste; (3) open space and parks;
(4) airports; (5) conservation and development of
the Bay and its shoreline; (6) transportation; (7)
sewage and waste water treatment and disposal; (8)
air pollution; and (9) criminal justice planning
and programs to supplement local law enforcement
programs.

1. The number of members and the interests to be
   represented would be determined by the executive
   committee under directives that the agency make
   extensive use of standing and special advisory
   commissions to be broadly representative of di-
   verse interests.
2. Standing advisory commission members would be
   appointed by the president from residents of the
   region subject to approval by the executive committee, except for carry-over members as described in B. below.
3. Advisory committees would be directed to report
   annually to the executive committee and on re-
   quest.
4. Chairmen of all standing advisory commissions
   would also serve as members, along with members
   appointed by the president with executive committee approval, of the standing commission on
   comprehensive regional planning.

B. Current members serving on the Bay Conservation and
   Development Commission (BCDC), the Bay Area Transportation Study Commission (BATS), and the Bay-
   Delta Technical Coordinating Committee (the latter
   two agencies went out of existence in 1969) would
   be retained as members of the relevant advisory
   commissions for 2 years, subject to removal by the
   original appointing agency.
C. Special temporary advisory commissions could be
   created by the executive committee to consider any
   matter of regional interest.
D. The president would be an ex officio member of all
   advisory commissions.
E. Technical advisory committees could be established

by the president. Members of such committees would
not be required to be residents of the Bay Area.
F. Special temporary advisory committees could be established by the executive committee to consider
any matter of regional interest.

X INITIATIVE, REFERENDUM AND RECALL (No provisions in the
bill)

POWERS AND DUTIES OF THE AGENCY

I FUNCTIONS
A. Functional jurisdiction would be limited to those
aspects of problems that are found to be regional
and that could not be solved by cities and counties
acting independently. The agency would have jurisdiction over the following mandatory functions:
(1) comprehensive regional planning, including
housing; (2) solid waste disposal; (3) open space
and parks; (4) airports; (5) Bay conservation and
development; (6) transportation; (7) sewage and
waste water treatment and disposal; (8) air pollution; and (9) criminal justice planning and programs
to supplement local law enforcement programs.
Agency planning would be advisory to local governments.
B. The agency would: assume the functions of BCDC,
BATS, and the responsibility for developing and operating the Bay Area component of the proposed Bay-
Delta water quality control plan; be responsible for
review and comment on applications for federal and
state grants; be authorized to carry out regional
studies and research; and be authorized to make
joint exercise of powers agreements.
C. The procedure to authorize new functions would include the following:
1. Filing of a "bill of particulars" with the agency
executive director by the executive committee,
any city council, or any board of supervisors.
2. The proposal would be discussed by Bay Area city
councils, boards of supervisors, and in public
hearings held by these agencies or by the agency
executive committee.

3. The detailed bill of particulars and public hearing results could be submitted for consideration at a subsequent general assembly meeting.
4. To assume the function, dual approval would be required by at least 60 percent of both councilmen and supervisors representing at least 60 percent of the total population in either the cities or counties.

II REGIONAL SERVICE AREAS
  A. Regional service areas could be established by the executive committee to administer regional policies and programs not applicable in the region as a whole. These could be initiated by the agency, any local government, or by petition of electors living in the affected subarea.
  B. Except for existing multicounty special districts, which could be designated as regional service areas, all other such areas would be administered by the agency, which could: (1) acquire, construct and operate facilities; (2) furnish governmental services; (3) contract with or cooperate with any public agency to carry out any regional or joint program or policy; (4) issue special bonds; (5) collect special taxes, subject to voter approval; and (6) collect special service charges and contract payments.

III RESPONSIBILITY FOR REGIONAL PLANNING
  A. Regional Plan Preparation
      The agency would be responsible for preparation of a regional plan for each of the mandatory elements.
  B. Regional Plan Adoption
    1. Following hearings on the plan held in the region, the agency would be authorized to adopt the Regional General Plan, to include authorized elements plus an element on housing needs.
    2. Adoption of the Regional General Plan in the general assembly would be by majority vote of official city and county representatives, voting separately.

C. Regional Plan Alteration
   Following adoption, changes could be made in
   the plan in the same manner as provided for
   adoption of the Regional General Plan.
D. Regional Plan Implementation
   1. Agency regional planning would be advisory only.
   2. The agency would be authorized to conduct con-
      ferences to consider special plan elements based
      on and conforming to the regional plan and con-
      taining policies and standards needed for its
      implementation.
   3. Following adoption of special plan elements,
      separate conferences would be required on each
      element, to include representatives of all gov-
      ernmental and private agencies having a respon-
      sibility for, or an interest in, the subject.
      The conferences would explore means of imple-
      menting the plan elements by the earliest and
      most efficient execution.
   4. Authorized procedures would include: develop-
      ment of a proposal for implementation by the
      staff to be submitted to the executive commit-
      tee; submittal of an implementation program to
      the general assembly by the executive committee,
      to include a finding that the problem is re-
      gional and outlining the area of benefit; and a
      vote on the program by the general assembly under
      the same procedures required for adoption of
      the regional plan.
   5. The agency could not make and enforce local zon-
      ing regulations, unless expressly required to
      do so by state law.
   6. Following adoption of the Regional General Plan,
      or any element of the plan, and adoption of a
      proposal for implementation in a special plan
      element, the agency would be authorized to
      undertake implementation of the regional aspects
      of the assumed functions.
E. Property Acquisition and Facilities Operation
   1. The agency would have the power of eminent domain
      for acquisitions declared to be in the public
      interest and necessity.

2. The agency could acquire real property necessary
for execution of the regional plan by purchase,
gift, condemnation or otherwise, only with the
consent of the city or county having jurisdiction, unless the acquisition comes under provisions for mandatory elements of the plan.
These require the agency to give 90 days' notice
of the need for such action following denial of
consent, and to obtain approval of the general
assembly by a 60 percent majority vote, tallied
separately for cities and counties, and representing 60 percent of the population.

3. The agency would be required to provide fair
compensation for the property or facilities acquired.

4. Following acquisition of the property, facilities operation and property improvement could be
carried out by contracts or with agency employees.

F. Intergovernmental Relations
1. Intergovernmental cooperation provisions would
allow the agency to accept contributions from
any public agency or private person or make contributions to any public agency. Such contributions could be in the form of money, labor,
materials, real or personal property, or construction, maintenance and operation of any facility.

2. The agency could cooperate with any other public
agency for the joint sharing of property, facilities, governmental data and information, and to
provide advice and assistance in the filing and
processing of applications for state and federal
grants.

3. Joint exercise of powers agreements could be
executed with any public agency to carry out any
powers common to the contracting parties.

4. The agency could undertake studies and make recommendations on any subject of regional concern.

5. Regional special districts would be given representation on standing advisory committees
dealing with plan elements of interest to them.

G. Review Over Other Agency Action
   1. The agency would be delegated authority similar
      to the jurisdiction, powers, and duties of the
      county local agency formation commissions for
      the supervision of proposed formation, annexa-
      tion, and exclusion proceedings involving terri-
      tory within the boundaries of existing or pro-
      posed multicounty special purpose districts.
   2. The executive committee would be authorized to
      hold hearings and make studies and recommenda-
      tions jointly with local agency formation com-
      missions in the Bay Area counties.
   3. The agency would be responsible for review and
      comment on other agencies' plans and proposed
      implementation with respect to conformity with
      the Regional General Plan. Specifically:
      a. *Multicounty special districts* would be re-
         quired to file plans affecting the agency's
         regional functions, plan elements, or land
         use, with the agency executive director at
         least 60 days before the district board's
         vote on the proposal. Following staff, ad-
         visory committee, and executive committee re-
         view of relevant data, plus results of public
         hearings, if any, the originating agency would
         be free to act, unless the proposal was de-
         termined to be in conflict with the Regional
         General Plan.
      b. *State agencies* active in programs affecting
         land use or construction of facilities would
         be required to follow the same procedures as
         specified above for regional special dis-
         tricts, with the additional requirement that
         the state Department of Finance and state
         Council on Intergovernmental Relations assist
         with this regional review.
      c. *City and county governments within the region*
         would be required to file with the agency for
         review copies of all proposals substantially
         affecting the Regional General Plan in the
         same manner as specified for regional special
         districts.

    d. *Federal agencies* that acquire Bay Area land
or construct and operate facilities would be
invited to submit such programs to the agency
for review and comment before final decisions
are made. The state Council on Intergovernmental Relations would assist the agency in
negotiating such agreements.

H. State and Federal Grant Review

The agency would be responsible for the state
and federal financial assistance review required
under state and federal statutes and regulations.
If any such grant application concerns a matter
substantially affecting an element of the Regional General Plan, the application would go to
the agency for review and comment before submittal to the granting agency.

FINANCING THE AGENCY'S OPERATIONS

I TAXING AUTHORITY

The operations of the agency would be financed
by a business privilege tax and a regional income
tax in the form of a surtax at a rate set by the
general assembly, not to exceed ½ of 1 percent
(.005).

II INDEBTEDNESS

A. The agency would be authorized to issue general
obligation bonds needed for implementation of
plan elements following approval by the general
assembly and the electorate in elections as specified in the state Public Utilities Code (Ch. 8,
Part 2, Div. 10).

B. The agency would be authorized to issue revenue
bonds and acquire property by special assessment
proceedings.

III OTHER REVENUE

The agency would have authority to impose service charges to cover the costs of performing authorized functions.

IV SUBVENTIONS TO LOCAL AGENCIES (No provisions in the bill)

TO ESTABLISH A REGIONAL GOVERNMENT OF THE BAY AREA
1969 PROPOSAL: AB 711

Ora Huth

*Introduced by Assemblyman John Knox on March 3, 1969.
Sent to the Assembly Committee on Local Government for
interim study by the 1969 Legislature. 124 pages.*

ORGANIZATION OF THE AGENCY

I AREA
  A. Agency jurisdiction would cover the same area as
     that included under the San Francisco Bay Area Re-
     gional Water Quality Control Board. This includes
     all of the City and County of San Francisco and
     most of the area in the 8 other Bay Area counties.
     It excludes northwest Marin, northern Sonoma, north-
     ern Napa, northeast Solano, eastern Contra Costa,
     eastern Alameda, southern Santa Clara and southern
     San Mateo counties.
  B. The agency would be authorized to provide service
     to subregions in the area.

II ESTABLISHMENT
     The agency would be established following authori-
     zation by a majority of the voters in the area at
     a special election.

III GOVERNING BODY
  A. Composition
        The 36-member board would be directly elected
        from substantially equal districts in odd

numbered years on a "one man, one vote" basis in nonpartisan elections to 4-year staggered terms. Procedures for nomination would require prospective trustees to be residents and voters in the area. Elections Code provisions for the nomination and election of assemblymen would apply to the nomination and election of trustees.

B. Executive Committee

The board would be required to appoint an executive committee composed of 6 to 10 agency members, plus the president, who would serve as the presiding officer. Executive committee members would be subject to removal by the board and would function under powers delegated by the board. Executive committee decisions would be subject to amendment or repeal by majority vote of the regional board.

IV COMPENSATION

A. Board members would receive a yearly salary of $6 thousand paid in equal monthly installments and a per diem set by the board, the total not to exceed the annual compensation provided for an assemblyman.

B. In addition to compensation as a trustee, the president would receive an annual stipend as fixed by the board, not to exceed $4 thousand per year.

C. Executive committee members, other than the president, would receive an additional annual stipend as fixed by the board, not to exceed $2 thousand per year.

V VACANCIES

A. In the case of an unexpired term over one year, the vacancy would be filled by special election in the election district called by the board within 30 days of the date of the vacancy.

B. In the case of an unexpired term one year or less, the vacancy would be filled by appointment by the board.

VI OFFICERS: PRESIDENT AND VICE PRESIDENT
  A. The president and vice president would be selected
     by the board from among the members. The president
     or the vice president would have one vote as a
     trustee and a second vote for tie-breaking purposes.
  B. The president or, in his absence, the vice presi-
     dent would be the presiding officer of the regional
     board and the executive committee.

VII PERMANENT COMMITTEES
  A. The executive committee would be responsible for
     matters delegated to it by the board.
  B. Initially there would be 5 standing committees, one
     for each mandatory element of the regional general
     plan: San Francisco Bay, transportation, environ-
     mental quality, regional parks and open space, and
     public service.
  C. Other standing and special committees could be es-
     tablished by the board.

VIII STAFF
  A. Officers appointed by the board would include the
     administrative officer, attorney, clerk, auditor
     and additional officers they might authorize.
  B. Employees appointed by the administrative officer
     would include the treasurer, planning director,
     and additional officers authorized and provided by
     the board.

IX CIVIL SERVICE
     The board would be authorized to establish a civil
     service system for the staff.

X RETIREMENT BENEFITS
     A retirement system available to all employees would
     be authorized. Benefits could be those available
     in any such system presently applicable to state or
     local employees.

XI ADVISORS AND ADVISORY COMMITTEES
     The agency could be authorized to employ consul-
     tants and appoint technical advisory committees and

public advisory committees that may include officers and employees of the agency. Committee members would receive compensation for necessary and
reasonable expenses.

XII INITIATIVE, REFERENDUM AND RECALL
The agency would be subject to standard provisions.

POWERS AND DUTIES OF THE AGENCY

I FUNCTIONS
  A. Functional jurisdiction would include responsibility
     for preparation of a Regional General Plan for the
     physical, social and economic future of the Bay
     Area, as well as suggesting programs for desirable
     development within the region, to include the fol-
     lowing mandatory elements: (1) San Francisco Bay
     conservation and development, (2) transportation,
     (3) environmental quality, (4) regional parks and
     open space, and (5) public service facilities.
     The agency would be responsible for development of
     ordinances for the above mandatory elements and for
     adoption of general standards and criteria that
     would be binding on local governments.
  B. The agency would: (1) assume the functions of the
     Bay Conservation and Development Commission (BCDC),
     the Bay Area Transportation Study Commission
     (BATS), the responsibility for developing and oper-
     ating the Bay Area component of the proposed Bay-
     Delta water quality control plan, and for operation
     and maintenance of regional parks and open space;
     (2) be responsible for designating regional trans-
     portation corridors and reviewing and commenting on
     proposed routes, construction and expenditures for
     regional highways; (3) be responsible for review
     and comment on applications for federal and state
     grants of regional significance; (4) function as a
     clearinghouse for information on job training and
     job placement programs; (5) be authorized to carry
     out regional studies and research; and (6) be au-
     thorized to make joint exercise of powers agree-
     ments.

C. Additional functions would be authorized only by state legislative action.

II REGIONAL SERVICE AREAS
   A. Regional service areas could be established by the agency to administer regional policies and programs not applicable to the region as a whole for: (1) making acquisitions or constructing facilities; (2) providing management, operation, or maintenance for any property or facilities; (3) furnishing governmental or proprietary services or products; and (4) cooperating or contracting with any public agency to carry out any regional or joint policy or program.
   B. The regional service areas could be initiated by the agency. In the event the agency fails to provide for such subareas, they could be initiated by any local government, by petition signed by 10 percent or more of the voters in the affected subarea, or by petition in an uninhabited area by owners of 10 percent of the affected land.
   C. In the regional service areas the agency could provide for: flexible boundaries and financing by bonding, special property taxes, service charges, and contract payments to the regional agency by public agencies or private persons.

III RESPONSIBILITY FOR REGIONAL PLANNING
   A. Regional Plan Preparation
      1. The agency would be responsible for preparation of a regional plan within a 5-year period and for development of a continuing planning process for each of the mandatory elements. The plan would be required to contain statements of objectives, policies, and standards to guide development in relation to the planning elements and for regional social and economic programs of the agency.
      2. The regional plan could also contain plans for any matters under the authority of local agencies. These components need not conform to local plans.

3. The plan would be required to include statements based on studies of the following factors, and to identify the problems connected with each: (1) population characteristics such as age, educational level, income and race; (2) amounts, types and locations of business activities; (3) amounts, types and locations of housing units; (4) location, extent and plans for major transportation, utility and regional facilities; (5) land uses and their interrelationships; (6) blighted areas and blight causes; (7) sites or buildings of aesthetic, historic, educational, or recreational quality or usefulness; and (8) natural resources, including air, water, forests, soils, rivers and other waters, waterfronts, shorelines, fisheries, wildlife and minerals.

4. To the extent reasonable, the plan would also contain advisory statements for: (1) specific public actions to be accomplished within 5 years of plan adoption, plus types of programs anticipated; (2) future public land acquisitions and estimates of the needs and provisions for relocation of displaced persons; (3) needed development controls and their implementation; (4) social and economic consequences of public actions and alternatives; and (5) assumptions regarding future development for public and private use on which the program of public actions is based.

B. Regional Plan Adoption

1. Following hearings, the board could, by ordinance, approve and adopt any authorized plan, portion of a plan or amendment, as filed or as changed by the board. Not later than 5 years after the first agency meeting, the board would be required to adopt a regional general plan containing the specified mandatory elements. At least one element would have to be adopted during each year of the 5-year period.

2. The agency would be authorized to prepare, adopt and amend specific plans based upon and conforming to the general plan in the same manner provided for the general plan.

3. Pending adoption of a comprehensive general plan
   the board could adopt plans for all authorized
   elements on an interim basis, not less than 30
   days or more than 270 days after the first agency
   meeting. The following specific plans would be
   automatically approved as interim plans: (1) the
   San Francisco Bay Conservation and Development
   Plan, (2) the Bay Area Transportation Study Commission Plan, and (3) the Bay-Delta Study Plan
   prepared by the State Water Resources Control
   Board.

C. Regional Plan Alteration

   Following adoption, the agency could repeal all
   or any part of the plan or change it, in the same
   manner as provided for adoption. The agency
   would be required to continuously review the plan
   and provide for public hearings on the plans and
   changes.

D. Regional Plan Implementation

   1. The agency would be authorized to implement and
      administer a San Francisco Bay Plan to be en-
      forced by a system of ordinances specifying de-
      velopment permit, variance and hearing proce-
      dures. To implement this plan the agency would
      have jurisdiction over Bay waters and immediately
      adjacent land.

   2. For effectuation of the remaining mandatory ele-
      ments, the agency could adopt ordinances pre-
      scribing standards and criteria for which com-
      pliance and conformity of local plans, ordinances
      and regulations are required. This would apply
      only to matters having a direct effect on the ob-
      jectives of the general plan. The agency could
      not exercise any powers vested in local govern-
      ments, but any local agency exercising such
      powers must comply with the rules, standards and
      criteria prescribed by the agency.

   3. The regional agency, by ordinance, may approve
      one or more model development ordinances and
      recommend their adoption by local agencies, when
      the ordinances relate to discretionary elements
      in the general plan covering matters authorized
      to be provided by local agencies.

4. Local agencies could adopt planning ordinances and would be required to adopt a comprehensive general plan. If such a plan has not been adopted, the regional agency may order adoption within a specified time, but allowing at least 180 days, after which it could prepare and adopt a general plan for the local agency at the latter's expense. Local agencies would be required to supply all requested data on plans.

5. Authority for *water quality control and management*. The regional agency could formulate and adopt long-range plans and implementing policies covering water pollution and water quality control that could be more stringent than those vested in existing agencies responsible for Bay Area water quality control. The agency could, by contract or condemnation, acquire, construct, maintain, operate and dispose of any water quality control facilities within or outside the region. Bay Area sewage disposal and treatment would be subject to control and regulation by the agency that is legally empowered to require that sewage collection connections be made. The agency could own and operate sewage collection facilities and, with prior consent of local agencies, could acquire their local sewage collection facilities by contract but not by condemnation.

6. Authority for the *regional highway system*. The regional agency would have the power to review and make recommendations on route locations, construction, and financing for California highways, county highways, and city streets included within the regional highway system. Final determination of such matters would be made by the California Highway Commission and, for county highways and city streets, by the local agency concerned.

7. Authority for *regional parks and open space*. The regional agency could own, establish, maintain and operate regional parks within the region, and by contract or condemnation acquire

property or an interest in property for regional park and open space purposes. The agency could acquire, maintain and operate needed facilities for such purposes, but only with the prior consent of local agencies owning and operating such facilities.

E. Property Acquisition and Facilities Operation
   1. The agency could acquire any real or personal property, or interest in such property, within or outside the region, by deed, purchase, lease, contract, gift, devise, condemnation or otherwise.
   2. The agency would have the power of eminent domain for condemnation of private property for public use. To exercise this power the agency would be required to adopt a resolution by a 2/3 vote of all board members and to provide fair compensation for the acquired property.
   3. Following acquisition, the agency could make contracts for any purposes necessary or convenient for the full exercise of its powers.

F. Intergovernmental Relations
   1. Intergovernmental cooperation provisions would allow the agency to accept contributions from any public agency or private person or to make contributions to any public agency. Such contributions could be in the form of money, labor, materials, real or personal property, or construction, maintenance and operation of any facility.
   2. The agency could cooperate with any other public agency for the joint sharing of property, facilities, governmental data and information, and to provide advice and assistance in the filing and processing of applications for state and federal grants.
   3. Joint exercise of powers agreements could be executed with any public agency to carry out any powers common to the contracting parties.
   4. The agency could undertake studies and make recommendations on any subject of regional concern. These could be carried out by employees or by

others under authorized contracts. The agency
would be authorized to provide for demonstration
programs to test the results of research and
development programs.
5. The agency would be required to collect, process,
maintain and disseminate information on Bay Area
job training, placement, and relevant matters.
For such purposes the agency could not duplicate
the powers, functions, or services of any public
or private agencies engaging in job training and
placement programs.
G. Review Over Other Agency Action
1. In making planning and policy decisions, the
agency would be required to consider and seek to
harmonize the needs and goals of the region, the
plans of local agencies, and the plans or planning activities of federal, state, and other governmental or nongovernmental agencies and organizations that affect regional planning and development.
2. The plans of all local agencies would be required
to conform to the mandatory elements in the general plan. Local action having a bearing on the
plan would be required to conform to agency standards and criteria except for discretionary elements.
H. State and Federal Grant Review
The agency would be responsible for the state
and federal financial assistance review required
under state and federal statutes and regulations.
If any such grant application concerns a matter
substantially affecting an element of the general plan, the application would go to the agency for review and comment before it is submitted
to the granting agency.

FINANCING THE AGENCY'S OPERATIONS

I TAXING AUTHORITY
A. The operations of the agency would be financed by
a business privilege tax and a regional income tax

in the form of a surtax at a rate set by the board.
The income tax would be required to be in multiples of one percent and could not exceed one percent
of the personal income taxes imposed by the state.
The regional business privilege tax, imposed at the
same level as the income surtax, would be required
to be in multiples of 1/100th of one percent of
gross receipts. Public agencies would be exempt
from paying the gross receipts tax and the agency
could provide exemptions to charitable, educational,
religious and benevolent organizations.
B. Taxes on all taxable property in the region could
be imposed and collected for debt service on bonds
or other evidences of indebtedness issued by the
agency and for expenses incurred for purposes of a
regional service area. The rate would be required
to be fixed as an even multiple of one cent computed
in mils.

II INDEBTEDNESS
A. The agency would have authority to issue general
obligation bonds subject to majority vote of the
voters in the region. The debt limitation would be
20 percent of the assessed value of taxable property in the region, with the debt to be paid by an
annual levy on the property tax.
B. The agency would be authorized to issue revenue
bonds and could also acquire and improve property
by special assessment proceedings.
C. The agency would be authorized to borrow money and
issue notes in anticipation of receipts during the
first 2 fiscal years of operation.

III OTHER REVENUE
A. The agency would be authorized to impose service
charges to cover the costs of performing authorized
functions to be established for the entire region
or within regional service areas.
B. The agency could impose and collect environmental
quality fees, Bay fill fees, water quality fees,
air quality fees, and contract with public or private sources to pay for regional studies and research.

IV SUBVENTIONS TO LOCAL AGENCIES

Within 60 days after the end of each fiscal year, the agency would be required to subvene and distribute to Bay Area local agencies surplus money in excess of an amount equal to 20 cents multiplied by the estimated population of the region. For this purpose the agency would include all available and unencumbered moneys but not including general reserve funds; or funds required to pay prior obligations, earmarked for debt service on bonds, or from funds established for regional service areas; other earmarked funds; gifts given for special purposes; or funds that cannot be legally expended for purposes of local agencies.

Appendix IV

TO ESTABLISH A CONSERVATION AND DEVELOPMENT
AGENCY OF THE BAY AREA
1970 PROPOSAL: AB 2310

Ora Huth

*Introduced by Assemblyman John Knox on April 3, 1970.
Died in the Senate Committee on Governmental Organization, August 21, 1970. 56 pages.*

ORGANIZATION OF THE AGENCY

I AREA
> Agency jurisidction would cover the 9 Bay Area coun-
> ties with borders touching San Francisco Bay: Ala-
> meda, Contra Costa, Marin, Napa, San Francisco, San
> Mateo, Santa Clara, Solano, and Sonoma counties.

II ESTABLISHMENT
> The agency would be established following authori-
> zation by a majority of the voters in the area at
> a special election.

III GOVERNING BODY
> A. Composition
>> 1. The 40-member board would be directly elected
>> from districts in odd numbered years on a "one
>> man, one vote" basis in nonpartisan elections
>> to 4-year staggered terms.
>> The measure would include provisions for filing
>> nomination papers.

2. There would be provisions for an 18-member regional districting commission appointed by the area supervisors and mayors. The commission would be composed of local government officials and would function to establish and define the boundaries of the 40 regional election districts. The districts would be substantially equal in population but would not necessarily conform to existing governmental boundaries.

B. Executive Committee (No provisions in the bill)

C. Compensation
Members of the board would receive a salary of $2,400 paid in equal monthly installments, and necessary travel expenses.

D. Vacancies
1. In the case of an unexpired term over one year, the vacancy would be filled by special election in the election district, called by the board within 30 days of the date of the vacancy.
2. In the case of an unexpired term of one year or less, the vacancy would be filled by appointment by the board.

IV OFFICERS: PRESIDENT AND VICE PRESIDENT
In the president's absence, the vice president would be responsible for performing various duties. There are no provisions in the bill for selecting these officers. The president or the vice president would have one vote as a trustee and a second vote for tie-breaking purposes.

V PERMANENT COMMITTEES
A. Executive Committee   (No provisions in the bill)
B. Standing Committees
Initially there would be 4 standing committees to provide one for each mandatory element of the agency resources plan: (1) San Francisco Bay, (2) transportation, (3) environmental quality, and (4) regional parks and open space elements. The committees would be directed to make recommendations to the agency board.
C. Other standing and special committees would be established as specified by the board.

VI STAFF
  A. Officers appointed by the board would include the
     agency administrative officer, attorney, clerk,
     auditor, and additional officers authorized by the
     board.
  B. Employees appointed by the agency administrative
     officer would include the agency treasurer, plan-
     ning director, and additional officers authorized
     and provided by the board.

VII CIVIL SERVICE
  The regional board would be authorized to establish
  a civil service system for the staff.

VIII RETIREMENT BENEFITS
  A retirement system available to all employees would
  be authorized. Benefits could be those available
  in any such system presently applicable to state or
  local employees.

IX ADVISORS AND ADVISORY COMMITTEES
  The agency would be authorized to employ consultants
  and appoint technical advisory committees and public
  advisory committees that may include officers and
  employees of the agency. Committee members would
  receive compensation for necessary and reasonable
  expenses.

X INITIATIVE, REFERENDUM AND RECALL
  The agency would be subject to standard provisions.

POWERS AND DUTIES OF THE AGENCY

I FUNCTIONS
  A. Functional jurisdiction would include responsibility
     for preparation of a regional resources plan for
     the physical, social, and economic future of the Bay
     Area and for suggesting programs for desirable de-
     velopment within the region to include the following
     mandatory elements: (1) San Francisco Bay conser-
     vation and development, (2) transportation,

(3) environmental quality, and (4) regional parks
and open space.

The agency would be responsible for development of
ordinances for effectuation of the above elements
and for adoption of general rules and regulations
that would be binding on local governments in the
region.

B. In addition the agency would: (1) be responsible
for review and comment on applications for federal
and state grants if such applications are related
to or affect mandatory elements of the resources
plan; (2) be authorized to carry out regional studies and research concerned with any subject matter
of the resources plan or matter determined to be of
regional concern by the agency; and (3) be authorized to make joint exercise of powers agreements.

C. Additional functions would be authorized only by
state legislative action.

II REGIONAL SERVICE AREAS   (No provisions in the bill)

III RESPONSIBILITY FOR REGIONAL PLANNING
A. Regional Plan Preparation
1. The agency would be responsible for preparation
of a regional plan within a 3-year period and
for development of a continuing planning process
for each of the assumed mandatory elements. The
plan would be required to contain statement of
objectives, policies, and standards to guide
development in relation to the planning elements
and the regional social and economic programs
of the agency.
2. The plan would be required to contain statements
based on studies of the following factors and to
identify the problems connected with each: (1)
population characteristics; (2) business activities; (3) information on housing; (4) the location, extent, and plans for major transportation,
utility and regional facilities; (5) land uses
and their interrelationships; (6) blighted areas;
(7) sites or structures of aesthetic, historic,
educational or recreational quality or usefulness;

and (8) natural resources, including air, water, forests, soils, rivers and other waters, waterfronts, shorelines, fisheries, wildlife and minerals.

3. To the extent reasonable, the plan would also contain advisory statements for: (1) a program of specific public actions to be accomplished within 5 years (or within a shorter period stated in the plan) of the adoption of the regional plan, plus types of future programs anticipated; (2) estimates of future public land acquisitions, public transportation, utility and other facilities, and information on relocation of displaced persons; (3) needed development controls and implementation; (4) costs of acquisitions, development, and enforcement of needed development controls and the public funds available; (5) social and economic consequences of public actions and alternatives; and (6) assumptions regarding future development for public and private use on which the program is based.

B. Regional Plan Adoption

1. Following hearings the board, by ordinance, could approve and adopt any authorized plan, portion of a plan or amendment, as filed or as changed by the board. Not later than 3 years after the first agency meeting, the board would be required to adopt a regional resources plan containing the specified mandatory elements. At least one element would have to be adopted during each year of the 3 year period.

2. The agency would be authorized to prepare, adopt and amend specific plans based upon and conforming to the resources plan in the same manner as that provided for the resources plan.

3. Pending adoption of a resources plan containing all of the specified mandatory elements, the regional board could adopt any or all of the plans and ordinances authorized, on an interim basis not less than 30 or more than 270 days after the first agency meeting. The San Francisco Bay Plan, as adopted and amended by BCDC,

would be automatically approved as an interim
plan.
C. Regional Plan Alteration
    The agency could repeal all or any part of the
    plan at any time and would be required to con-
    tinuously review the plan and provide for pub-
    lic hearings.
D. Regional Plan Implementation
    1. For the mandatory elements, the agency could
       prescribe rules and regulations that must be
       complied with in any local agency plan, ordi-
       nance, or regulation relating to planning or to
       the regulation and control of development. This
       would apply only to matters having a direct ef-
       fect on the objectives of the resources plan.
       The agency could not exercise any powers vested
       by law in local agencies, but any local agency
       exercising such powers would be required to com-
       ply with the rules and regulations prescribed
       by the agency.
    2. The agency board could authorize the planning
       director to specify data that must be used by
       local agencies in the preparation of local plans
       and ordinances. Local agency plans must only be
       consistent with agency rules and regulations.
       Agency planning could not preclude the adoption
       of any local agency plans, ordinances, or regu-
       lations affecting the mandatory elements of the
       resources plan.
    3. Local agencies would be required to comply with
       the regional agency's request for information
       on the nature and extent of all existing local
       plans, ordinances, and regulations relating to
       planning and development that could have a sub-
       stantial effect on matters covered by the man-
       datory elements of the resources plan.
E. Property Acquisition and Facilities Operation (No
    provisions in the bill)
F. Intergovernmental Relations
    1. Intergovernmental cooperation provisions would
       allow the agency to: (1) accept contributions
       such as money, labor and materials from any

public agency or private person; (2) cooperate with any other public agency for the joint sharing of property, facilities, governmental data and information; and (3) provide advice and assistance in the filing and processing of applications for state and federal grants.

2. The agency could execute joint exercise of powers agreements with any public agency to carry out any powers common to the contracting parties.

3. The agency could undertake studies and make recommendations on any subject matter of the resources plan. Such studies could extend to any subject considered to be of regional concern by the agency board. These studies could be carried out by employees or by others under authorized contracts. The agency would be authorized to provide for demonstration programs to test the results of research and development programs.

G. Review Over Other Agency Action

1. In making planning and policy decisions, the agency would be required to consider and seek to harmonize the needs and goals of the region, the plans of local agencies, and the plans or planning activities of federal, state and other governmental or nongovernmental agencies and organizations that affect planning and development in the region.

2. The plans of all local agencies would be required to be consistent with the mandatory elements of the resources plan; local agency action having a bearing on the resources plan would be required to conform to agency rules and regulations.

H. State and Federal Grant Review

The agency would be responsible for the state and federal financial assistance review required under state and federal statutes and regulations. If any such grant application concerns a matter substantially affecting an element of the resources plan, the application would first go to the agency for review and comment before submittal to the granting agency.

FINANCING THE AGENCY'S OPERATIONS

I TAXING AUTHORITY

The agency could impose a business privilege tax set at a level not to exceed ¼ of 1 percent of the personal income taxes assessed against taxpayers in the region. This tax would be required to be in multiples of 1/100th of 1 percent of regional gross receipts.

A minimum could be established without regard to the amount of gross receipts received. Public agencies would be exempt from paying this tax and the agency could provide exemptions to charitable, educational, religious and benevolent organizations.

II INDEBTEDNESS

The agency would be authorized to borrow money and issue notes in anticipation of receipts during the first 2 fiscal years of operation.

III OTHER REVENUE (No provisions in the bill)

IV SUBVENTIONS TO LOCAL AGENCIES (No provisions in the bill)

Appendix V

THE METROPOLITAN COUNCIL OF THE TWIN CITIES AREA

Stanley Scott

I FUNCTIONS AND RESPONSIBILITIES
  A. Regional Planning
       This function was taken over from the preexisting
       Twin Cities Metropolitan Planning Commission.
  B. Power to Implement Plans
       1. Authority to review the proposals and projects
          of independent commissions, boards or agencies
          whose plans have a multicommunity effect. This
          includes the power to suspend any plan found in-
          consistent with the Metropolitan Council's plan.
       2. Authority to review all comprehensive municipal
          plans in the area, to comment on and criticize
          them, but not to veto them.
       3. Authority to review plans and proposals submitted
          for support from federal funds ("section 204" and
          other similar federal review requirements). This
          power is reinforced by state legislation also
          specifically requiring such a review. The re-
          view requirement also includes a veto power in
          the case of open space land acquisition propo-
          sals.
       4. Responsibility for preparing a statement of pro-
          gram recommendations on metropolitan area needs,
          for submission to the state Legislature. In
          effect the Legislature appears to have said to
          the Metropolitan Council: "If you agree among
          yourselves that you want something done, and if
          it doesn't conflict with general state policy,
          we'll give you the authority to do it." In pre-
          paring its statements of program recommendations,

the council is sponsoring a program of research
in the following subject areas: air pollution
control, water pollution control, solid waste
disposal, acquisition and financing of major
parks and open spaces, long-range planning, fiscal resoures and tax equalization, assessment
practices, consolidation of common services of
local governments, and advance land acquisition
for development purposes. Each study is to include recommendations as to the governmental
organization or agency best suited to discharge
the functions in question.

5. Additional responsibilities delegated in 1969.
Under 1969 state legislation sponsored by the
Metropolitan Council, a number of levels of
government were delegated new responsibilities
as follows:

--Parks and Open Space: A 7-member Metropolitan Park Board appointed by the council, was created to act as a service commission under the Metropolitan Council,
which appoints the board's membership.
The park board will place strong emphasis
on open space--and on less-than-fee land
acquisition around water bodies, and along
streams and trails--as well as on parks as
such.

--Solid Waste Disposal: The Metropolitan
Council was directed to draw up a comprehensive solid-waste disposal plan, and
the county governments were instructed to
prepare reports on how they will implement the plan.

--Regional Sewage Disposal: A 7-member Metropolitan Sewer Board was created to act
as a service commission under the Metropolitan Council, and to implement the council's plans for regional sewerage collection, treatment and disposal. The Metropolitan Council appoints the board's membership.

--Airport Zoning: The Metropolitan Council
was authorized to adopt criteria and guidelines for land-use development within 3
miles of the site selected for the new regional airport. Local governments must
then adopt controls in accord with the council's guidelines.

--State Zoological Garden: A State Zoological Board appointed by the governor will
plan, construct and operate a state zoological garden in the metropolitan area. The
board's site and development plans must be
approved by the Metropolitan Council.

C. Council Activities in 1970

The council chose as its first priority item
in 1970 exploring the multi-faceted problem
of metropolitan finance and recommending ame-
liorative actions.

In all the council is now concentrating on 9
major issues: metropolitan finance, the
Metropolitan Development Guide, centers, airport work, sewer implementation, thoroughfare
and transit systems, open space implementation, health and housing.

The council has completed its metropolitan
open space plan and has published the metropolitan sewer plan and the metropolitan solid
waste plan.

The transportation work is being done in conjunction with the council's transportation
planning unit, with formal active participation from the Metropolitan Transit Commission, the Minnesota Highway Department and
the metropolitan counties and municipalities.[1]

---

[1] Metropolitan Council of the Twin Cities Area, *A
Metropolitan Area...A Metropolitan Council to Organize
its Growth* (St. Paul: 1970), p. 13.

II COMPOSITION

The 15-member Metropolitan Council body is appointed by the governor, one member being selected from each of fourteen 100 thousand-plus population appointive areas, formed by grouping two state Senate districts (approximately). The governor makes his appointments in consultation with two state senators and four state representatives from each appointive area. The fifteenth member, who is also the chairman and executive officer, is appointed by the governor, at large.

III ESTABLISHMENT

The Metropolitan Council was created in 1967 by state legislation, without a referendum. (*Minnesota Session Laws 1967*, ch. 896)

IV REVENUE

A. The Metropolitan Council may levy a property tax of not more than 0.7 mil per $1 assessed valuation (7 cents per $100.00).
B. Council activities are also supported by general planning grants from the federal government, by federal grants for specific programs and by special contracts.

Appendix VI

CHOOSING REPRESENTATIVES FOR A BAY AREA
UMBRELLA AGENCY: ANOTHER POSSIBILITY

Stanley Scott

I A BRIEF DESCRIPTION OF THE SUGGESTION
  A. The Governing Body
    The governing body of the umbrella agency would
    have 40 members. Eighteen would be chosen from
    districts (called electoral units) according to
    a constituent-unit formula. Eighteen would be
    chosen from districts by members of the Bay
    Area state legislative delegation. Four at-
    large members would be chosen by the governor.
  B. The Six Electoral Units
    Each of the 5 largest counties would constitute
    an electoral unit (see Table I). The 4 north-
    ern counties would be grouped into one electoral
    unit. Regional representatives would be distri-
    buted among the electoral units in proportion
    to population. The arrangement shown in Table
    I would seem to be acceptable, as it conforms
    rather closely to the distribution of both popu-
    lation and registered voters.
  C. Selection of Representatives
    1. One-half of the representatives of each elec-
    toral unit would be chosen by majority vote of
    members of the ABAG Executive Committee from
    that electoral unit (see Table II).
    2. One-half of the representatives of each elec-
    toral unit would be chosen by majority vote of

TABLE I

ELECTORAL UNITS FOR A BAY AREA UMBRELLA AGENCY

Electoral Unit No.	County	Population (% of Bay Area) (1970 estimate)	Registered voters (% of Bay Area) (1970)	Regional Representatives	
				Total=36	(% of Bay Area)
1	Alameda	23.19	23.74	8	22.22
2	Contra Costa	12.11	12.31	4	11.11
3	San Francisco	15.33	17.21	6	16.66
4	San Mateo	12.01	12.32	4	11.11
5	Santa Clara	23.21	20.29	8	22.22
6	Marin Napa Solano Sonoma	14.13	14.10	6	16.66

the state senators and assemblymen from that electoral unit (see Map 1, Map 2 and Table II).[1]

---

[1]Three Senate districts and one Assembly district cross the proposed electoral unit boundaries. The following provisions (a,b,c and d) would seem to take care of this problem:

a. Senate District No. 1 extends to the Oregon line, but nearly half of its 189 thousand registered voters reside in Sonoma County. Thus the senator from that district presumably should participate in the selection of regional representatives of Electoral Unit No. 6.

b. Senate District No. 2 contains only a very small amount of Bay Area territory. Although it has a total of 169 thousand registered voters, only 2,638 are within the Bay Area (in a small northeastern portion of Solano County). Because of the small numbers involved, this Senate district presumably should be excluded from the voting on regional representatives from Electoral Unit No. 6.

c. Senate District No. 14 has a total of 252 thousand registered voters, 58 thousand in Alameda County and 194 thousand in Santa Clara County. Because of the comparatively large numbers of voters involved, it would seem justifiable for that senator to participate in both electoral units.

d. Assembly District No. 2, which extends to Eureka, has 52 thousand registered voters in Sonoma County. Thus that assemblyman should participate in the voting on regional representatives from Electoral Unit No. 6.

After reapportionment in 1971 these special provisions can be modified to take the new Senate and Assembly district boundaries into account.

TABLE II

1971 BAY AREA LEGISLATIVE DELEGATION AND ABAG EXECUTIVE COMMITTEE

COUNTY		LEGISLATIVE DELEGATION	ABAG EXECUTIVE COMMITTEE
	District		(Official Representative)
Alameda		Assemblymen:	County Representatives:
	13	Carlos Bee (D) Hayward	Supervisor Joseph P. Bort[1] (District 4, Berkeley)
	14	Robert W. Crown (D) Alameda	Supervisor Robert E. Hannon[1] (District 2, San Leandro)
	15	March K. Fong (D) Oakland	Cities Representatives:
	16	Ken Meade (D) Oakland	Mayor Jack D. Maltester[2] (San Leandro)
	17	John J. Miller (D) Oakland	Councilman Donald F. Dillon[2] (Fremont)
		Senators:	City of Oakland:
	8	John W. Holmdahl (D) Oakland	Vice Mayor Joshua Rose[2]
	11	Nicholas C. Petris (D) Oakland	Councilman Felix F. Chialvo[2] Councilman Fred Maggiora[2]
	14	Clark L. Bradley (R) San Jose	

County	No.		Representatives
Contra Costa	10	Assemblymen:	James W. Dent (R), Concord
	11		John T. Knox (D), Richmond
	7	Senator:	John A. Nejedly (R), Walnut Creek

County Representative:
Supervisor James P. Kenny[2]
(District 1, Richmond)

Cities Representatives:
Mayor Louise Gierschl (Antioch)
Councilman Donn L. Black[2] (Lafayette)

Santa Clara	22	Assemblymen:	Richard D. Hayden (R), Los Gatos
	24		John Vasconcellos (D), Campbell
	25		Alister McAlister (D), San Jose
	13	Senators:	Alfred E. Alquist (D), San Jose
	14		Clark L. Bradley (R), San Jose

County Representatives:
Supervisor Ralph H. Mehrkens[1] (District 4, San Jose)
Supervisor Victor Calvo[1] (District 5, Mountain View)

Cities Representatives:
Councilman Frances Dias[2] (Palo Alto)
Councilman Edward Rogers[2] (Campbell)

City of San Jose:
Mayor Ronald R. James[2]
Councilman Kurt Gross[2]

| San Mateo | 26 | Assemblymen: | Dixon Arnet (R), Redwood City |
| | 27 | | Leo J. Ryan (D), So. San Francisco |

County Representatives:
Supervisor Jean Fassler[2] (District 5, Pacifica)
Supervisor Gerald F. Day[1] (District 3, Belmont)

COUNTY	District	LEGISLATIVE DELEGATION	ABAG EXECUTIVE COMMITTEE
			(Official Representative)
San Mateo, cont'd	12	Senator: Arlen F. Gregorio (D) San Mateo	Cities Representative: Councilman R. David Martin[1] (Burlingame)
San Francisco	18 19 20 23	Assemblymen: Willie L. Brown, Jr. (D) Leo T. McCarthy (D) John L. Burton (D) John Francis Foran (D)	County Representatives: Supervisor Dianne Feinstein[1] Supervisor Terry A. Francois[1] City Representatives: Mayor Joseph L. Alioto[2] Mr. Thomas J. Mellon, CAO[2,3] Supervisor Ronald Pelosil
	9 10	Senators: Milton Marks (R) George R. Moscone (D)	
Marin, Napa, Solano, and Sonoma	2 5 7	Assemblymen: Frank P. Belotti (R) Eureka John F. Dunlap (D) Vallejo William T. Bagley (R) San Rafael	County Representative (Marin) Supervisor John F. McInnisl (District 1, San Rafael) Cities Representative: Councilman Holmes S. Norville[2] (Corte Madera) County Representative (Napa) Supervisor Dewey K. Andersen[1] (District 5, Napa)
	1 4	Senators: Randolph Collier (D) Yreka Peter H. Behr (R) San Rafael	Cities Representative: Mayor Ralph Trower (Napa)[2]

(Solano County is not a member of ABAG)

Cities Representative:
Councilman Arne Digerud[1]
(Fairfield)

County Representative (Sonoma)
Supervisor Arthur "Art" Ruonavaara[2,4]
(District 4, Healdsburg)

Cities Representative:
Mayor William R. Lucius[1]
(Healdsburg)

[1]Term of ABAG office: July 1, 1969--June 30, 1971

[2]Term of ABAG office: July 1, 1970--June 30, 1972

[3]Chief Administrative Officer

[4]President: Supervisor Ignazio A. Vella, Sonoma County, is also a voting member of the Executive Committee.

D. Eligibility for Selection
  1. Membership on a city council, county board of supervisors or special district governing body would not render an individual ineligible for appointment to the umbrella agency. The enacting legislation could contain a specific finding to this effect.
  2. Thus the ABAG Executive Committee members in each electoral unit would be free to choose councilmen and supervisors residing in that unit, or lay citizens, at their discretion. The state senators and assemblymen would have the same discretion.
E. Protecting Racial and Other Minorities
  1. The interests of minority populations could be protected by the following language:

> In making their selections, each appointing authority shall give due consideration to the distribution of population within its electoral unit, and to such factors as socioeconomic level, and racial and ethnic composition. The appointing authority shall weigh such other considerations as it may see fit for the purpose of appointing persons who are reasonably representative of the voters of the electoral unit.

  2. A special residential requirement would probably be appropriate in the case of Electoral Unit No. 6 because of its large size. Thus the legislation could specify that each of the 4 member counties should have at least one resident among the 6 representatives chosen from that electoral unit.
F. Interim Establishment and Subsequent Review
  The umbrella agency could be established under the formula for an interim period of 2 to 5 years. At the end of this period, the agency could be reviewed both as to (1) its substantive accomplishments and (2) its performance as a representative body.

II REASONS FOR MAKING THE SUGGESTION

A. To Get On with the Job and to Gain Experience

There seems to be a substantial consensus that the Bay Area needs a regional umbrella agency to oversee certain activities and implement certain programs that cannot be handled effectively at the local level.

But we have not yet achieved consensus on how the members of such an umbrella agency should be chosen. Three possibilities are (1) direct election, (2) an ABAG formula, or (3) a combination of these two.

The current suggestion is a fourth alternative that would enable us to get on with the job on an interim basis and to gain experience, without making irrevocable commitments to any formula.

B. To Defer a Decision on Direct Election

There are several persuasive reasons to defer a decision on the inclusion of direct election in the umbrella agency's representational formula. The interim arrangement suggested here would make it possible to move ahead with a workable interim representational device, while postponing until later a decision on direct election.

C. To Build on What We Have

There are many ways of representing the public: direct election, constituent-unit representation, ex officio representation, and an almost infinite variety of appointive methods.

In the Bay Area we already have two groups of elected officials, each of whom represents the public and is also legitimately concerned with the problems and future of the region. These are: (1) state senators and assemblymen, and (2) county supervisors and city councilmen.

The current suggestion would involve both of these groups in the selection of representatives to a regional umbrella agency. It would build on what we now have and enable us to get on with some of the regional jobs that need to be done, while holding open the options for adopting

different representational formulas in the
future as we gain experience.

D. To Help Provide a Representative Cross Section
Some Bay Area observers believe that the ABAG
formula needs to be supplemented if all the
various interests of the public in the Bay
Area's future are to be represented adequately
and in proportion to population. They have
been seeking alternative representational arrangements to help express minority and other
interests that, they believe, could otherwise
be overlooked. Perhaps this suggestion can
help achieve that objective.

MAP I.

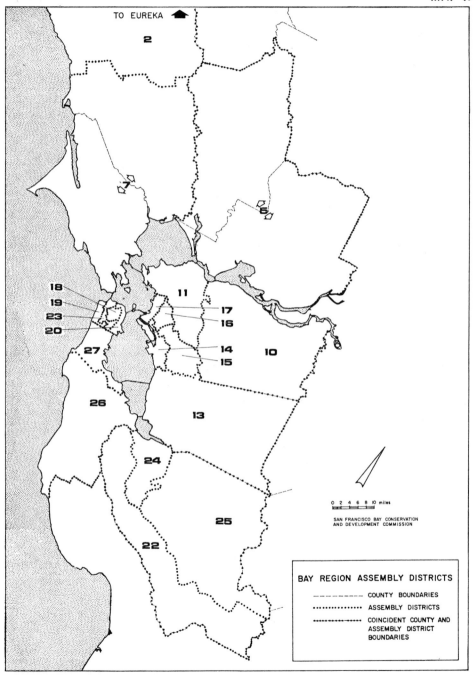

TO EUREKA

2

7

6

18
19
23
20

11

17
16

27

14
15

10

26

13

24

25

22

0 2 4 6 8 10 miles

SAN FRANCISCO BAY CONSERVATION
AND DEVELOPMENT COMMISSION

BAY REGION ASSEMBLY DISTRICTS

— — — — — COUNTY BOUNDARIES

· · · · · · · · · ASSEMBLY DISTRICTS

· · · · · · · · · COINCIDENT COUNTY AND
ASSEMBLY DISTRICT
BOUNDARIES

MAP 2.

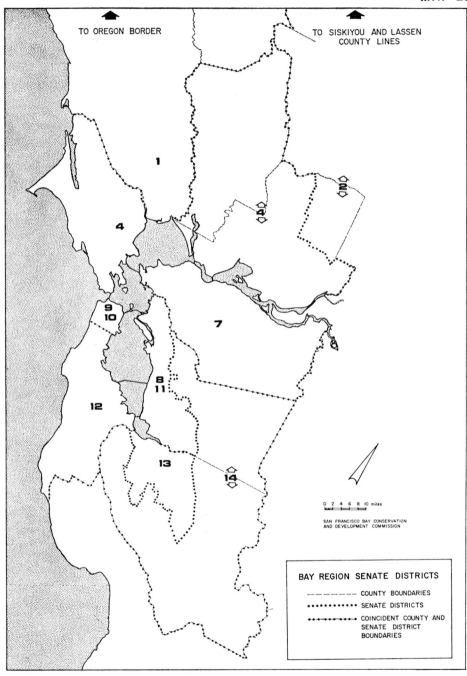

TO OREGON BORDER

TO SISKIYOU AND LASSEN
COUNTY LINES

0 2 4 6 8 10 miles

SAN FRANCISCO BAY CONSERVATION
AND DEVELOPMENT COMMISSION

BAY REGION SENATE DISTRICTS

— — — — — COUNTY BOUNDARIES
• • • • • • • • • • • • SENATE DISTRICTS
•–•–•–•–•–• COINCIDENT COUNTY AND
SENATE DISTRICT
BOUNDARIES

Appendix VII

A BAY AREA "REGIONAL BUDGET"

Approximate Governmental Expenditures
in the 9-County Bay Area

PART I

I LOCAL GOVERNMENTS (1967-68)
   Cities $ 708,941,000
   Counties   505,981,000
   School districts (estimate, based on population)   973,000,000
   Other special districts[1]   152,452,000
                                                    _____

   TOTAL LOCAL GOVERNMENTS   2,340,374,000

II MAJOR REGIONAL DISTRICTS AND AGENCIES (1967-68)
    A. Operating and Control Agencies

        Bay Area Air Pollution Control Districts   1,259,000
        Golden Gate Bridge & Highway District   3,707,000
        East Bay Regional Park District   7,298,000
        East Bay Municipal Utility District   30,028,000
        Alameda/Contra Costa Transit District   17,282,000
        West Bay Transit District   259,000

Appendix VII Part I, cont'd

Marin County Transit District	49,000
S.F. Bay Area Rapid Transit District	2,443,000
Regional Water Quality Control Board (statewide average)	325,000
TOTAL REGIONAL OPERATING AND CONTROL AGENCIES	62,650,000
B. Planning Agencies	
ABAG	700,000
BCDC	225,000
BATS (per year average rate)	750,000
Bay-Delta Water Quality Study	4,400,000
TOTAL REGIONAL PLANNING AGENCIES	6,075,000
TOTAL MAJOR REGIONAL DISTRICTS AND AGENCIES	$68,725,000

---
[1]The special district figure excludes funds expended by the regional and sub-regional districts included under "Major Regional Districts and Agencies."

Appendix VII   PART II

I	FEDERAL GOVERNMENT[1] (1966-67)	$2,910,000,000
II	LOCAL GOVERNMENTS[2] (1967-68)	2,340,374,000
III	STATE GOVERNMENT[3] (1967-68)	409,944,000
IV	REGIONAL ORGANIZATIONS (1967-68)	

A. Operating and control agencies	$62,650,000	
B. Planning agencies	6,075,000	68,725,000

TOTAL ALL GOVERNMENTS $5,729,043,000

[1]The federal figures are for fiscal year 1966-1967, and exclude (1) military prime contracts, (2) payments in connection with social security, old age and survivors insurance, and disability insurance, and (3) FHA-insured home mortgages. These figures were excluded because they are very large items (totaling $2.2 billion) that do not represent normal governmental operating or capital outlay expenditures. Nearly $1 billion of the $2.2 represents military prime contracts in Santa Clara County, alone. *Source:* Office of Economic Opportunity, *Summary—Federal Programs for the State of California, 1967* (no date).

[2]*Source:* California, Controller, *Financial Transactions* for the various types of local governments.

[3]Local assistance payments of $2.1 billion are excluded from the state totals because this kind of support is reflected in the local government figures. *Source:* California, Governor, *California State Budget.* The $409,944,000 represents the San Francisco Bay Area's prorata share of the state total, based on its proportion of the state's population.

Appendix VIII

REPRESENTATIVE LOCAL GOVERNMENT:
FROM NEIGHBORHOOD TO REGION[1]

Victor Jones

*Professor of Political Science
University of California,
Berkeley*

If we could recall the image that we held in 1959 of the challenge of the Sixties, and of the likely responses of local government, we would be chagrined to realize that we did not foresee the direction of the civil rights movement, the rise of Black Power, the upheaval among students and the beginning of reform in all parts of our educational system, the Vietnam War, the rising expectations and frustrations of millions of formerly quiescent people, the realization that public welfare is a degrading and humiliating way of life, the development of impatient leadership cadres among minority groups, and widespread postures on all sides of intransigency often accompanied by demonstrations and physical violence.

Looking backwards it is clear that the challenge of the Seventies is almost unchanged from the challenge of the Sixties: to develop a system of government and

---

[1]Also published as *Public Affairs Report*, vol. 11, no. 2, April 1970 (Berkeley: Institute of Governmental Studies, University of California).

politics which will deliver goods and services and administer regulations efficiently, effectively and justly, *and at the same time* provide, through representation and citizen participation, genuine popular control of the direction of governmental activity and a sense of communal membership.

I should like to raise several questions by making some more or less positive assertions.

1. We cannot put the disquietude of the past decade to rest and return to the status quo ante that existed when only a few professors questioned the representativeness of local government, as it was organized in the United States.

We have lived through a noisy, impolite, violent, irrational decade, a decade of "maximum possible misunderstanding." But out of it has come a political agenda of basic issues we must address during the next decade. Hopefully we can approach the task ahead with *maximum mutual understanding*, because it is a prerequisite for the institutional reconstruction, the policy decision, and the administrative actions we are facing.

We can also hope that nonnegotiable demands--except when used in the rhetoric of the hustings or as a ritualistic approach to reasoning together--will be replaced by open participation and negotiation, both by those out of power and those in power. Even so, the processes of politics, of getting attention, of securing and maintaining a following, of influencing the electorate, will frequently seem vulgar, threatening, and sinister to those who remember the Fifties.

The basic responsibility lies with people of power and influence to listen and to consider the goals, and means of achieving goals, that are pushed upon them from the outside. But again the responsibility is mutual--once those in power have been brought around to listening, demands must be translated into policies acceptable to a congeries of interests.

2. Nor can we return to the status quo ante that critics of municipal reform during the past fifty years would have us believe would bring government back--from the impersonal and ponderous bureaucracy and the power structure at city hall--to a warm and personal government in the neighborhoods.

In the first place, the current image of earlier machine politics in the ward and at city hall is highly romantic. Party bosses and party workers have had latent functions of social service, mediation between people and power, and coordination of fractionated government for both legal and illegal purposes. Most institutions, we now recognize, have latent as well as overt functions, and certainly the political machines around the turn of the century were not exceptional in this respect. But do we know that the older political machines maintained open channels of advocacy and protest?

In the second place, even if ward politics had all the virtues now retroactively ascribed to it, we must ask if it, and the administrative agencies which it controlled, would be able to deliver services today in a manner and a quality to satisfy the so-called politically deprived people of our cities. Furthermore, there is much historical evidence that corruption and personal self-serving were systemic.

Is it necessary to return to a past that never existed, in order to provide means of political access to groups that do not, or think they do not, have such access under local government as it is now organized? As Alex Gottfried has written:

> Machine politics is not yet dead, even in the invidious sense. There have been major transformations; there will be more. But the need for organizations, for leadership, and for political responsibility has increased in the contemporary world. Some promising new organizational forms are

developing. They coexist side by side with
the remaining weakened and modified older
forms and with the still developing structures in the troubled Negro, Puerto Rican
and Mexican-American ghettos. Perhaps we
are now wiser than we were fifty years ago.
Perhaps we can devise structures that will
permit access and integration for those
groups which are still dispossessed, without paying the enormous price we have paid
for ineffective and often venal local
governments.[2]

Finally, any attempt to restore machine politics
based on the ward system is probably hopeless, because
of changes that have occurred in American society since
the heyday of machine politics.

*3. Unless we have a revolution in the old-fashioned
sense of the word, institutional changes will occur
slowly.*

This does not mean that changes will not be made
quickly and abruptly, here and there, but nowhere will
the whole system of local government be replaced by
another whole system. Nor will any given modification
of a part of the system be adopted simultaneously in all
local communities.

In many instances social changes must first be made
before we can even identify the consequences to the immediate participants and certainly to the innocent by-
standers. It is desirable, therefore, to evaluate substantive changes, social institutions and practices before they spread widely and irrevocably.

---

[2]Alex Gottfried, "Political Machines," *International
Encyclopedia of the Social Sciences* (New York: The Mac-
millan Company and The Free Press, 1968), 12:248-252.
See p. 252.

There are so many uncertainties, for instance, in
the imminent decentralization of schools in New York City
that all groups interested in educational decision making
would be wise to wait for a short time, at least, to observe and analyze the New York City experiment. All elements of communities all over the United States can prof-
itably learn from the results of this attempt to decentralize a school system in a city of eight million
people. But such decentralization, as a Movement to be
universally embraced at once, can polarize the country,
without negotiating the reform it seeks.

A plea for time, of course, can be a tactic to slow
down or to avoid compliance, or even consideration of
needed change. But recognition of this fact does not
alter the other fact that time is an element of institutional change. The wisdom, if not indeed the necessity,
of "all deliberate speed" should not be rejected because
so-called deliberation without perceptible movement has
characterized other reform efforts.

*4. Local government as it is now organized and as
it now operates is being questioned and challenged from
many sides.*

Congressional committees, special Presidential commissions (e.g., the National Commission on Urban Problems
and the National Advisory Commission on Civil Disorders),
national organizations (e.g., the Committee for Economic
Development and Urban America), governors and state legislators, and many special-purpose advocacy groups (e.g.,
conservation groups), as well as civil rights groups,
black power groups, and the professional neo-reformers
associated with community action programs--all these and
many others have doubts about the capacity or the will-
ingness of local government to meet the problems of
cities and suburbs. Many of them, black and white, rich
and poor, government official and businessman, see local
government as unrepresentative in structure, parochial
in orientation, overly concerned with petty matters, unable to make hard decisions where the public interest is
opposed to local interests (as defined by supporters of

regional services and controls), or where justice and
equality is opposed to private gain or prejudice.

I myself have heard state legislators in the San
Francisco Bay Area speak in this manner of elected city
and county officials. Strictures such as these may be
deserved in some instances; they are certainly not deserved by most local officials. Many of them are equally
applicable to state and federal officials, and to neighborhood leaders. In fact, they may be applied to any
organized group of people. But the fact of life is that
local government is widely criticized in such terms, and
that the criticism is growing, to the point of condemnation.

5. *American federalism--and, of course, American
politics--is changing in style, direction, and structure.*

Such changes, but at a different rate and scope,
may have been going on from the beginning of our national
history. But the rate and magnitude of change now make
the historical differences one of kind as well as quantity.

Local government has become one of three operational
partners in the new federalism. Despite all efforts of
state governments to return to a two-level federalism,
irreversible patterns of give-and-take, and sharing of
functions and power are operating, for better or for
worse, through frequent formal and informal relationships
among state and federal and local governments and agencies.

This has been accomplished by local governments going
to Washington, and by federal agencies going into the
local communities. But more important, this intermin-
gling has been supported, and at times demanded, by many
collections of interests. As a consequence, federal constituencies have been built up in the metropolitan areas
of the country, which overlap state and local constituencies.

The most startling and far-reaching change in American federalism is the emergence of the national government as the focus for discussion of urban and metropolitan affairs. It is now the leader in formulating urban programs, and in using the grant-in-aid to elicit intergovernmental cooperation among local governments in our metropolitan areas.

The political base of the active involvement of the national government in metropolitan and urban affairs must be emphasized. One could conclude from the cries of "home rule" and "states rights" that the state and national governments are hostile foreign powers. We should remember that from the beginning of our history individuals and groups have habitually and constitutionally turned to other governments, and within a government to other branches and agencies, whenever they have been unable to get what they want from the particular level or agency with which they first dealt. In fact, there are interests within our local communities, such as organized labor, racial and ethnic groups, and many influential businessmen and professional people, whose orientation is typically national. They find it easier and more natural to look to state and federal governments to satisfy their interests directly or, at least, to influence local organizations of concern to them. Thus either the state or national government may, in their view, be "closer to the people" than local government.

6. Therefore, the governance of metropolitan America will be a mixture of the actions of public and private groups. Within the public sector, it will be a mixture of federal, state, and local governmental actions.

Under these circumstances, conflict and disagreement in metropolitan governance would not be eliminated, and neither would the need for cooperation and coordination, even if all local governments within each metropolitan area were consolidated. Furthermore, in most metropolitan areas, certainly for the larger, more heterogeneous, multicounty, in some instances multistate, metropolitan areas such consolidation of local government is not likely to occur.

On the other hand, local government as now organized in metropolitan areas is unable to execute programs of the federal and state governments on a regional basis, much less to participate as an equal partner in formulating programs and in adapting them to local needs, desires and conditions.

7. Concomitant with the thrust toward metropolitanization is another powerful thrust toward smaller areas where influence, control and other objectives of political participation may be realized.

Although either neighborhood decentralization or metropolitan centralization (or both) of certain governmental activities may be undesirable, a movement in both directions at the same time is not necessarily contradictory. Movement in both directions at once is the essence of federalism--I say "directions" because we are certainly not compelled by federal principles to seek continuously for either smaller or larger units of political decisionmaking.

The creation or development of either a regional agency or a number of neighborhood agencies, or both, will increase the decision-making points in a system of metropolitan governance. A regional agency should reduce the dysfunctional effects of the governmental fragmentation of the metropolitan area. Neighborhood agencies, along with the continued existence of relatively small suburban municipalities, should reduce the dysfunctional effects of very large governments now existing or soon to be created. All this makes the problem of structural linkages among governments in and out of the metropolitan area very crucial.

8. Linkages between municipal government and neighborhood "governments."

Some social reformers and activists want no link between the neighborhoods and city hall. Nothing less than the breaking up of the big city into many autonomous governments will satisfy them. Undoubtedly others

want nothing that suggests a division of authority between the city government and organized groups in subareas of the city. Neither of these will be satisfied
with the changes that are already occurring in local
government, or with those that are beginning to be proposed.

Certainly in some parts of the country there will
be varying degrees of decentralization, but it will be
done by, and not to, local leaders and municipal officials. We are still not out of the period of "maximum
feasible misunderstanding," but it is now clear that
change will have to come about through normal political
means.

This makes all the more remarkable the fact that
the Los Angeles City Charter Commission provides in its
recommended charter for

> the formation of self-initiating neigh-
> borhood organizations, [with populations
> between 5,000 and 30,000] with an elected
> board and an appointed neighborman, as a
> new institutional mechanism for communi-
> cating neighborhood needs and goals, in-
> volving citizens in city affairs, and re-
> ducing feelings of alienation.[3]

A Neighborman would be the formal link among the
elective Neighborhood Board, the residents of the neighborhood, and city hall. He would be selected by the
Neighborhood Board, exempt from civil service, and paid
by the city a salary no less "than the salary of a field
deputy of a member of the [city] council."

The Neighborhood Board, of not less than seven members, elected by and from the registered voters of the
neighborhood, could draw up bills of complaints and

---

[3] Los Angeles City Charter Commission, *City Government
for the Future* (July 1969), p. 19.

otherwise advise and recommend action to the appropriate
public authorities. It would be the duty of the Neighborman to follow up on the action of the Neighborhood
Board.

There would be a formal linkage, then, between
neighborhood and city hall. In addition, many informal
relationships will develop not only between city hall
and individual Neighbormen, but probably among Neighbormen and therefore between them as a group and city
hall.

Another relevant proposal, lost for a dozen years on
the library shelves, was made by the late Don Larson in
his study of city-county consolidation for Sacramento.[4]
The feature of primary interest here is the formal linkage, and the other possible informal linkages, between
the general government of the area and the governments
of subunits. The Sacramento proposal is illustrative of
the many ways in which this might be done in a large
city or complex metropolitan area.

Larson proposed to consolidate the Sacramento city
and county governments under a metropolitan Council of
eleven members--six to be elected at large and five by
districts or boroughs. In addition to serving as election districts for members of the Metropolitan Council,
each borough would elect a Borough Council of five members.

> The Borough Council, as a unit, would be
> essentially a formal advisory link between
> the people of each area and the Metropoli-
> tan Council. *To put teeth into this func-
> tion, the charter should provide that any
> request or recommendation made by*

---

[4] Public Administration Service, *The Government of
Metropolitan Sacramento* (Chicago: 1957), pp. 115, 132-
136.

resolution of a Borough Council would
have an automatic place upon the agenda
of the next Metropolitan Council Meeting.
[emphasis supplied]

The Borough Council would also provide another
"official bridge," in that the chairman of each council
would serve on an 11-member Metropolitan Planning Commission, and the other four members of each council
would serve on one of the other metropolitan boards--
Parks and Recreation, Health and Welfare, Public Works
and Public Safety.

The boroughs were also envisaged as administrative
units, with "sub-city halls" or "sub-civic centers,"
where agents of the metropolitan government could dis-
pense services and as quasi-autonomous units to which
government functions could be decentralized. Even in
the Fifties, neighborhoods were not overlooked. Larson
pointed out the possibility that even the boroughs might
in time be broken up into "neighborhoods" with

"neighborhood councils" which would be
defined as smaller advisory or action
organizations covering several square
miles and a few thousand people.

I have quoted from the Sacramento Report to help
bring it down from the library shelves and once again
into public view. Our organizational imagination is
limited, and it is important that we not overlook a
single proposal that addresses the problem of linking
organizations in metropolitan areas.

If the ward or district system is used to elect
members of the local legislative body, a link between
the people living within the subarea and the central
government is automatically provided. The desirability
of making a district councilman a little mayor of his
district is an open question. But if this approach is
taken, it still will not provide for formally organized
participation at the neighborhood level, unless the size
of city councils is drastically enlarged.

9. Linkages among governments at the metropolitan or regional level.

During the past decade, with the open entrance of the national government into metropolitan affairs, and with increased interest in metropolitan planning on the part of local officials, the prospect of formal metropolitan decision making and execution is brighter than ever. Most local officials, but not all, insist that such governmental arrangements permit them to participate in the making and administration of metropolitan policies. On the other hand, some local officials in many metropolitan areas, and most local officials in a few metropolitan areas, favor a directly elected metropolitan body, with no formal linkages to city and county governments.

Insistence upon an all-directly elected regional government will make it impossible to develop a formal and workable scheme of metropolitan governance in most of our large and complex metropolitan areas. The Twin City Region in Minnesota is an exception--a referendum would probably not be required, and almost all local officials in that area favor direct elections.

In the San Francisco Bay Area the issue seems to be drawn sharply, with strong combatants who are now in agreement that there should be some form of multipurpose but limited regional government--and with a good chance that the issue may be settled by compromise at the present legislative session.

The Bay Area has two large (or at least vocal) groups, heterogeneous in their make-up, one of which has taken a firm stand in favor of a directly elected regional government, while the other supports the creation of a regional governing body selected by and from elected city and county officials. Bills were introduced in the 1969 session to create a multipurpose regional agency along each of these lines (AB 711 and AB 1846). Neither bill was reported out of the Assembly Committee on Local Government because the Committee, both houses of the

Legislature, and many proponents of regional government were completely involved in the legislative struggle to strengthen and make permanent the Bay Conservation and Development Commission.

It now appears that high political leadership in both the Legislature and in the Association of Bay Area Governments will develop and sponsor a compromise bill to create a limited-purpose but wide-ranging regional agency. It is understood that the proposed regional agency would have a governing body selected by and from elected city and county officials (the ABAG proposal) but with functions, duties, and powers as provided in Assemblyman Knox's bill. Assemblyman Knox has made it clear that he considers the new proposal a means of testing local officials, to see if they can make the hard decisions of regional governance. If they fail to measure up, the bill will provide for the reopening of the whole question of the composition of the regional governing body. In addition, there is speculation about a suit to force the new government, if established by the Legislature, to comply with the one person-one vote decisions of the United States Supreme Court.

Certainly, the whole matter of representation will be argued vigorously during Committee hearings on any bill that may be introduced. In the past, both groups have come down squarely on the side of principle. On one hand, it is maintained that a directly elected regional body, on which city and county governments are not represented, would destroy local government and home rule. It is alleged that the regional body would be a distant metropolitan supergovernment. On the other hand, the proponents of direct election hold this to be the only way to secure a democratic, responsible, responsive, and effective government.

As might be expected in a constitutional debate, a Connecticut Compromise has been proposed, but both sides thus far seem to find it uninteresting. I want to argue that, apart from the political realism of a compromise, the proposal to mix the two bases of representation--

direct election, and representation of local govern-
ments--deserves consideration on its own merits:

    (1) Mayors, city councilmen, and county supervisors
        should participate in regional policy making
        through membership on the governing body, be-
        cause

        a. They represent tough, ongoing, legitimate
           local governments with organizational and
           representational interests in metropolitan
           affairs;

        b. Cities and counties are more likely to co-
           operate by willingly carrying out regionally
           adopted policies, if they participate in the
           formulation and adoption of regional poli-
           cies; and

        c. City and county officials can probably de-
           feat any other proposal in a referendum.

    (2) It is not true, however, that *all* interests
        within a metropolitan region such as the San
        Francisco Bay Area are represented by mayors,
        councilmen, and county supervisors. At least
        it is a matter to be inquired into. Otherwise,
        one must hold that everyone is virtually repre-
        sented under whatever system is in effect.

    (3) Direct election from districts, as a means of
        supplementing mayors, city councilmen and county
        supervisors on the governing body, can increase
        the representativeness of the regional agency.
        Not only is a combination of direct election
        with representation of local governments a means
        of obtaining the virtues of both systems, it is
        actually likely to increase the representation
        of various minority groups--such as Blacks
        Mexican-Americans, conservationists, and Demo-
        crats.[5]

---

[5] Stanley Scott and John C. Bollens show that the city
and county representatives in ABAG are "only 37 percent
Democratic, representing a population that is over 60
percent Democratic." *Governing a Metropolitan Region:
The San Francisco Bay Area* (Berkeley: Institute of Governmental Studies, University of California, 1968), p.
158.

In any event, the presence of city and county officials on the regional governing body would provide formal linkages to city and county governments. Steps should also be taken to link state and federal governments into the governance of the metropolitan region.

10. Minority representation may be enhanced by a mixed system of representation on the regional governing body.

A mixed system would provide representation of groups in the region that might not be represented among the city and county officials selected to sit on a regional governing body. Suggesting that the ABAG system of representation needs to be supplemented is, however, in no way an admission that it needs to be replaced.

But direct election alone is not likely to assure the widespread election of Blacks and other members of minorities. The division of the Bay Area into 36 electoral districts would yield districts of 123.5 thousand inhabitants. If the population of the Bay Area increases as projected, the average population of 36 regional election districts will increase to 170 thousand or more inhabitants within 10 to 15 years. Such districts would be small when compared with State Assembly districts, but they would still be relatively large. The problem of size is compounded by the unknown factor of where the district boundaries are to be drawn.

Based on districts of 123.5 thousand people, one must conclude it to be unlikely that more than two Blacks would be elected from the nine districts in Alameda County; or more than one, if any, in Contra Costa County. Perhaps one member representing Mexican-Americans would be found among the eight representatives elected from Santa Clara County. Probably two members of minority groups would be elected out of six in San Francisco. None would be elected in Marin, Sonoma, Napa and Solano counties. Thus only six out of 36 directly elected members might be expected to be Blacks and Mexican-Americans.

The number could be increased if there were also
city and county representation on the regional governing
body. Perhaps there would be no increase in the proportion of such members, but 12 out of 72 will provide better representation than 6 out of 36. There will be
more voices to speak, more bodies to participate in committee work, more hands to help or to listen to constituents.

Under a system where cities and counties were also
represented, it would be possible to have minority group
members, elected to the regional body by the city councils of at least San Francisco, Oakland, Berkeley and
Richmond. Such a selection from the Alameda County Board
of Supervisors is not at all unimaginable. And the likelihood increases with time. Undoubtedly there would already be more Black representatives to the ABAG General
Assembly and Executive Committee if Black members of
city councils and boards of supervisors had shown greater
interest in participating in regional affairs.

*11. If compromise is not considered to be ideologi-
cal capitulation, political leadership can exercise its
historical role of developing and legitimating institutional and behavioral adaptations to the new tasks of
federal, state and local governments.*

An outstanding example of political leadership is
now being exhibited by Assemblyman John Knox and his
colleagues in the Assembly and by the Executive Committee
of the Association of Bay Area Governments. Hopefully,
other interested groups in the Bay Area will approach
the review and evaluation of the compromise bill in the
same spirit. Proponents of either form of representation
can undoubtedly keep the other side from establishing
its preferred style of regional government. But both
sides should ask themselves, which is more important,
the establishment of a multipurpose but limited regional
agency that can be reformed as experience and changing
regional desires suggest, or unyielding insistence on a
principle not shared by everyone?

Intransigence will prevent the creation of any regional multipurpose agency. This does not mean that we will not have metropolitan government. We have it now, in the form of many single-purpose districts and authorities. Unless a multipurpose regional agency is developed, we shall also have many more special districts in the Bay Area.

12. *The Supreme Court of the United States has not ruled that the governing bodies of multipurpose regional agencies must be directly elected.*

It has maintained, in other cases affecting the method of selecting local governing bodies, that it

> is aware of the immense pressures facing
> units of local government, and of the
> greatly varying problems with which they
> must deal. The Constitution does not re-
> quire that a uniform strait jacket bind
> citizens in devising mechanisms of local
> government suitable for local needs and
> efficient in solving local problems....[6]

13. *Nevertheless, Supreme Court decisions, agitation for neighborhood government, and widespread uneasiness about the quality and democracy of our system of local government, suggest the need for a systematic reevaluation of the theoretical bases of local governmental structure.*

---

[6] *Avery v. Midland County*, 390 U.S. 474 (1968); see also *Sailors v. Bd. of Education*, 387 U.S. 105 (1967) and *Dusch v. Davis*, 387 U.S. 112 (1967). See the symposium "One Man–One Vote and Local Government" edited by Robert G. Dixon, Jr., in *George Washington Law Review* (May 1968)-- including an article by me entitled "Metropolitan Detente: Is it Politically and Constitutionally Possible?" (pp. 741-759).

Regardless of whether Mr. Justice Frankfurter was correct or not in warning the Court that it was being asked by the plaintiffs in *Baker v. Carr* "to choose among competing theories of political philosophy--in order to establish an appropriate form of government,"[7]--we outside the Court must face that choice in adapting local government from the neighborhood to the region to current expectations and perceptions of justice, democracy, effectiveness, security and community.

14. Furthermore, this task must be approached with the full realization that it is extraordinarily complex.

Local governments and politics are systems of social organization interdependent upon other overlapping social systems, some with territorial imperatives smaller than that of the local government, and with many spilling over into the larger and more inclusive society. Local government is not socially autonomous, if indeed any institution is, and its capabilities are often limited by the behavior of other institutions within its environment. Any conservationist should understand this ecological truism.

As an institution, local government is both tough and delicate. Its toughness has been demonstrated by the proliferation and survival of thousands of local governmental units, and by the slowness of *structural* reform. It is a delicate institution, however, that can be replaced or by-passed by impatient advocates of any given goal--hence, the easy creation of special districts for the special purposes of special groups. Given such pressures, governments could wither away, while remaining alive only in a most formal sense.

Even more terrifying is the possibility of destroying the important role of city governments, a role being assumed increasingly by county governments, of managing

---

[7]369 U.S. 186, 300 (1962).

the resolution of conflict within the community--at least
of providing a legitimate place for attempts to resolve
conflict. This role has inestimable symbolic value.

The danger is present and great that local government and the associated local political system will be
converted into an engine to stifle dissent and to manage
conformity. It would then cease to be a general government and become in fact a very special kind of special
authority. There is great danger today that extremists
of either side could bring this about.

Under these circumstances, and with the full realization that structural reforms are important, but not
all-important, we should pick up where the Supreme Court,
perhaps properly and wisely, left off.[8] What kind of
system or systems of representation do we want? What
are likely to be the consequences of the continued use,
or increased use, or discontinuance, or modification of
the appointed executive, elected executive, small council, nonpartisan elections, local elections isolated
from state and national elections? Do we know, for instance, that the manager plan is necessarily incompati-
ble with a large partisan council elected by districts?

How a responsive and responsible reevaluation can
be staged is another matter. But clearly many features
of local government and politics are being evaluated

---

[8]See the excellent essay by Malcolm E. Jewell, "Local
Systems of Representation: Political Consequences and
Judicial Choices," *George Washington Law Review* (May
1968), pp. 790-807; Robert G. Dixon, Jr., "Local Repre-
sentation: Constitutional Mandates and Apportionment
Options," ibid., pp. 693-712; Dixon, "Reapportionment
Perspectives: What is Fair Representation?" 51 *Am. Bar.
Assoc. Journal* (1965), pp. 319-324; and Dixon, *Democratic
Representation: Reapportionment in Law and Politics*
(New York: Oxford Univ. Press, 1968), pp. 23-57, 544-
588.

without reference to each other, or to the system as a whole. In the meantime local government as we have known it may actually be withering away.

Agencies: alternative ways of organizing, 91-104, 123-126; coordination of, 6, 201, 202, 286; directly elected, *see* Election, direct; financing of, 22, 24, 70, 221-223, 236-237, 248-250, 258; functions of regional, 5-7, 20-60, 91-92, 112-114, 125-128, 135, 150-151; legislative proposals for alternative, 211-223, 225-237, 239-250, 251-262; neighborhood, 278-297; services, 167-168, 176, 179-180, 181; tax base of, 118, 120, 169-173, 180-198; umbrella, 91-95, 124, 127, 140, 145, 193, 205

Agencies. *See* Association of Bay Area Governments; Bay Area Air Pollution Control District; Bay Area Mass Transit Group; Bay Area Rapid Transit District; Bay Area Regional Organization; Bay Conservation and Development Commission; Bay-Delta Water Quality Control Program; California Toll Bridge Authority; East Bay Regional Park District; Golden Gate Bridge, Highway and Transportation District; Housing and Urban Development, Department of; Metropolitan Council of the Twin Cities Area; Metropolitan Transportation Commission; San Francisco Bay Open Space Commission

Air pollution, 12, 20, 28, 43-45, 61-68, 92, 128, 133, 172

Alioto, Joseph, 190, 206

Alquist, Alfred, 27, 42, 46

Andersen, Ralph, 175-176, 183-185, 188-189, 194-195

Area Planning Organization (APO), 53-54

Assembly Bills*(AB) 1969: *711*, 23-24, 31, 32, 35, 97, 205, 211-223, 239-250, 289; *1846*, 31, 60, 205, 211-223, 225-237, 289; 1970: *16*, 43; *108*, 43; *215*, 44; *357*, 44; *363*, 39, 40, 72, 73, 75; *387*, 44; *477*, 44;

---

* Bill numbers are italicized.

478, 44; *479*, 43; *493*, 49; *640*, 46, 47; *641*, 43; *642*,
44; *647*, 41; *684*, 37; *725*, 40, 41; *730*, 47; *818*, 47,
48; *1200*, 35; *1247*, 47, 48; *1310*, 32, 33; *1771*, 36;
1942, 48-49; *1971*, 36; *1984*, 41; *2077*, 45; *2131*, 47,
49; *2310*, 31-32, 33, 35, 60, 82, 99, 203-205, 211-
223, 251-258; *2345*, 33, 35, 60; *2348*, 33; *2459*, 41;
2463, 49
Assembly Concurrent Resolutions (ACR) 1970: *26*, 42; *40*,
41; *41*, 44; *97*, 42; *182*, 25, 43
Association of Bay Area Governments (ABAG), 13, 20-23,
35, 38, 41, 73, 88, 89, 102, 103, 125, 126, 141, 149,
152, 154-155, 170, 181, 201-202, 204, 276, 290, 292;
executive committee, 21, 23, 58, 59, 96, 266-269,
293; formula for alternative organization, 95-104,
137-140, 142-145, 155, 263, 265, 270; general assembly, 20, 21, 96; and minority representation, 98, 99,
101, 149, 156-159; regional plan, 38, 41, 51, 53, 59,
89, 143; as review agency for federal assistance, 20,
50-58, 59, 60, 191-193. *See also* AB *1846*. *See also*
Constituent-unit system of representation

Bagley, William, 21, 37. *See also* AB *1846*
Bay Area Air Pollution Control District (BAAPCD), 12,
14, 28-29, 43, 44, 45, 97, 157
Bay Area Council, 131-132, 135, 136
Bay Area Mass Transit Group (BAMTG), 22-23
Bay Area Rapid Transit District (BART), 29, 40, 41, 42,
72-73, 74, 80, 97, 124, 157, 167
Bay Area Regional Organization (BARO), 13, 23-25, 88,
164
Bay Area Transportation Study Commission (BATS), 22, 24,
39, 96, 102, 215, 231, 242, 276
Bay Conservation and Development Commission (BCDC), 13,
14, 19, 21, 24, 27, 31, 32, 33, 35, 36, 38, 46, 68,
88, 102, 131, 135, 136, 215, 231, 242, 255, 276, 290
Bay-Delta Water Quality Control Program, 24-26, 32, 33,
37, 215, 231, 242, 276
Beckett, John C., 71-75, 83
Bee, Carlos, 40
Beilenson, Anthony, 49
Belotti, Frank, 41
Bodovitz, Joseph E., 68-71, 78-79, 83, 140

Bolton, Herbert E., 9
Bort, Joseph P., 142-146
Brave New World (Huxley), 12
Briggs, John, 47, 48
Britschgi, Carl, 42
Brown, Willie Jr., 14, 43, 44, 90, 142, 158, 159
Budget, regional, 175-187, 275-277. *See also* Fiscal base
Bureau of the Budget, 50-51, 57
Burgener, Clair, 49
Burton, John, 44
Business: and conservation, 130, 135-136; and regional organization, 106, 131-134

California Constitution (1879), 10, 15
California Environmental Protection Program Fund, 39, 49
California Toll Bridge Authority, 40-42, 69-70
Carbert, Leslie E., 163-173, 176-177, 181-182, 184-188, 190-191, 195-197
Carrell, Tom, 45
Citizen participation, 19-20, 38, 51-54, 55-57, 108-109, 158, 280. *See also* Representation
Conservation: and business, 130, 135-136; coastal, 46-49; and Development Commission. *See* Bay Conservation and Development Commission. *See also* Environmental issues
Constituent-unit system of representation, 95-101, 125, 137-140, 141, 143-146, 155, 156, 201-202, 204-205, 263-265, 270-272
Constitutional issues, 15, 294-297
Coordinating Council for Higher Education, 84
Council on Intergovernmental Relations, 33, 34, 35, 174
County, and municipal government, 15, 97, 107-108
Crandall, Earle, 43
Crown, Robert, 42

Decentralization, 283, 285-289
Demonstration Cities Act (1966), 206-207
Direct election. *See* Election, direct
Dolwig, Richard, 42
Dunlap, John, 36, 49

Earthquake hazards. *See* Seismic safety
East Bay Municipal Utility District, 31, 65
East Bay Regional Park District, 30, 45, 46
Education, and regional government, 70, 76, 83-84, 148,
    178, 187-188, 192, 206
Edwards, Don, 45
Election, direct, and regional government, 35, 97-101,
    103, 110-111, 117, 125, 129, 135, 139-140, 144, 145,
    155, 157, 196, 204-205, 288-295; minority representa-
    tion in, 98-99, 101, 129, 141, 142, 157, 291-293; and
    partisanship, 140-142, 145. *See also* AB *711* and *2310;*
    Umbrella agency
Employment, 77, 120, 148, 152-153, 192
Environmental issues: and citizen pressure, 19-20, 38;
    and governmental levels, 62-68; planning for, 33-35,
    57-58, 71; and political parties, 108. *See also* Air;
    Open space; Sewage; Water
Expenditures, governmental, in Bay Area, 275-277

Fazackerley, Don, 130-136
Federal grant requirements, 49-58
Federalism, 283-288
Financing regional organizations, 21-25, 70, 174-181,
    221-223, 236-237, 248-250, 258, 275-277. *See also*
    Taxes. *See also* AB *1846, 711, 2310*
Fiscal base, of regional organizations, 70, 163-173,
    186-187; budget, 174-186; collection of revenues, 176,
    179-182, 203; sources of revenues, 169-173, 175-182,
    183-198; unified base, 170-172, 177, 182
Foran John, 13, 39, 41, 72, 82

Gentry, Curt, 3-4
Golden Gate Bridge, Highway and Transportation District,
    29-30, 41-42, 72, 74. *See also* Transportation
Gottfried, Alex, 280-281
Government, regional: local structure and, 154-155, 170,
    172, 191, 278-288; powers of, 5, 24, 91-92, 112-114,
    125, 128, 135, 150, 151; proposals for, 211-223. *See
    also* AB *711, 1846,* and *2310;* services of, 167-168,
    174, 176, 179-181; tax base of, 70, 118, 120, 169-
    173, 180-198. *See also* Taxes
Great Frontier (Webb), 9, 11

Henderson, Mary W., 136-140, 154-156, 158-159, 202
Hetland, James L. Jr., 105-122, 144, 155
Heyman, Ira M., 123-126, 136, 158, 159
Home rule, 60, 71, 143, 151, 183-184, 225-237, 290
Housing: and regional organizations, 76-77, 120, 148,
    192; and Urban Development, Department of (HUD), 20,
    22, 40, 50-59, 193, 206, 207
Huth, Ora, 19-60, 225-237, 239-250, 251-258

Jackson, Henry M., 59
Jobs. *See* Employment
Joint Exercise of Powers Act, 20, 55
Jones, Victor, 99-101, 136-137, 278-297

Kent, T.J. Jr., 38, 126-130, 140, 145
Ketchum, William, 43
Knox, John T., 12, 15, 23, 31-32, 33, 35, 43, 44, 45,
    60, 72, 78, 82, 99, 135, 151-153, 184, 193, 203-205,
    206, 207, 290, 293. *See also* AB *711, 2310*

Lagomarsino, Robert, 49
Lands, tidal and submerged, 37, 49. *See also* Open space
Lanterman, Frank, 12
Larson, Don, 287-288
Last Days of the Late, Great State of California
    (Gentry), 3
League of Women Voters, Bay Area, 57, 97, 135
Lee, Eugene, 3-7, 8, 10, 61, 68, 82-84, 140-142, 154,
    156-158, 159, 201-203, 208
Legislative proposals, 31-49, 81-82. *See also* Assembly
    bills, Senate bills; for alternative agencies, 211-
    223. *See also* AB *711, 1846, 2310,* Metropolitan Coun-
    cil of the Twin Cities Area

McCaffrey, Stanley E., 61-62, 68, 75, 78, 80, 82
McCarthy, John, 36
McCullum, Donald P., 146-151, 152, 153, 177, 191
MacDonald, Ken, 41
Marks, Milton, 13, 36, 38, 39, 49, 82
Metropolitan Council of the Twin Cities Area, 93-95,
    103, 105-122, 144, 152, 259-262

Metropolitan Transportation Commission (MTC), 23, 35, 39-40, 41, 72, 73, 75. *See also* Transportation
Milias, George, 46, 47
Miller, John J., 76-78, 83, 158
Minority groups: attitudes towards regional organizations, 146-151; and direct elections, 98-99, 101, 129, 141, 142, 157-158, 291-293; participation in policy making, 51-56, 119-120; representation in ABAG, 98, 99, 101, 149, 156-159, 292
Mulford, Don, 41, 72
Municipal government, 107, 114, 119, 120

Negative Income Tax plan, 177-178
Neighborhood agencies, 280-288
Neighborman, provision for, 286-287
Nejedly, John, 37, 41, 44, 47, 48
New York City, 190-191, 282

Open space, 13, 20, 24, 34-35, 37-39, 68, 78, 87-88, 92, 114, 118, 128, 153, 169, 189, 196-197, 246-247
Organization, regional. *See* Agencies

Parks, 20, 24, 30, 45-46, 70, 87-88, 92, 246-247
Patman, Wright, 53
Petris, Nicholas, 46
Policy decisions, of regional organizations, 4-5, 64-68, 70-75, 105, 134; and partisan politics, 130, 141, 146
Politics, machine, 280-281
Pollution. *See* Air; Sewage; Waste; Water
Powers: of regional agencies, 5, 20-49, 91-92, 112-114, 128, 135, 151, 215-221, 231-236, 242-248, 253-257
Population density, 77-78, 80-81. *See also* Open space

Regional organization. *See* Agencies, Legislative proposals
Regional problems. *See* Open space; Pollution; Sewage, Transportation; Water
Regional Transportation Planning Committee (RTPC), 22-23
Representation: by appointment, 96, 102-104, 110-112, 117, 118, 126, 149, 150, 202. *See* ABAG; Constituent-unit system; AB *1846*. by direct election. *See* Election, direct; of minority groups. *See* Minority groups

by mixed system, 95-96, 99-101, 125, 126, 202, 204-205, 289-293; in planning organizations, 53-57; and revenues, 194-196; in umbrella agencies, 263-270. *See also* AB *711, 2310*
Revenue: collection of, 176, 179, 180-182, 203; sources of, 169-170, 175, 183-198, 275-277
Rolph, Earl R., 177-178, 179-181, 187-188, 190, 196, 206
Romney, George, 206

San Francisco Airport Commission, 23
San Francisco Bay Conservation and Development Commission. *See* Bay Conservation
San Francisco Bay-Delta Water Quality Control Program. *See* Bay-Delta
San Francisco Bay Open Space Commission, 37-38. *See also* Open space
San Francisco Planning and Urban Renewal Association (SPUR), 60
San Francisco Public Utilities Commission, 65
San Francisco Regional Water Quality Control Board, 27-28
Schrade, Jack, 48
Schultz, George, 177
Scott, Stanley, 87-104, 123-125, 127, 129, 205, 259-262, 263-274
Seismic Safety, Joint Committee on, 26-27, 46
Select Committee on the Environment, 13
Senate Bills*(SB) 1970: *48*, 41; *62*, 44-45; *77*, 45; *86*, 37; *187*, 37; *262*, 39, 49; *277*, 37; *331*, 42; *371*, 47, 48; *687*, 47, 48; *708*, 42; *793*, 42; *980*, 46; *1055*, 33; *1082*, 49; *1110*, 36; *1321*, 49; *1354*, 49; *1400*, 37, 38, 39
Senate Concurrent Resolutions (SCR) 1970: *24*, 42; *60*, 27, 46; *70*, 27, 46
Senate Joint Resolution (SJR) 1970: *35*, 36
Senate Resolution (SR) 1970: *225*, 36
Sewage, 13-14, 24, 25-28, 63-68, 118, 166, 189
Sherman, Lewis, 35, 42
Sieroty, Alan, 47, 49
Solano County Board of Supervisors, 21

---

*
Bill numbers are italicized.

Sonoma County Board of Supervisors, 41-42
State, control of decisionmaking, 6, 10, 64-68, 79-80, 202-203
Stead, Frank M., 60, 62-68, 79, 82, 83
Stockfish, Jack, 181
Supreme Court, and direct election, 294-295

Taxes: equity of, 172, 182, 184-185, 187; income, 24, 70, 173, 182, 184, 186-187, 189; of regional agency, 70, 118, 163-173, 180-198; payroll, 170, 172, 182; property, 24, 70, 168, 172, 180, 182, 184, 189; sales, 182, 184, 186, 189, 206. *See also* Financing
Train, Russell, 57, 58
Transportation, 13, 21, 22-24, 29-30, 35, 39-43, 71-75, 80-81, 87, 88, 95-96, 103, 118, 120, 124, 133, 172, 189, 191, 245; Regional Transportation Planning Committee, 23, 39, 58
Turner, Frederick Jackson, 9

Umbrella agency: functions of, 91-95, 124-129, 140, 145, 193, 205; representatives for, 263-274. *See also* Metropolitan Council of the Twin Cities Area

Valley Community Services District, 31
Vasconcellos, John, 36, 44
Vella, Ignazio A., 8-11, 82, 153-154, 192-193, 196, 205-208

Waste, solid, 60, 62-67, 87, 88, 92, 114, 116, 133, 166, 189
Water: pollution, 20, 25-26, 28, 62-67, 87, 92, 133, 172; quality, 25-26, 32, 37, 246; resources, 26, 36, 37, 47, 62-67, 115, 118. *See also* Bay-Delta Water Quality Control Program
Webb, Walter Prescott, 9, 11
Wheaton, William L. C., 174-175, 178-179, 186-187, 189, 190, 191-192, 193, 195-198
Wilson, Pete, 47

Zoning, 77-78